WHAT EVERY AMERICAN SHOULD KNOW ABOUT WHO'S *REALLY* RUNNING AMERICA

Former *National Geographic Traveler* columnist, "pop subculture" corre-spondent for *Newsweek*, and biographer of Courtney Love, award-winning journalist MELISSA ROSSI changed career course after the 9/11 attacks. Since then, she's been gallivanting across the globe bringing geopolitics to the masses in her What Every American Should Know (WEASK) series for Plume. Kicking off with *What Every American Should Know About the Rest of the World*, the collection includes *WEASK About Europe*, *WEASK About Who's Really Running the World*, and *WEASK About Who's Really Running America*. She is also the co-author of *Think India* (Dutton, 2007). Rootless Rossi suffers from urban deficit disorder—she can't focus on one city for long—but is often spotted in exotic corners of Europe or Asia.

WHAT EVERY AMERICAN SHOULD KNOW ABOUT WHO'S _REALLY_ RUNNING AMERICA

AND WHAT YOU CAN DO ABOUT IT

MELISSA ROSSI

A PLUME BOOK

PLUME
Published by Penguin Group
Penguin Group (USA) Inc., 375 Hudson Street, New York, New York 10014, U.S.A.
Penguin Group (Canada), 90 Eglinton Avenue East, Suite 700, Toronto, Ontario, Canada
M4P 2Y3 (a division of Pearson Penguin Canada Inc.)
Penguin Books Ltd., 80 Strand, London WC2R 0RL, England
Penguin Ireland, 25 St. Stephen's Green, Dublin 2, Ireland
(a division of Penguin Books Ltd.)
Penguin Group (Australia), 250 Camberwell Road, Camberwell, Victoria 3124, Australia
(a division of Pearson Australia Group Pty. Ltd.)
Penguin Books India Pvt. Ltd., 11 Community Centre, Panchsheel Park,
New Delhi – 110 017, India
Penguin Group (NZ), 67 Apollo Drive, Rosedale, North Shore 0745, Auckland,
New Zealand (a division of Pearson New Zealand Ltd.)
Penguin Books (South Africa) (Pty.) Ltd., 24 Sturdee Avenue, Rosebank, Johannesburg
2196, South Africa

Penguin Books Ltd., Registered Offices: 80 Strand, London WC2R 0RL, England

First published by Plume, a member of Penguin Group (USA) Inc.

First Printing, June 2007
10 9 8 7 6 5 4 3 2 1

Ⓟ REGISTERED TRADEMARK—MARCA REGISTRADA

LIBRARY OF CONGRESS CATALOGING-IN-PUBLICATION DATA
Rossi, M. L. (Melissa L.), 1965-
   What every American should know about who's really running America : and what you
can do about it / Melissa Rossi.
      p. cm.
   Includes bibliographical references and index.
   "A Plume book."
   ISBN 978-0-452-28820-1
  1. Business and politics—United States. 2. Corporations—United States—Political
activity.   3. Power (Social sciences)—United States.   4. Elite (Social sciences)—United
States.   5. Pressure groups—United States.   I. Title.
   JK467.R65 2007
   322' .30973–dc22   2006036632

Printed in the United States of America
Set in Helvetica and Grotesque Black

To Melik Boudemagh, the demigod of information

Acknowledgments

This book would be a pile of fragmented notes and a torrent of tears were it not for my dream come true of an editor, Emily Haynes, and the patience of Plume's guiding light, Trena Keating. As everyone—from production editor Lavina Lee to production queen Norina Frabotta to copy editor Sheila Moody to proofreader John Morrone to interior designer Eve Kirch and cover designer Melissa Jacoby—knows, this baby was a hair-puller and I thank them all deeply for tending to it with care and fitting the pieces of this puzzle together. I'm also forever indebted to Zac Petit, who along with my advisor, researcher, guru, social life, and source of food, Melik Boudemagh, loaded me up with fantastic information. I was elated to have the chance to interview so many fascinating people for this book, including some of DC's weightiest voices. Grover Norquist of Americans for Tax Reform, political commentator Linda Chavez, Coushatta whistle-blower David Sickey, Public Citizen's Joan Claybrook and Taylor Lincoln, Union of Concerned Scientists' Dr. Edwin Lyman, Wikipedia's Jimmy Wales, energy expert Michael Klare, *National Geographic Traveler*'s Sheila Buckmaster, front group exposer Sheldon Rampton, and physicist Lawrence Krauss are but a few whose insights were invaluable. Website wizard Greg Landry was a huge help, and Khun Jo and Chairit made my life so much sweeter.

And, as usual, my family helped pull me through this, along with the always optimistic words of my agent, Bill Gladstone.

Contents

WHAT EVERY AMERICAN SHOULD KNOW ABOUT WHO'S _REALLY_ RUNNING AMERICA

Introduction

This book may break your heart, because this book is about a beautiful idea that has gone tragically wrong, or so it certainly appears at the moment. It's about the government of the United States of America, and what the hell has happened to it. This is about how thugs took over the steering wheel of our country—but they didn't yank it by force, they won it with money. This is a book about how our government has been corroded inside and out. And this is about what you can do about it.

The seventh year of the twenty-first century—AD 2006—was an alarming one. Granted, things had been pretty strange since we'd turned the corner into the new millennium, whether you were talking about tsunamis and hurricanes or terrorism and American politics. But 2006 was the year the curtain dropped on DC, pulled down when a man widely admired as the capital's slickest lobbyist took a tumble and tripped up the cord. And when Jack Abramoff took his final dive, he revealed a gang of money-hungry scoundrels running our country and pawning it off to the highest bidder. Just as frightening as what they were doing—namely, selling out the country to corporate interests—much of what they were doing was perfectly legal. Abramoff and his cronies just took it a little too far.

Access, favors, and backslaps are for sale—anybody who opens their wallet wide enough can rate a photo op or handshake with a VIP or can figure out a way to legally buy a new law that can help them rake in millions. Far too many of the elected officials we've pointed toward DC have largely bombed in their "represent the people" mission or in their ability to get anything done. Dead and gone are most of our distinguished statesmen with lofty ideals and high IQs—the people's representatives who were capable of compromise, debate, and accomplishment. The lawmakers of the twenty-first century now juggle roles as corporate reps who cut deals for the companies that fill up campaign coffers—and as salesmen for their state's local big boys for whom they snatch multimillion-dollar federal giveaways—as well as backslappers of the special interest groups who turn out most to the polls.

It's not just Congress that's turned into an auction house. The executive branch now defines conflict of interest: it's teeming with former lobbyists who loosen and snip regulations that might tie up Big Business. The Bush administration joyously appoints those who work to destroy from within: the Environmental Protection Agency ignores the advice of its own experts as it keeps dropping the bar, Secretary of the Interior Gale Norton worked to open protected land to oil drilling, Labor Secretary Elaine Chao steamrolls unions, and our former United Nations ambassador John Bolton appeared hell-bent on weakening, if not entirely ruining, that institution.

Our judicial branch is under attack—with legislators and the White House eroding the courts' power—passing laws that sidestep rulings, as in the Terri Schiavo case. Attorney General Alberto Gonzalez warns judges to stifle any constitutional concerns they might have, including ones over laws that allow the practice of holding "enemy combatants" without charge. Livid that courts made abortion legal and kicked prayer out of schools, conservative religious groups are trying to stack the courts with judges whom they believe will overturn landmark rulings, while Big Business throws millions into electing state and federal judges who favor business concerns over those of consumers.

It's tempting when looking at the mess in DC to deeply sigh, shrug, and hightail it out for a beer. But there are reasons to look this beast in the eye. It's our money that's being frittered away on costly and dangerous projects—be they no-end-in-sight wars that are costing a billion dollars every two days or elaborate sci-fi schemes for security that so far have proved to be money-burning boondoggles. It's our world that's destroyed when environmental concerns are thrown out the window, and those are our rights that keep getting shredded. While Congress and the White House bow down to Big Business, the people's concerns aren't being addressed—be they for alternative energy cars or for reining in a ravenous credit card industry that wallops us with ballooned interest rates or for health care and prescription drugs that we can afford.

The antics of the sort that are now being exposed in DC shake our belief in government as a relatively honest, transparent, and accountable institution—all the more given an administration that chronically deceives and snarls and resorts to name-calling whenever an objection is raised. While some misdeeds are finally being addressed in Congress, the White House is off-limits; whenever unethical practices and lies are uncovered, the response is frequently a shrugged, "Yeah, whatever."

There seems to be but one solution: the people have to get back into the game, keep an eye on our lawmakers, and let them know just what we think. We need to vote—only half of us do—and we need to vote in the local elections, even those for school boards, where turnout is so piddly an extremist can win if he gets all of his extended family out to the booths. We need to make noise—by writing letters to the editor, calling up talk radio, attending utility meetings and those at city hall—and by calling up our representative's office, and sending our elected crew in Congress handwritten letters and faxes, since they've stopped reading most of those messages that are e-mailed in. We need to follow legislation and to form groups with our family and friends to make our personal lobbying effort louder, and we very much need to swell the membership of our valuable watchdog groups, and give them more teeth.

Most of all, we need to remember that even though money talks, so does the vote. And we've got to figure out how to use our votes, our voices, and our pens to let the government know that we will not tolerate what has happened to be repeated again.

CHAPTER 1

Something Stinks

Background on the Mess in DC

"What a great time to be a Republican in Washington, DC."

—Speaker of the House Dennis Hastert in November 2004[1]

When trying to decipher what is happening to America, and who's doing it, and how, simply gaze toward Washington, DC. The river-hugging city of column-wrapped monuments, park-lined boulevards, graceful domes, and the granite finger of that trademark obelisk rising up not far from tenement towers, Washington looks

Lobbying and freebies aren't always bad: for twenty-four years, travel writer Eliza Scidmore lobbied for cherry trees in DC until First Lady Harding gave a nod in 1909; favor-seeking Japan donated the blossoming beauties as a gift.

stately and respectable—especially in postcards, which block out the eyesores and show the city bursting with cherry blossoms.

Not shown in airbrushed photos, and hard for the naked eye to discern, are the hidden channels of money and influence snaking through our capital—the epicenter of the twenty-first century American power machine—where a cadre of a few hundred elite make and shape the decisions that affect all of our lives, even the lives of those in distant countries. And a fair amount of these brass-plated power seats in DC are occupied by those who bought their way in; others simply buy the decisions the inner circle makes. How intertwined corruption had become with everyday business became shockingly obvious in the recent crash of lobbyist-shyster Jack Abramoff, whose downfall pulled plenty more with him and exposed the framework of how the national rip-off factory works.

MEGALOMANIAC MAGNET

The gleaming marble architecture, the treasure-laden museums, and the pink petals that flutter down streets in spring aren't what bring visionaries and madmen, the civic-minded and extremists, the needy, the greedy, and the angry—and those who desire to inflict their ideas on the country—swooping into the nation's capital. The allure of DC is the concentrated power stuffed within twelve city blocks: this weighty core holds the potent symbols of the three branches of our federal government, namely:

- The **White House**, which heads the *executive branch*, including fifteen all-important departments—from Agriculture to Energy to Education to Defense
- The columned **Supreme Court Building**, where nine judges appointed for life head the *judicial branch* and have the final say on matters constitutional
- The domed **Capitol Building**, which houses Congress, our *legislative branch*, and its two chambers—the 435-member House of Representatives and the 100-member Senate

In an area smaller than downtown Des Moines, a mighty group of some six hundred legislators, officials, cabinet heads, department directors, and judges—the tip of our government—shape, make, and sometimes break our laws.

Just as important, a small subgroup among them directs the flow of the trillions of dollars that sweep in and out of the U.S. Treasury, deciding exactly to whom multizeroed checks will go. Some who come to DC aspire to be part of this mighty elite, but they are outnumbered by those drawn to the gleam of the Treasury, a portion of which they hope will end up in their own pockets.

Moneywise, the United States runs the world's biggest government outfit, and it commands the largest budget. In 2005, taxes kicked in $2.3 trillion to the Treasury,[2] which for the fourth year in a row ran in the red, spitting out $2.48 trillion for expenses ranging from Medicare to homeland security, public education to military bases. Of that $2.48 trillion, about one-third—$843 billion—was "discretionary spending," bureaucratese for

Torched by the British in 1814, the U.S. Capitol is now being destroyed by the raging greed within.

"approved and apportioned by Congress—come on down!" And that's
when the fun begins: everybody from corporations to church groups,
city governments to university science departments, wants a federal
handout—and they swarm the House and Senate appropriations committees, which divvy up the greenbacks. The legislators decide not only
how much to fund departments and agencies, but in every bill they pass
lawmakers tack on funding for thousands of pet projects that benefit
contributors, friends, and their state.

To give an accurate, twenty-first century picture of DC, those fetching
postcards of our cherished capital should come with a wide scratch 'n'
sniff strip, and the scent that emerges should not be of flowers. Once
held up as an icon of justice, democracy, and liberty, the capital stinks to
high heaven of corruption, greed, and insider dealing, no matter how
much air freshener they spray. From House Majority Leader Tom "I did
nothing wrong" DeLay to Representative Bob "the booze made me do it"
Ney, lawmakers are self-ejecting from the Hill—with at least some looking at a few years behind bars—while those who've clung to their seats
in Congress shudder, aghast that such dastardly deeds have been happening under their very noses.

NOT ALL THAT DIFFERENT

The many criminal acts of Jack Abramoff triggered the ongoing corruption sweep in Congress, but in many ways he was just a typical
lobbyist. As we will explore through this book, the profession isn't
particularly clean-nosed or honorable these days. The problem: lobbyists are now an integral part of the election finance system. They
steer huge wads of money toward politicians' contribution kitties,
and, in exchange, legislators frequently grant lobbyists and their corporate clients the power not only to shape legislation, but to literally
write our laws. Lobbyists can also grab multimillion-dollar federal
projects for their clients, whom they direct to make extremely generous donations to the charities of the lawmakers whose help they
need. Lobbyists may also suggest that their clients take congressmen on exotic vacations. What Abramoff did was far shadier—and

more complicated than that. His multi-tentacled scheme included moving millions of dollars through nonprofit organizations—to avoid being traced. It involved trickery and deception—and playing clients against clients—and creating bogus companies. Many of the practices that Abramoff employed—such as paying experts to write editorials that helped his clients or lavishly giving to the foundations and election campaigns of legislators whose vote he wanted—may indeed be bribery, but they are just how the game is played these days in DC. Abramoff's scandalous behavior—as well as that of fallen Rep. Randy "Duke" Cunningham—brought to light how corroded the system has become.

More of the capital's bigwigs are sure to fall soon, because the culprits are pointing fingers. Pleading guilty to six criminal counts, including conspiring to bribe public officials, mail fraud, and tax evasion in January 2006, former DC superstar Jack Abramoff is now cooperating with authorities, agreeing to name the names of exactly who in Congress succumbed to his bribes. Nearly two dozen lawmakers and congressional staff may be ensnared—and by October 2006, one congressman (Bob Ney, R-Ohio) and three former Capitol Hill staffers who tangoed with the lobbyist were heading for prison. But Abramoff accounts for but one slimy incident in the capital's very recent history: Congressman Randy "Duke" Cunningham (R-California) pleaded guilty in November 2005 of taking millions in defense contractor bribes, and the case is leading investigators in new directions, including toward the CIA and the agency's card-playing, stogie-smoking, stripper-lovin' (says *Vanity Fair*) former number three, "Dusty" Foggo.[3] The hasty departure of CIA Director Porter Goss in 2006 reportedly may be linked to Cunningham's corruption scandal,[4] which some say reaches further and deeper than Abramoff's in showing "the mafia" running parts of our government. And federal investigators have yet to fully throw the book at former House majority leader Tom DeLay (R-Texas), whose antics elucidate how rotten DC's core really is; hit with a money-laundering charge in Texas, DeLay slithered out of the House of Representatives in June 2006, leaving behind a malodorous trail of slimy deals and creative money-moving techniques that bring to mind the workings of organized crime.

Sickened by the antics and ineffectiveness of the scandal-rocked 109th Congress, most of us summed it up in one word: *yech*. By fall 2006, only one in four Americans mildly approved of the job our legislators were doing[5] and only 3 percent regarded them as trustworthy.[6] It was just everyday news when Republicans shut out Democrats from key discussions and Dems blocked Republican moves—and not a whole lot got done in those ninety-five days or so a year that representatives in the House actually showed up for the job.[7]

As campaign costs soar, keeping politicians running from fundraiser to fundraiser in their home states, our legislators—particularly the People's Representatives, with those brief two-year terms—spend far less time in DC: for most of 2006, the House had a two-day week, typically arriving on Tuesday afternoon and taking off on Thursday. The Senate met less than 130 days—and with their staggered six-year terms, only a third of them had the House's campaigning excuse.[8]

SPRING CLEANING THE HOUSE: A FEW OF THE RECENTLY DEPARTED

- **James Traficant** (D-Ohio, 1985–2002): The former sheriff with the puffy toupee, garish fashion sense, and penchant for ending floor comments with "Beam me up," was tried for bribery back in 1983— getting off back then after arguing that he took mobster money (nearly $200,000) merely to follow the scent of corruption. When accused of taking bribes as a congressman, he wasn't so fortunate, being convicted in 2002 of ten felony counts of bribery, racketeering, and tax evasion. His employees at the House must have been pleased when he was booted from Congress: he'd forced his staff to hand him part of their salaries—and made them slave on his farm. Now serving an eight-year term in federal prison.

- **Bob Ney** (R-Ohio, 1995–2006): Cosponsor of the "freedom fry" movement to delete the word "French" from the American vocabulary, Ney chaired the House Administration Committee, overseeing ethical conduct with lobbyists, which is a laugh. Ney was palsy-walsy with Abramoff, whose generous contributions (as well as those of his clients) so swayed Ney that he added Abramoff-desired amendments to bills and cast aspersions on a Florida businessman—denouncing him in the Congressional Record—when Abramoff wanted to buy up the Floridian's gambling boat biz. Tossing aside rules that mandate that former staff can't lobby their bosses for one year, Ney tried to make the wishes of his former aide Neil Volz come true, and he accepted lavish gifts from lobby-

Hitting up Abramoff's Indian tribes to pay for ritzy European vacations to elicit his yea was one act of straying on the far side of legality that got Rep. Bob Ney (R-Ohio) nayed out of Congress and into prison.

ists, including Jack's infamous 2002 golf trip to Scotland. These, along with the massive contributions Abramoff and his Indian tribe clients were making to his campaign kitty, convinced Ney to intervene on behalf of the tribes. After a lucky night—funded by a felon who wanted to sell plane parts to Iran—at a London casino (Ney took home more than $50,000), the congressman lobbied Colin Powell to drop restrictions on trade in the land of the ayatollah. Ney tumbled with Abramoff, who named him as "Representative Number 1" in ongoing Justice Department investigations. In 2006, Ney pleaded guilty to two counts of conspiracy to commit fraud and making false statements and is looking at a maximum of ten years in federal prison. With any luck, he'll end up rooming with fellow Buckeye Traficant.

- **William Jefferson** (D-Louisiana, 1991–present): The FBI videotaped him accepting $100,000 allegedly to help make the case for an Internet company—money that the FBI found in his freezer when agents stormed his house and his office in Congress in May 2006. Not found in the deep freeze was Jefferson's demand that he be made owner of the company[9] or the beaucoup bucks that his wife and daughter had made as consultants to the company, a keep-it-in-the-family technique employed by plenty of others. His former aide Brent Pfeffer, now a Kentucky businessman, pleaded guilty to attempts to bribe Jefferson and was sentenced to eight years in prison, but as of November 2006, Jefferson remains on the happy side of the bars.

- **Mark Foley** (R-Florida, 1995–2006): The five-term representative may not have done anything illegal, but he won the congressional creep award in September 2006. The self-proclaimed protector of youth, who in 2002 loudly accused the Supreme Court of "siding with pedophiles over children,"[10] for not closing down child pornography websites, was the chairman of the Missing and Exploited Children's Caucus and crafted bills to protect kids from sleazebag adults. He resigned in September 2006 after ABC broke the news that he was a sleazebag himself. A former House page, whose complaint was echoed by others, notified the media that Foley had sent him "sick" e-mails requesting photos. "Do I make you a little horny?" Foley asked in one. The congressman was far more lewd and graphic in others. The embarrassment that the homosexual, youth-fawning Republican created for the GOP—whose leaders have sought to ban gay marriage and to paint true Republicans as the guardians of decency and family values—was nearly palpable, and cries for Speaker of the House Dennis Hastert, who was accused of ignoring warnings, to step down were deafening. As testimony to his clout—Boeing is said to have relocated its Seattle headquarters to Illinois simply to be in his district[11]—Hastert (who shares his DC townhouse with his two top male aides[12]) easily won reelection.

Golfing matters—it matters a lot. Billions of dollars' worth of deals are casually struck on the greens—and the industry club, the Professional Golfers' Association, was rather dismayed to find that its reputation had been indirectly chipped by the Abramoff affair, which involved quite a few holes in Scotland. That's why in summer 2006 the PGA hired a few lobbyists to professionally point out to our lawmakers (perhaps along with a few checks for the election campaign) that golfing—who knew?—actually putts $62 billion into the economy every year. Driving home the all-Americanness of the wealthy businessman's favorite sport, the House of Representatives adopted House Resolution 471, honoring the PGA for ninety years of excellence. The ceremony was held in Palm Beach, Florida, presided over by the man who'd introduced the resolution and represents the PGA's district in the Sunshine State—Rep. Mark Foley, who nobody knew at the time would resign from the House the next day. We don't want to think about how many millions the PGA will now have to sink into lobbying and PR to shine up its newly tainted image.

Across Washington, you could almost hear dominoes falling starting in 2005, but after two years of nonstop scandals, it's clear that as they crash we are getting only a small glimpse of the truth. What's coming to light in shrieking neon colors is that the swampland that George Washington designated as the country's capital in 1791 has turned into a sleazy pay-to-play racket, and it leads from the lobbying racket known as K Street to Congress right up Pennsylvania Avenue, where big-time campaign contributors land plum appointments and shape projects in progress, be they wars on the drawing board or energy plans. To be dealt into the executive-level poker game, it helps to be a Pioneer—a Bush supporter who has raised campaign contributions of $100,000 or more— a list that begins with Jack Abramoff, who raised more than $200,000 to elect and reelect Bush and kicked millions to others in the GOP.

"The president does not know [Jack Abramoff] nor does the president recall meeting him," Scott McClellan insisted at a White House press briefing in January 2006, as the Abramoff scandal was snowballing.[13]

> *The White House went on a mission to destroy any pictures of*
> *George W. Bush with Jack Abramoff, although photos soon emerged,*
> *including some published in* Time.

PRESIDENTIAL PAYBACKS

Ante up big in the presidential pool, and you could win a jackpot: President George W. Bush, whose campaign contributions topped all records, tapped thirty of his heftiest contributors as ambassadors to foreign countries, despite a glaring lack of diplomatic experience.[14] Another twenty-five of his big-time backers rated top department appointments, even though many knew about government bureaucracy only from the other side, most being company owners, corporate CEOs, or lobbyists.[15] In fact, according to the *Washington Post*, 104 of the 246 fundraisers identified as Pioneers in the 2000 election landed a job in the Bush administration during the first term[16]—and the practice continued into the second.

Among the best known of handsome campaign contributors (Pioneers are starred) who scored a job:[17]

- *Defense Secretary Donald Rumsfeld*
- *Attorney General John Ashcroft*
- *Defense Department number three man Douglas Feith*
- *Environmental Protection Agency head Christine Todd Whitman*
- *Homeland Security Secretary Tom Ridge**
- *Department of Labor head Elaine Chao**
- *Commerce Secretary Donald Evans**
- *Special appointee to develop Iraq's private sector Thomas Foley**

Those who paid their dues to the Bush administration witnessed all sorts of miracles: laws they'd long lobbied for suddenly passed, federal cases against them suddenly dropped, regulations and standards for their industries quickly relaxed.[18] And Pioneer Jack Abramoff got his wishes granted too: in 2002, when it came to light that he was the subject of a federal investigation on Guam, a U.S. territory in the Pacific, the prosecutor was suddenly yanked from the case. President George W. Bush fired him.[19] And the investigation was dropped.

Just as there's nothing illegal about a president rewarding his contributors with high-ranking jobs—President Clinton did it too, although not quite as much[20]—there's also nothing illegal about many other screwy DC practices that appeared to turn lawmaking and government policy into a sold-to-the-highest-bidder business.

> *"The White House is like a subway. You have to put in coins to open the gates."[21]*
> *—Johnny Chung in 1996, speaking of how China perceived the U.S. government. Chung had illegally dumped more than $300,000 into the Democratic Party coffers and attempted to bribe public officials in what was dubbed "Chinagate." Back then, some may have thought the Taiwan-born businessman was merely confused as to how things really worked around here. Turns out he understood the system better than we did.*

Take, for instance, the common practice among lobbyists to underscore the case they are making—perhaps that Congress should block less expensive pharmaceutical drugs coming in from Canada or it should open up more federal lands for oil exploration—not simply by picking up lunch or by handing over a report, but by forking over a check for the next election. Sure, that may resemble bribery—but up to $2,000 is entirely copacetic. And in the course of persuading our congressmen and officials, lobbyists can do so much more, including helping them raise hundreds of thousands of dollars for campaigns—again, legally—which is one reason the industry ain't looking lily-white, even when all the rules are followed to a T, which lately they frequently don't seem to be.

The right to petition the government—in essence, lobby—is guaranteed by the First Amendment.

President Ulysses S. Grant, the story goes, first coined the term that's now synonymous with egg-on-his-face Abramoff. Every time the nineteenth-century president slipped off to the grand Willard Hotel to puff

on a cigar (the missus forbade him from lighting up at the White House)
he was swarmed by a small pack of men waiting in the foyer hoping to
bend his ear. Their persistent presence in the hotel's lobby prompted
Grant to slap on the term "lobbyists." If Grant found the top-hatted gentlemen taxing back then, good thing he isn't in Washington now. From
a handful back in the 1950s, to six dozen in the 1960s, the number has
dramatically swelled: now there are thirty-five thousand registered
lobbyists[22]—about seventeen thousand of which showed up in the past
six years as the lobbying craze hit and as Capitol Hill staffers, legislators, and department heads realized that their connections were gold if
they moved over to K Street. Lobbying—once a derided sideline—is now
alluring as a potentially multimillion-dollar-a-year profession: Washington
lobbying firms are now pulling down more than $2 billion a year, and the
numbers keep soaring.

Anybody can lobby—from a hunched-over grandma upset about rising medical costs to a teenager who wants federal funds to help build a
skateboard park. But most professional lobbyists are Gucci-clad
lawyers, toting reports and embossed cards, and most now work in DC
law firms, many located near the boulevard of bland, glass box buildings
known as K Street. Here one finds internationally famous names like
Barbour Griffith & Rogers (actually located on Pennsylvania Avenue) or
Patton Boggs (actually on M Street), where attorneys are paid $500 an
hour as "persuaders for hire" for clients ranging from cigarette manufacturers to the American Medical Association. Top-shelf clients often want
to change laws already on the books or to shoot down (or support) bills
being debated in Congress. But about half of the lobbying work from K
Street—as the lobbying business is collectively known—has one goal:
getting a cut of the federal budget.

Lobbyists are popping up from all corners, grabbing congressmen's
arms in parking lots, squeezing into elevators for a quick word, hovering
in restaurants, passing on reports and requests via chiefs of staffs. In
this world where you're only as good as the names in your BlackBerry,
face familiarity is so crucial that some lobbyists first rack up experience
working in the Senate cloakroom just to forge introductions. Because to
really score in this field, one needs access to the big boys, particularly

committee chairmen and those sitting on Congress' budget boards, the powerful appropriations committees. That's why many firms scoop up staff fresh from Capitol Hill—they come with fat Rolodexes and knowledge of the legislature's complexity and who's doing what, and, above all, boast name recognition.

And that's where things start getting even dirtier.

According to the Center for Public Integrity, more than 2,200 of those who previously worked for the government—whether as a Senate staffer or secretary of labor—are now working the government as lobbyists, including more than two hundred former members of Congress and forty-two former agency heads.[23] Realizing the value of their "access abilities," some former legislators, officials, and staffers leave simply to start their own lobbying firms, promising clients that they'll be able to score impressive results with their former colleagues and bosses on the Hill.

LOBBYING DELAY-STYLE

Until recently, one of K Street's most brazen, thuggish, and successful lobbying houses was Alexander Strategy Group, which was conflict of interest personified, although not illegal, by definition at least. Hatched in 1998 by weaselly Edwin Buckham—DeLay's pastor and chief of staff who led the daily prayer meetings in the congressman's office—Alexander Strategy Group lured other DeLay aides such as Tony Rudy to quit Congress and join up as lobbyists. Even DeLay's wife, Christine, was dealt into the action: the congressman's better half was paid more than $100,000 as a political consultant for the firm.[24] Attracting grade A clients—Microsoft, the Magazine Publishers of America, and the well-muscled drugmaker trade group PhRMA, to name but a few—Alexander Strategy Group soon was pulling in millions. One problem: the firm's hardball tactics amounted to extortion, some say. One Republican insider described its lobbyists' sales pitch as "Either you hire me or DeLay is going to screw you."[25] Working closely with their former boss, the lobbyists also were entwined in Abramoff deals, sharing some of the same clients. Alexander Strategy Group hastily shut down in January 2006 due to the uproar over the smirking congressman and the besmirched lobbyist—and at news that

Abramoff's prosecutors were looking its way. However, excessively close ties between former aides and certain legislators—and seemingly unethical acts such as putting spouses on the payroll—still pervade both Capitol Hill and K Street.

"Tom DeLay sent Buckham downtown to set up shop and start a branch office on K Street. The whole idea was, 'What's in it for us?'"
    —Former Republican majority leader Dick Armey, who is now a lobbyist
        for Piper Rudnick [26]

While legislators can be overwhelmed by the sheer number of those elbowing in, some lobbyists very much warm a lawmaker's heart. Besides presenting congressmen with insightful research and reports (slanted to make their clients' cases), the K-Streeter can make a lawmaker's life oh so much easier. They wine, they dine, they present gifts (theoretically valued under fifty dollars), they provide legislators with invitations to exclusive see-and-be-seen dinners with VIPs. They cajole with offers to travel to far corners of the world (expenses paid by the lobbyist's client). But those are just appetizers.

Congressmen took more than $50 million worth of free trips between 2000 and 2005. Major "free getaway" sponsors included the Nuclear Energy Institute, the Aspen Institute, and the American Israel Education Foundation (linked to powerful AIPAC, America's pro-Israel lobby). [27]

K Street's paid-to-persuade gang plays another much more pivotal role for the elected: lobbyists are also candidates' campaign backers, and they control millions of donation dollars. As part of their work, lobbyists loosen their clients' purse strings: they tell the moneyed, be they high-rolling bankers, Indian tribes, or chemical makers, which lawmakers they should toast by hosting $500-a-plate election fund dinners—where the legislators are served up envelopes stuffed with checks. They

Two of DC's heroes, Senators John McCain (R-AZ) and Russ Feingold (D-CA), tried to tidy up the electoral finance mess with their 2002 election reform law. Try again, guys.

recommend which lawmakers' "charitable causes" their clients should help out. Lobbyists direct and deliver the money collected from groups of employees and friends, who "bundle" checks via "political action committees," since the ka-ching has a stronger memory impact when lawmakers are presented with checks totaling $10,000 or more.

The election reform law passed in 2002 appears to have had negligible effect, except to pump up the importance of political action committees (PACs), which now dole out about half the money used in congressional campaigns. A vehicle to move cash legally to a candidate's election coffers, PACs are "collective piggy banks" made up of contributions from a company's employees, family, and friends, who collectively chip in to help elect candidates. Politicians may also start up a PAC, with the money in it going to help out other lawmakers, who will then be indebted to their colleague and more inclined to vote his or her way. Individuals who contribute to PACs don't necessarily kick in all that much—they may pony up only a couple hundred or a couple thousand—but it adds up. PACs of the National Association of Realtors or the Association of Trial Lawyers or

AT&T shovel millions of dollars into elections. Theoretically voluntary, PACs sometimes become a legal cover for the boss to fork over a huge wad of money that isn't the company's, since businesses can't legally give directly to candidates; employees may be pressured to contribute to the candidate that their boss favors.

A FEW TRICKS OF THE PERSUASION TRADE

Lobbyists for wealthy clients commonly pull these tricks out of their briefcases:

- *How 'bout dinner?* It's easy to get to a politician's heart through his stomach, when companies, law firms, and industry trade associations endear themselves to candidates by throwing $1,000-a-plate fundraiser dinners for them.

- *What a heartwarming cause!* Since corporations are banned from directly contributing to legislators, they often donate very, very generously to their foundations and charities—Lockheed Martin, for instance, donated a million bucks to the foundation of then Senate majority leader Trent Lott for the Trent Lott Leadership Institute at the University of Mississippi.[28] But sometimes these charities appear to be fronts, with "administrative costs" like buying pricey furniture and going on Parisian vacations eating up most of the donations (see box "Give to the Needy, Help Out the Greedy?" on page 20). And since these are tax-exempt nonprofit organizations, they don't have to list their contributors, making them an ideal way for corporations to get their money to a candidate surreptitiously.

- *Our workers just love you.* Lobbyists or other representatives hand politicians hundreds of thousands of dollars raised through employee donations to PACs—a crucial funding mechanism for candidates. Handily, lobbyists are often PAC treasurers.

- *A change of scenery would do you good.* Whether they want legislators to see nuclear plants in France, meet top military brass in Israel, or speak at mountaintop conferences, groups who want results often invite lawmakers and regulators on all-expenses-paid trips. Lobbyist Abramoff said it all in an internal memo at law firm

Preston Gates & Ellis, where he once worked, describing overseas trips as "one of the most effective ways to build permanent friends on the Hill"[29]—and Abramoff made it a trademark.

- *Buying opinion.* Another trick of Abramoff's—and other lobbyists, whose law firms may work with on-site public relations companies—is to pay experts and think tank fellows to submit favorable articles and op-ed pieces to editorial pages, a practice that is alarmingly common. Sleazily, PR firms often write the pieces—asking only that the "expert" use his or her name as the byline and send it in to newspaper editors as an original work.

- *Stop by for a drink.* Whether they're K Street law firms pouring out fine brandy or conservatives serving up bagels, power groups often hold weekly networking meetings over coffee or cocktails, where the up and coming can meet the already there. If you're anybody in DC—or at least anybody right of center—you'd better be seen at Grover Norquist's invitation-only Wednesday meeting.

Friends with access to deep pockets are a necessity in an age when campaigning is frighteningly expensive: a run for the House rings in at over $1 million, a Senate run is seven times that. Which helps explain how the relationship between some lawmakers and some lobbyists became so incestuous, and why many are screaming that the lobbying system needs fixing, starting with barring lobbyists from raising money for candidates. Between 1997 and 2005, lobbyists and lobbying firm PACs ladled out more than $100 million to the congressional campaign funding tureen—spoonfeeding congressmen nearly $34 million in 2004 alone.[30]

Through their hired hands on K Street—and the palm greasing that comes in the form of donations—corporations and wealthy special interest groups, from the NRA to the Chamber of Commerce, have become so cozy with Congress that they do more than dictate laws to the lawmakers; now their lobbyists actually write the bills. It's common practice these days to allow lobbyists to pen parts of legislation, amendments, and earmarks: the paid persuaders hand their gang in Congress a copy of the bill with the precise wording of sections that are relevant to them, and the lawmakers often cut and paste it right in.

Given the leeway they already have, it's alarming that so many lawmakers, lobbyists, staffers, and officials have overstepped the wide bounds in what lately appears to be a three-ring circus of bribery, corruption, and money juggling. Working the power of their yea or nay, their ability to introduce laws, and perhaps most important their ability to toss a government-funded project at those dropping jack into their campaign baskets—perhaps a $3 million deal to a wireless contractor to install antennas in House offices—some lawmakers employ dodgy practices that smack of money laundering. And one of the cheapest tricks involves charities.

GIVE TO THE NEEDY, HELP OUT THE GREEDY?

A few of the many congressmen's charities that may have more than altruism at heart:

- **The DeLay Foundation for Kids and Rio Bend:** With three foster children of his own, Tom DeLay loves to show up for the photo ops as he presents checks to the orphaned kids whom his charities help. To raise money for his do-gooder nonprofits, DeLay frequently hosted golf getaway fundraisers, where the rich (from Bill Gates to the heads of AT&T and ExxonMobil) could meet the powerful (DeLay and his congressional buddies) face to face on the greens. The fundraisers were fabulously successful, raising some $7 million dollars[31] between 2001 and 2005—and of that about $80,000 went to organizations that worked with kids; more money was set aside to build a housing division for foster families. Meanwhile, more than $600,000 went to holding the fundraisers.[32]

- **U.S. Family Network:** Set up by DeLay's right-hand man Ed Buckham in 1996, when Buckham was still the congressman's chief of staff, this nonprofit group created to advocate for family values, economic prosperity, and the well-being of the United States got its very first check—for $15,000—from one of Jack Abramoff's tribal clients, and more kept coming: Russian oil tycoons kicked in a million alone.

Over five years, $3 million was raised, a third of which went to Buck-ham and his wife for, well, hmm, they did lobby to shoot down a bill that would have further regulated cigarettes (R. J. Reynolds quickly coughed up a $100,000 donation to the nonprofit)[33] and they bought a few radio spots (denouncing Democrats) and oh, yeah, they did a lot of traveling—more than a quarter million dollars' worth—and a fair amount of decorating too, dropping $20,000 for a vase, another $60,000 for a painting.[34] After the Federal Elections Commission started sniffing them out in 2001, suspecting the nonprofit of funnel-ing money from the national Republican Party, the USFN hastily shut down. In 2004, the commission slapped the National Republi-can Congressional Committee with a $280,000 fine for shooting $500,000 into this nonprofit, which used the money to attack Demo-crats.[35]

- **World of Hope:** Heart surgeon/Senate Majority Leader Bill Frist, who is so beholden to (or should we say deeply appreciative of the fine work of) certain pharmaceutical companies that he slipped an amendment into the USA Patriot Act shielding drugmaker Eli Lilly from lawsuits for a defective vaccine linked to autism, set up his charity World of Hope for a most worthy cause: to battle AIDS. The charity took in $4.4 million at a 2004 fundraiser (conveniently held at the Republican convention) and gave some $3 million of that mostly to evangelical AIDS groups that preach abstinence.[36] No surprise that one of the most generous donors to Dr. Frist's cause was Eli Lilly. Guess it shouldn't be a surprise either that the charity employs the wife of a congressional colleague, and that the charity also paid $450,000 to political consultants—who are appar-ently necessary these days to help battle HIV, although they might also come in real handy for shining up Frist's image for a possible run in the 2008 presidential election.[37]

Giving to charities may indeed stem from altruism, but more and more often it's just another way for lobbyists and corporations to grease the wheels of the government. Firms might present a heavily zeroed check to a lawmaker's favorite cause when lobbying for changes to the laws that benefit their clients; donations to congressmen's charities may also help to grab a slice of the federal fund pie. The most common way to score a project is to propose it to a legislator—perhaps with an envelope of checks. And legislators may then slip in funding for special projects as "earmarks" in the budget—setting aside millions of dollars for unauthorized projects that benefit a legislator's district, his most generous contributors, or his pals.

Lobbyists who have a knack for snatching money during the divvying up of the annual budget can quickly grow wealthy. Specifically, what they're angling for is that earmark: a short amendment tacked on a bill during budget meetings that allots money for a specific project—maybe $140,000 to program the White House computers, maybe $80,000 for a University of Michigan science program, maybe a million for a shrimp farming experiment in Oregon, maybe $60,000 for a community pool. These grants and awards for contracts are slipped in the back door with little scrutiny, and they eat up billions of taxpayer dollars a year. According to the government Congressional Research Service in 2005, earmarks—15,877 of them—cost taxpayers $48 billion. But even though we were paying for those freebies, until recently it was hard to track down who was getting earmarks or how much they were for. And budget bills are laden with stinkers:

- $500,000 of transportation budget awarded for a teapot museum in Sparta, South Carolina[38]

- $4 million of defense budget to study the genes behind hibernation[39]

- $1 million of defense budget to study the brown tree snake[40]

- $5.5 million of defense budget to improve waste removal of the boondoggle C-135 transport[41]

- $3 million for New York's Center for Grape Genetics[42]

- $196,000 to control geese in New York[43]

- $400,000 to study bear DNA (the fourth time the project was awarded a federal grant)[44]

- $250,000 to research turf grass in West Virginia[45]

- $380,000 to help protect sunflowers in the Dakotas from black-birds[46]

- $50 million for an indoor rain forest in Coralville, Iowa (that was never built)[47]

- $5.2 million for Philadelphia's Please Touch Me Museum[48]

- $950,000 for a museum parking lot in Nebraska[49]

- $50,000 for the Capitol Hill baseball and softball league[50]

The 2006 winner of the eyebrow-raising earmark award: $2.1 billion for ten cargo planes—Boeing's C-17—that the Department of Defense doesn't want. Passed in September 2006 as part of an emergency defense spending bill, the ten planes were apparently earmarked simply to help out Republican senator Jim Talent from Missouri, where Boeing makes those aircraft. His reelection was looking iffy, so fellow Republicans helped him score with his people back home.[51] All those billions were in vain: Talent still lost the 2006 race.

The sixty-five legislators who sit on appropriations committees in the House and the twenty-eight "appropriators" in the Senate rake in more campaign funding than the average lawmaker—as so many interests want lawmakers to see things their way and slip their projects into the budget. Desirous outsiders also send in thousands of lobbyists to cajole lawmakers with free trips or contributions, whatever it takes.

And the lobbyists' job is to increase the odds that their clients' projects are picked. They often hit up legislators from their clients' state—since legislators wave these federal grants around to show the folks back home what a great job they're doing. Then again, it always helps if a lobbyist is friendly with, say, the chairman of an appropriations committee or subcommittee—so powerful they are dubbed "The Cardinals"—and lately they sure seem swayable. Take, for instance, Alaska's grandfather-like senator, Ted Stevens. (See "Shoveling Dough into the Great White Hole," page 25.)

Rep. Don Young (R-Alaska), who heads the House Transportation and Infrastructure Committee, single-handedly stuffed the 2005 transportation bill with nearly $1 billion worth of unauthorized projects, mostly benefiting Alaskans.

Newt Gingrich had a hand in creating the current tide of lobbyists washing up on Capitol Hill: earmarks had been around before— Ronald Reagan protested that nearly 150 littered the transportation bill—but back then many projects were actually assigned through the relevant departments. Gingrich opened the door to flagrantly using these giveaways as a political tool. When the Republicans took over Congress in 1994, Gingrich, who as Speaker of the House was the chamber's most powerful leader, directed the House Appropriations Committee to add more earmarks, particularly from GOP lawmakers who faced a tough race—and the number has skyrocketed since. From about 4,126 earmarks in 1994 when the boom began, there were almost 16,000 earmarks in 2005. The amount of money jumped as well—from $30 billion in 1994 to more than $47 billion in 2005.[52]

SLICING UP THE PORK

Lawmaking is rarely neat and tidy. As Germany's first chancellor, Otto von Bismarck, warned, "It's best not to see either laws or sausages being made." But the budget ordeal boggles the mind—and it eats up months of every year as legislators debate the details of the federal budget, all of which ultimately come weighted down with earmarks. To put it very simply, the process begins the first Monday in February when the president submits a budget request to the House. Twelve appropriation subcommittees on matters from homeland security to agriculture begin debating in the House over the budget amounts and the projects, and then they punt their suggestions to the Senate, which does the same and punts it back. Then the subcommittees in both chambers haggle over the exact amounts again—tacking on earmarks along the way—and then both the House and Senate committees meet in a congressional conference, where a dozen battle over differences and add thousands more pet projects. Then the hammered-out version of this bill is voted on in both House and Senate and shot back to the president to sign into law.

By the time final drafts of the budget bills arrive for that final vote in Congress, sometimes running over a thousand pages and weighing over ten pounds, nobody really knows or cares what's in them anymore, particularly with regard to earmarks. And that means many billions of dollars go out the door with a yawn and a shrug.

Making lawmaking even more of a crapshoot: most of these grants and contract awards are inserted only just before the floor vote, and our elected representatives don't have time to read them. Predictably, the public isn't informed of what these projects are. A new law, signed in September 2006, begins to rectify that problem: the Coburn-Obama Transparency Act requires that the federal government create an Internet website that spells out exactly who are the beneficiaries of earmarks, and how much funding they are receiving for their projects. The bad news: with the likes of Ted Stevens running around, who knows how much of a difference that law will make.

SHOVELING DOUGH INTO THE GREAT WHITE HOLE

Ted Stevens, the diminutive Republican from Alaska, has been tottering around the Senate since 1968. His big break came in 1997: he's chaired or co-chaired the Senate Appropriations Committee ever since, and also heads the appropriations subcommittee with the biggest budget—defense. He's most famous for his "Bridge to Nowhere"—along with Alaska Representative Don Young, he earmarked $223 million of federal funding for a bridge to a sparsely populated Alaskan island, even though the ferry ride takes but seven minutes; he became infamous for threatening to quit the Senate if anybody diverted that nonessential bridge funding to aid post-Katrina reconstruction. And the odd thing about Stevens, say Congress watchers, is that as he's

become one of the most powerful men in the Senate, he's become quite well-to-do.[53] Thanks perhaps to his seat on the appropriations committee, the man who long struggled with money seems to be getting rich, and so does his son; his lobbyist brother-in-law is also apparently better off than before. A few questionable moves:

One of the Capitol's biggest oinkers, Sen. Ted Stevens (R-AK) funnels billions of gold to Alaska, and wants to let telecoms dictate the Internet.

• The Ted Stevens Foundation, a tax-exempt, nonpartisan charity founded by Ted Stevens simply to "assist in educating and informing the public about the career of Senator Ted Stevens," is headed by a lobbyist who happened to be treasurer of Stevens' 2004 senatorial campaign. In an event coordinated by over a dozen K Street lobbyists, the foundation raised some $2 million at a recent $5,000-a-plate fundraiser, which, the *Washington Post* noted, had the "air of a shakedown." Asked the *Post*, "What lobbyist with an interest in appropriations matters would fail to give to Mr. Stevens' charity?" since he had the Senate's final say in doling out federal checks.[54]

• Ted Stevens' Northern Lights PAC impressively contributed almost $200,000 to Republican campaigns in 2004; however, it took more than $400,000 to run it.[55]

• After Stevens kicked $450 million to a housing contractor, the contractor graciously brought Stevens into future deals—making the senator over $700,000 in profits.[56]

• A tribal company that showered it with millions in federal funds moved into a building owned by the senator. Yearly rent: $6 million.[57]

• After handsomely rewarding companies that employed his son as a six-figured consultant for years, Stevens tossed $29 million to the Alaskan Fisheries Marketing Board, which his son chaired.[58]

(Ben Stevens has indirectly benefited from so many of Pappy's earmarks that the FBI recently raided Ben's office—in the Alaskan Senate, where he's now president.)[59]

- When senators Barack Obama (D-Illinois), Tom Coburn (R-Oklahoma), and John McCain (R-Arizona) sponsored a bill in 2006 that demanded that the public be notified of any earmarks that senators were adding to legislation, Stevens secretly blocked it, causing such a ruckus by bloggers and consumer groups that Stevens finally fessed up.

In 2006, Stevens introduced what became known as the "Net neutrality" bill, Internet-rearranging legislation that would have essentially blocked access to websites that didn't pay up to the telecom pipers—a bill that enraged bloggers and companies from Yahoo! and Google to Microsoft and Amazon.com. Illustrating his expertise in Internet matters, an area overseen by the commerce committee, which he heads, Stevens complained that "an Internet was sent" by his staff, but took five days to arrive because "the tubes" were clogged up: "The Internet is not something you just dump something on. It's not a big truck. It's a series of tubes," he patiently explained. "Those tubes can be filled and if they are filled, when you put your message in, it gets in line and it's going to be delayed by anyone that puts into that tube enormous amounts of material."[60]

Senator Ted Stevens isn't under investigation for any ethical misconduct—this is just day-to-day life on the Hill. The guy on appropriations who everybody's looking at is Rep. Jerry Lewis (R–California), the man who looks like a cosmetically touched-up Steve Martin, with an arched eyebrow twist, who now heads the appropriations committee in the House. Now he's ducking for cover in the fallout of the Randy Cunningham conviction, which has led Congress into a collective panic attack, since it has both the public and the Department of Justice looking much more closely at how our budget sausage gets made.

"Mr. Cunningham broke the law in the most egregious way possible for an elected official. He admitted to taking bribes in exchange for

getting special treatment for those who bribed him. He betrayed his oath of office, his constituents, and his fellow members of Congress. I have never been as angry toward anyone in my entire career. Mr. Cunningham was never a close friend, but he was a colleague I trusted to serve the interests of his country. I am grateful that our system worked, and he was caught and is now paying the price for those crimes."

> —Rep. Jerry Lewis in May 2006,[61] apparently forgetting his F-22 maneuvers with Cunningham (see below) and his dizzying entanglement with defense lobbyists in Bill Lowery's law firm (see page 67)

KAMIKAZE CONGRESSMAN RANDY "DUKE" CUNNINGHAM (1991–2005)

The Vietnam fighter pilot who boasted that he'd inspired *Top Gun* was actually discovered by GOP talent scouts: Cunningham's booming commentaries as CNN correspondent during 1991's Persian Gulf War convinced some Republican strategists that the heavy-boozing divorcé belonged in DC; along the way to the House, Cunningham found the Lord. The decorated hero took the 1990 election with the slogan "A Congressman to be proud of"—although "A Congressman to be afraid of" might have fit better, since he got into fisticuffs with colleagues and was known for strong-arming.

Envelopes bulging with cash, boozy nights on yachts, and debauched poker parties were part of the fab life that bribery brought fighter pilot Cunningham after he turned Christian congressman; he recently went crashing through the gates of prison.

Even before 1997, when Cunningham won a spot on the Defense Appropriations Subcommittee, he'd befriended Brent "Mr. Stag Party" Wilkes, a tall, pale, and balding accountant turned defense contractor who hankered to get into document management for the government; defense projects in particular could bring in seven figures or more. Oh, it took a little convincing, but between attending Wilkes' crazy "poker parties" in swanky hotels and jetting around on Wilkes' private plane (and not forgetting the sneaky financial deals—be it cash, contribution, or courtesan, Wilkes dropped $630,000 wooing the Rep.),[62] the congressman shot Wilkes millions in defense projects by writing them into defense spending bills, including one for scanning old documents in Panama, an unneeded project foisted on the Department of Defense. When Wilkes wanted $10 million more, DoD balked, and before you knew it there was hulking Cunningham—alongside California congressman Jerry Lewis, then powerful chair of the defense subcommittee—in front of the TV cameras, making a surprising announcement: out of the blue, they were slashing DoD's budget for a new fighter plane—the adored F-22—by $1.8 billion.[63] It was a waste of taxpayers' dollars, the congressmen said.[64] Defense got the hint, Wilkes got his money, and the duo in the House restored funding for the plane.

What took Cunningham down: defense contractor Mitchell Wade, ex-Pentagon intel man, who bought the Rep's house for $800,000 more than its value and kept him well supplied with Persian rugs and nineteenth-century armoires in return for contracts, including a $140,000 gig for Wade's company to program White House computers—for which Wade rewarded Cunningham by (among other things) letting him live on his forty-four-foot yacht. Someone got wise to Wade's presents and the occasional envelope of cash slipped to Cunningham: under pressure, Wade turned state informant, and everything for Cunningham nosedived from there. "The Congressman to be Ashamed Of" pleaded guilty in November 2005 to accepting bribes of $2.4 million, and was sentenced to eight years and four months in prison, which for Cunningham, now dying of prostate cancer, will probably be a life sentence.[65]

And as with Abramoff, the Cunningham scandal appears to be leading to a much bigger one. Among those whom the feds have great interest in: Congressman Jerry Lewis, now wielding more muscle than ever as chair of the entire House Appropriations Committee.

Now that's an understatement: "No other entity in the Congress has done more to reform earmarks than the House Appropriations Committee."
    —Rep. Jerry Lewis (R-California), who heads the powerful committee

*that turned in more than 15,000 earmarked projects with the 2006
budget.[66] Lewis considers himself a reformer because he's limited
the number of earmarks to five per congressman per bill.*

*"There are some perfectly fine earmarks. The fundamental problem is
that nobody knows if [an earmarked project] is a good idea or a bad
idea. And that is not an accident. Congress doesn't want to know."*
—*Winslow Wheeler, former defense appropriations aide to Sen. Pete
Domenici (R-New Mexico)[67]*

For years, almost everybody ignored the slime oozing across Capitol
Hill. Congressmen appeared not to notice how some lawmakers' charities were being used as personal piggy banks and vehicles to pay
spouses and how money was moving in mysterious ways through tax-
exempt organizations. How laws were being passed and investigations
begun, only to benefit generous campaign contributors. How certain
lobby firms appeared to be running rackets with certain congressmen.
How Jack Abramoff was working the House, handing out box seats to
basketball games and flying lawmakers on overseas golf trips to persuade them to vote for his clients in ways that smacked of bribery. How
certain GOP leaders were stepping on lobbyists to cough up more cash,
and threatening ruin for those who donated much to Democrats. In
short, how the House was being strong-armed by something that very
much resembled a mafia. And Tom DeLay, the majority leader from Sug-
arland, Texas, was one who appeared to be very much involved.

But we might never have learned what Majority Leader DeLay or his
dear friend lobbyist Jack Abramoff were up to had it not been for two
people: a congressman who had been gerrymandered out of a job and
a twenty-five-year-old in Louisiana who was mystified when he looked
at his tribe's accounting books.

TOM DELAY

You can call DeLay many things, but wimp isn't one of them, and when
the five-foot-seven, blue-eyed Texan with a winsome smile is ticked off
he shows it. And that's why the evangelical exterminator put down his

rat poison: in 1984, he rolled into DC to kill the vermin in the capital, starting with the Environmental Protection Agency—"the Gestapo," he called it after the EPA banned his favorite pesticide. And "the Gestapo" was but one symbol of the regulation-happy rule of Democrats he sought to erase. A hard-core "New Republican," DeLay hatched plots for GOP ascendancy, gerrymandered Texas voting districts to favor Republicans, and helped the White House get almost everything that it wanted, including the war in Iraq. Just as important, along with lawmaker Newt Gingrich, political strategist Grover Norquist, and lobbyist Jack Abramoff, he helped create the GOP steamroller—transforming the party from a dissatisfied outsider

The most ballsy of the House slimesters, "gangsta' Rep." Tom DeLay helped make the House a sewer of sell-outs, while preaching that he walked with the Lord.

to a ball-breaking insider, determined to keep the hold on power, even if it took financially slamming the Democrats' kneecaps to do it. DeLay didn't much hide his closeness with paid persuaders, and he tried to rule them—and to some extent did: his demands rang out loud and clear. First, they had to toss into the kitty: he badgered lobbyists to fork over big checks if they wanted to feast at his or any Republican's table, sounding rather *Godfather*ish as he admonished, in the mid-1990s, when the GOP ruled both sides of Congress, "If you want to play in our [Republican] revolution, you have to live by our rules."[68] And second, he demanded that paid persuasion become an exclusively GOP profession. He insisted that lobbying firms hire only Republicans—those firms that didn't go 100 percent GOP would be denied access to congressional power players, he warned, and he tried to push GOP legislators into opening the door only to lobbyists from the party. And the so-called K Street Project (see page 100)—which hasn't yet died—became yet another means both to tighten the power circle and to strangle the money to Democrats, this time by shutting off income from lobbying, the profession that bred overnight millionaires.

Beyond boosting the party, DeLay pumped up his personal clout and funding abilities, warmly inviting those with deeply corporate interests to guide the lawmaking process along (and it sure didn't hurt that they tossed in checks to his PAC or his charity or did something that made it worthwhile: "It's sort of, 'Scratch my back, and I'll scratch yours,'" he told the *Washington Post* in 1999).[69] He brazenly held a 2002 fundraiser on a golf course with energy execs while Congress was considering energy legislation, and he flew a few dozen of his favorite lobbyists to Las Vegas to thank them for all the dough they'd shot his way. He outrageously cajoled a fellow congressman, Rep. Nick Smith, promising generous support for his son's upcoming run for a House seat if Smith switched his vote on Medicare.[70] Even if DeLay was loud and reckless, he had a gift for attracting big money. According to Democracy 21, he raised $12.6 million between 2000 and 2002 alone.[71] Over the years, DeLay scared up hundreds of millions to fund campaigns for other Republicans, particularly those at serious risk of losing a race. The underdogs who were elected were thus indebted to him and fueled his rise. As majority whip in 1995, he hammered Republicans to vote as a unified GOP bloc. As majority leader from 2004 to 2006 he could help determine which bills made it to the floor (technically the bailiwick of the House Speaker) and ensure that projects of his pals were federally funded. Supporting the White House, he tried to strip the courts of power by trying to weaken their word—the rejection of a court ruling regarding the Terri Schiavo ordeal being but one stab at the judicial branch—and he openly expressed his desire to Christianize the United States,[72] right down to holding daily prayer meetings in his House office.

And given the money and favors that Jack Abramoff brought his way, he helped oust the lobbyist—in fact, some say that Abramoff's winning card was DeLay, whose vote he could count on and who was happy to champion the lobbyist's cause. To aid one of Abramoff's clients, a Republican running for the governor's seat in Guam, DeLay demanded that the Department of the Interior launch an investigation of the incumbent governor, whom he asserted was crooked.[73] After Abramoff flew DeLay to the Mariana Islands to meet with a clothing manufacturer accused of running sweatshops, DeLay helped to kill a bill that would have boosted the island's minimum wage and enforced labor laws. He blocked legislation that would have slapped more taxes on tribal casinos, and he campaigned on the part of Abramoff— or rather the Coushatta tribe—not to allow a nearby tribe to open a competing casino.

The list goes on, but what tripped up DeLay was his habit of funneling money from one pot to another: he was burned when he moved corporate money from his PAC to fund elections for Republicans in Texas, which bans corporate money in elections. But his creative financing methods might have continued to be ignored had not DeLay decided to remap the voter districts in Texas in 2003, a move that brought five additional Texas Republicans to Congress the next year. But in the process he erased the district of a Texan Democrat, who loudly cried foul. (See "Indicting DeLay," page 35.)

Despite chronic rule breaking, shady dealing, and monkey business that was becoming harder to ignore, particularly in the House, the ethics committee in that chamber didn't take any action against DeLay or anybody else (except James Traficant, widely disliked by both parties) and there was a reason. A gentlemen's agreement had been struck several years before to ignore the grimy practices so entwined with modern politics. And the disastrous effects of that "ignore screaming conflicts of interest" agreement have been most pronounced in the House of Representatives since Speaker Dennis Hastert (R-Illinois), the flabby-faced GOP hard-liner, took over the coop in 1999, encouraging congressmen to look the other way and bend rules—whether the problems were an indicted leader of the House[74] or a congressman who was "overfriendly" with House pages.

Big surprise that the House turned darker and dodgier under Hastert's guiding light: his own ethics have been questioned. Take, for instance, his involvement with Jack Abramoff, whose restaurant Signatures was site of a June 2003 Hastert fundraiser, where Abramoff's Indian tribe clients shucked out over $21,500 for the Speaker. The next week Hastert wrote a letter to the Interior secretary requesting (as Abramoff had asked him to) that the department block the Jena, a rival tribe, from opening a casino.[75] That wasn't the only time campaign contributions may have influenced his actions, alleges ex-FBI translator Sibel Edmonds. She says that agency tapes of wiretapped Turks contained repeated references to Hastert (calling him Denny Boy) and says that the Turks donated tens of thousands to his campaign, in small amounts, in return for favors, such as Hastert blocking a bill in 2000 that sought to designate the Turkish massacre of Armenians in the 1920s as genocide.[76]

Gagged and Bound to Fail

To get anything done (well, to the extent that they do), both the Senate and House break down into committees and subcommittees overseeing different areas from taxes to natural resources. Lawmakers are always elbowing each other in the race to sit on powerful ones, such as Appropriations or Ways and Means, which controls taxes. But of all the dozens of committees that a legislator can end up on in all of Congress, the most unglamorous and burdensome is the ten-person Committee on Standards of Official Conduct—half Republican, half Democrat—that oversees ethics in the rowdy House of Representatives.

Unlike the theoretically more serious and dignified Senate, the House—chamber of "the people"—is filled with almost-always campaigning legislators, since their terms last only two years. And on this side of Congress, the south side of the Capitol, you find more of the hotheads and loudmouths—which is why nobody really wants to be on the parental board of reining them in. Sitting on the House ethics committee has been even more dreadful lately, since it's become a bipartisan board of eye shutting and ear plugging that illustrates what has gone wrong in the House, even if it turns the stomach. Even though the last few years have been among Congress' most corrupt, the committee hasn't done a whole heckuva lot, having pulled on an impenetrable "hear no evil, see no evil" hood: according to CNN, leadership of both parties made a deal—in 1998.[77] That was the year that loose cannon House Speaker Newt Gingrich (R-Georgia)—the general of 1994's dramatic "Republican Revolution"—slunk out of Congress, after an ethics committee brouhaha over how he was paid for a series of propaganda-like motivation tapes for Republican domination. And the irony was that a decade before the ethics committee did him in, Gingrich had used the ethics committee to shame then House Speaker Jim Wright (D-Texas) out of Congress.

After that they made a pact: the Republicans would not file ethical complaints against the Democrats, and the Democrats would return the favor. And Dennis Hastert made sure the deal stuck.

Indicting DeLay

Chris Bell, a former radio reporter whose long face Is topped with a receding Brillo pad of gray hair, wasn't there for that handshake back in

1998. The Democrat from Texas took a seat in the House of Representatives in 2003, rapidly ascending the ranks to become assistant Democratic House whip (the right hand to the Democrats' number three man) and rating a spot on four committees. But Tom DeLay quickly pulled his plug. In 2003, DeLay went back to Texas for a few days and, with Republicans in the state legislature, he redrew the state voting district map—in a manner that favored Republicans. Bell's voting district was merged with another Democrat-heavy district that usually voted black and did so again in the primaries of 2004, which Bell lost.

The name of Chris Bell (D-TX), doesn't ring one because DeLay redistricted the first-term congressmen out of a district, but Bell blew the whistle.

Gerrymandering, as partisan-motivated remapping of a state's voting districts is called, has one goal in mind: reduce the number of districts the opposition party is able to take. DeLay and other Republicans redrew Texas' twenty-six voting districts—each of which send one congressman to DC—in a manner that slashed the number of

> *Democrats that Texans could send to Congress. DeLay and the gang did this by using one of two techniques: redrawing the voting map so that Democrats became a distinct minority in a given district, or merging two Democrat-dominant districts into one district, with the result that instead of sending two Democrats to Congress, the combined district could send only one. The latter technique was employed on Chris Bell's district, which was redrawn with another Democrat district; in the next primary, the other Democrat took the election.*
>
> *Redrawing the map requires approval of the majority of those in the state legislature. In 2003, when DeLay controversially engineered the redistricting of Texas, many Democrats in the state legislature flew out of Texas, trying to derail the gerrymander by ensuring that the number of votes on the matter weren't enough to make the vote valid. However, DeLay called the FAA, tracked them down, and had them arrested. DeLay's use of a federal agency in a partisan matter was one matter that later brought a slight rap on the wrist from the House ethics committee.*

The remapping of Texas was only one of the things that distressed the freshman congressman about DeLay, whom he considers "the most corrupt politician in America today."[78] He'd already had a good whiff of how DeLay was running his government business, and he had information that, among other stinky deals, DeLay had accepted a $25,000 contribution to one of his PACs from a Kansas energy company called Westar, to which he'd promised "a seat at the table" when a law it was worried about was drawn up.[79] So Chris Bell called up Melanie Sloan, former assistant United States attorney in the District of Columbia, who was so disgusted by what was happening across the capital that she'd started her own organization—Citizens for Responsibility and Ethics in Washington. And she helped him draw up a 187-page complaint against DeLay, formally delivered to the House ethics committee in June 2004.

The June 2004 complaint alleged that Tom DeLay:[80]

- "illegally solicited and accepted political contributions in return for official action"

- "laundered" corporate contributions for the purpose of legislative races in Texas (where corporate contributions are banned)

- "improperly used his office to urge federal agencies to assist in a partisan objective wholly unrelated to his official duties"

When Bell brought that complaint about DeLay to the ethics committee, he did more than break the vow of silence. He turned the spotlight on Congress, which he said was under attack and rife with "serious criminal acts including bribery, extortion, fraud, money laundering and the abuse of power."[81] The complaint at first had little impact—DeLay hollered back that it was all about party politics and that the attempted "character assassination" had "no substance."[82] The majority leader shrugged it all off, saying, "I have ultimate confidence in the ethics committee in doing the right thing"[83]—a fancy way, perhaps, of saying that he was sure they would do nothing, which is precisely what the ethics committee did—at least for the first four months.

In October 2004, the committee finally rebuked Tom DeLay. House Speaker Dennis Hastert soon ousted the committee chair, Joel Hefley (R-Colorado), and replaced several other members with trusted Republicans who more strongly toed the party line.

Even though the complaint received little news play, and GOP leaders laughed it off as a prank of the liberals, Representative Bell and Melanie Sloan had pulled one thread of the tapestry of foul practices that covered not just Congress but much of DC. Shortly thereafter, when a Democrat prosecutor in Texas decided to pursue one of the items in their complaint—about the use of corporate money in the Texas campaign—and began investigating DeLay for money laundering, the thread unraveled that tapestry a bit further.

In September 2005, DeLay was indicted on money-laundering charges in Texas. House rules required that he step down as House majority leader. However, under pressure from the GOP power boys, the ethics committee changed the rules, allowing him to retain his number two position in the House. That caused such a flap that eventually DeLay removed himself from the position.

At around the same time, a young American Indian in Louisiana was poring over a stack of papers, trying to piece together the trail of what had happened to $32 million. He would soon yank on yet another thread that would cause the whole shroud of corruption and deceit to unwind and would shake up—and wake up—the country in the process.

[What You Can Do]

Never mind that some of the most offensive exploiters have been booted. The existing system is the problem. Demand changes—through letters to Congress and op-eds to newspapers and by joining groups that are working for reform. Support the watchdogs:

- **Common Cause** (www.commoncause.org). "We want public officials to have literally millions of American citizens looking over their shoulders at every move they make."

  Started in 1970 by Republican John Gardner (Secretary of Health, Education and Welfare under President Lyndon Johnson), this nonpartisan government watchdog organizes e-mail campaigns that let Congress know when the public is ticked off. Following issues from government reform to ethical breaches to media ownership, Common Cause keeps voters up to date with its reports on the latest eyebrow-raising actions of Congress and the White House.

- **Taxpayers for Common Sense** (www.taxpayer.net). This nonpartisan budget watchdog targets earmarks and questionable congressional appropriations and effectively blows the whistle at ethically challenged moves by lawmakers of both parties.

- **Citizens for Responsibility and Ethics in Washington (CREW)** (www.citizensforethics.org). Started in 2004, Melanie Sloan's outfit is noisy and aggressive and hated by the House of Representatives, which has barred it from filing complaints there. Frustrated that consumer groups weren't achieving enough solid action, the former assistant U.S. attorney slaps lawsuits and formal complaints right and left—as well as hard-hitting reports. Some say she overdoes it, but CREW gets results and ends up with information before anybody else does: CREW sent "Foley page" e-mails to the FBI months before the scandal came out. Sloan also helped pressure DeLay out of office and put the spotlight on Congress' lame ethics committee. Officially nonpartisan, CREW is said by other watchdogs to be funded by Democrats, although feisty Sloan takes whacks at them too.

- **Public Citizen** (www.citizen.org). The nonpartisan government watchdog founded by Ralph Nader tracks money and corruption in the pay-to-play capital. Puts out dozens of stellar reports—documenting exactly what stinks and who's done it—that are required reading for those wanting to understand our current political quagmire. Take a bow.

- **Democracy 21** (www.democracy21.org). Often cited as DC's hardest-working lobbyist to clean up campaign finance, this nonprofit that works "to eliminate the influence of big money in American politics" certainly has its work cut out for it.

- **Citizens Against Government Waste** (www.cagw.org). Founded in 1984, and representing more than one million Americans, this nonprofit is the loudest and most effective in tracking pork-barrel spending and ludicrous earmarks. Best known for its annual *Congressional Pig Book*, it points out all sorts of bizarre uses of taxpayer dollars—from that $234,000 grant to the National Wild Turkey federation (ostensibly to promote hunting the fowl) to the $13.5 million the U.S. gives to Ireland (where the economy was booming the last time we looked) for such projects as running chef schools, to $5.6 million handed over to the alcoholism-studying Gallo Center—funding that mysteriously comes out of the defense budget. One caveat: the group inadvertently points out some projects that sound hilariously wasteful—like the ones for research into waterless toilets—which actually might be beneficial. While admirably documenting secret expenditures about which the public has long been kept in the dark, the book inadvertently illustrates that although government waste is astounding and the lack of scrutiny in handing out grants and noncompetitive federal contracts breeds corruption, not all projects that receive earmarked funds are a joke. The problem remains the noncompetitive manner in which these funds are handed out.

CHAPTER 2

Lobbying Pays

I t may not have the palm trees, the old theaters, and the movie lots, but Washington, DC, can feel a lot like Hollywood. Whatever corner you turn, whether dashing out for croissants on Dupont Circle or strolling along the grassy mall, you're always running into celebrities—the think tank analyst you saw last night on CNN, the official on the cover of that day's *Washington Post*, the senator who was just getting grilled by Bill O'Reilly, or maybe O'Reilly himself. Lately your chances of bumping into a living legend in DC are far better. After making that final shove away from their government desks, politicians and officials don't seem to be leaving: many are now professional persuaders with DC law firms, fattening up their wallets by championing causes of the very corporations and industries they used to lord over, regulate, and legislate. Two decades ago, 3 percent of our former lawmakers became lobbyists; now more than one in three do. According to Public Citizen's Congress Watch, of the legislators who left the Hill since 1998, a whopping 43 percent are now hired guns.[1]

Frenetic by day, when swanky restaurants are brimming with VIPs, and lawmakers and lobbyists, watchdogs and reporters descend upon Capitol Hill, the center of the city mostly clears out at night, since many government employees head for Virginia and Maryland after work. The allure of the suburbs rose sharply during the 1960s when DC's streets swelled with millions of protesters. Martin Luther King led peaceful marches on Washington, starting in 1963, demanding equality for blacks, but the calm he commanded vanished in the riots of 1968, which erupted when King was shot down. In DC alone, that year's riots destroyed twelve hundred buildings, injured over one thousand people, and left twelve dead—and much of the downtown was left in rubble for decades. Flag-burning Vietnam protesters also marched on the capital, hurling insults at officials and lawmakers every time they ducked out; in March 1971, radical students of the Weather Underground Organization detonated a bomb in the Capitol Building to protest the growing Vietnam War, and the next year they exploded another in the Pentagon. Crack cocaine rattled the city in the 1980s and '90s—even Mayor (now Congressman) Marion Berry was popped—and homicides soared: Washington became known as the murder capital of the world. No longer the world's most dangerous city—although the 9/11 attack made it feel like more of a terrorist target—its vibrant nightlife is beckoning some to move back. But DC remains split into posh areas interspersed with the dodgy. The northwest, which contains the villagelike Georgetown of colonial-style red-brick townhouses along shaded lanes, is the trendiest zip code in town, and the deep southeast is the riskiest.

As you stroll along K Street—a boulevard a few blocks northwest of the White House where a long line of bland 1960s-style box buildings is now broken up by swanky bars and posh white-linen restaurants—you might see Bob Dole, the former Senate majority leader from Kansas who was agribusiness' big boy on the Hill. He's now a lobbyist for countries from Malawi to Indonesia, even going to bat for Dubai Ports—but not to worry: he's promised that he's not using his position to sway his wife, Elizabeth Dole, who now holds a Senate seat.

According to the Boston Globe, *two bills before Congress in 2003—Medicare and energy—were so important to vested interests that corporations, businesses, and special interest groups "spent a staggering $799,091,391 in efforts to influence lawmakers, frequently employing former members of Congress, former staff members, and relatives of lawmakers to lobby on the bills."[2] Tellingly, those who spent the biggest money usually got what they wanted.*

AW, COME ON, PLEASE DADDY, MOMMY, HONEY

What do the son of Sen. Barbara Boxer (D-California), the daughter of Rep. Curt Weldon (R-Pennsylvania), the brother of former representative Tom DeLay (R-Texas), the wife of Sen. Ted Stevens (R-Alaska), and the three sons and son-in-law of Sen. Harry Reid (D-Nevada) have in common? Along with the offspring, wives, husbands, and in-laws of more than two dozen other legislators, they're lobbyists.

- **Rep. Roy Blunt** (R-Missouri): His son represents Philip Morris (now called Altria since the tobacco company merged with Kraft Foods) and so does his lobbyist wife—and Roy's been helpful to the company, his largest campaign contributor; he even tried to tack on an amendment to the Homeland Security bill to prevent cigarette sales over the Internet.[3]
- **Rep. John Murtha** (D-Pennsylvania): His brother's lobbying firm had a banner year in 2005, pulling in more than $20 million worth of contracts for its defense clients.[4] By the way, Murtha sits on the House Appropriations Committee and the Subcommittee on Defense.
- **Sen. Trent Lott** (R-Mississippi): Son Chester works for the hotshot Livingston Group, representing telecoms and utilities.
- **Rep. Billy Tauzin** (R-Louisiana): His son Billy Jr. is an in-house lobbyist for BellSouth, which isn't such a big deal now that Billy Sr. left his seat in the House, but what was pretty screwy is he tried to hand over that seat to Junior.
- **Rep. Curt Weldon** (R-Pennsylvania): The FBI found it fishy that daughter Karen, twenty-eight, was paid $1 million by Russian businessmen when she was green to the game. Raided her home weeks before Dad's election; Pops lost.

Former attorney general John Ashcroft recently set out his lobbying shingle with the Ashcroft Group. After the former head of the Department of Justice lobbied his former underlings at the Department of Justice, they gave a bright green light for a big-time acquisition to his client Oracle. Now his group also represents data-mining firm ChoicePoint (linked to the 2000 Florida elections flap), defense company General Dynamics, an Israeli aircraft company, and more than a dozen more.[5] In what is now a bona fide trend, Spencer Abraham—U.S. energy secretary until 2005—now lobbies for energy companies and he also rah-rahs for French nuclear firm Areva, which cashed in big time from his decisions as the Department of Energy's nuclear-promoting head; the energy outfit was so taken by Abraham's work when he was an official that Areva now pays him handsomely to sit as chairman of its board. And owlish Robert Blackwill, who resigned from his gig as ambassador to India, is now making far more representing the country as president of lobbying firm Barbour Griffith & Rogers.

SPIN, BABY, SPIN: THE REVOLVING DOOR

Never mind that it's a raging conflict of interest—the people who make laws or hold high office keep on spinning out into the arms of the people they once regulated (or vice versa) in the quickly revolving door that is further blending business with government and making DC even smellier. Just a few who moved from the Capitol to lobby firms:

- **Bob Livingston** (R-Louisiana): Chairman of the House Appropriations Committee starting in 1995 when the GOP-run House first began going earmark crazy, he bolted out of the House in 1998, after *Hustler* magazine got wind of Livingston's extramarital affair, which sort of weakened the case to impeach President Clinton over his tryst with an intern. The next year, Livingston started up the Livingston Group, quickly filling its offices with a half dozen former representatives. Arms manufacturers drop huge wads of money on this experienced general of the battle over defense earmarks, who represents, among others, Northrop Grumman. He spreads the wealth, but, true to the ideals of the K Street Project (see page 100), he keeps the riches within the GOP. Between his family and his firm's two PACs, he showered Republican candidates with half a million dollars between 2000 and 2004.[6]
- **Bill Paxon** (R-New York): A big GOP supporter—he and lobbyist wife Susan Molinari have contributed more than $173,000 to congressional candidates[7] (all Republican)—as well as a boon to Sen. Ted Stevens' noble causes, the former Republican congressman from New York (a role also held by Molinari) was also a Pioneer in

the 2004 Bush-Cheney campaign. It all helps him and his firm, Akin Gump Strauss Hauer & Feld, to successfully battle against army base closures across the country. Defense is another specialty: Boeing's signed him up. He could be in trouble if Newt Gingrich makes a run for the White House and takes it: Paxon led a rebellion against Gingrich in 1997 and when it failed, Paxon made a quick career change.

- **Tom Daschle** (D-South Dakota): The once-powerful Senate majority leader was shoved out of his seat in 2004 (the U.S. Chamber of Commerce took credit) and swung over to K Street, where his wife, Linda, a former top FAA official, has been flying high for years, representing, among others, Lockheed Martin.
- **William Lowery** (R-California): Winner of the Most Bounced Checks Award—he and his wife wrote over three hundred rubber ones on the House bank when he was a representative—Lowery lost his seat to Randy "Duke" Cunningham in 1992. But he maintains a very close friendship with Rep. Jerry Lewis, who now chairs the all-important House Appropriations Committee. Besides vacationing with his congressman friend, Lowery also made sure Lewis got a big chunk of the more than $200,000 Lowery contributed to congressional campaigns from 1998 to 2005, of which 99.5 percent went to Republicans.[8]

And there are hundreds of others, from Vic Fazio (D-California) to Sen. J. Bennett Johnston (D-Louisiana, Johnston & Associates); and at least fifty of these former lawmakers lobby for defense companies and are making more than ever thanks to the skyrocketing federal defense budget.

Former members of Congress have more going for them than face recognition. They have more access than anybody else heading up to Capitol Hill because they retain their old privileges. These lobbyists can chat up their former colleagues in the gym or the dining room or even on the floors of both chambers.

A snoozy and unglamourous zip code until the 1990s, K Street and environs is now flash, class, and glitz with designer eateries and deluxe steak houses that draw the town's platinum Amex club. In front of the caricature-wrapped walls at the Palm, you might find good old ex-congressman Billy Tauzin (R-Louisiana) digging into a lobster or juicy steak, much easier to afford with his new job. The heavy-browed Cajun from Louisiana chaired the House Energy and Commerce Committee, most famously ushering through the 2003 Medicare bill—for which he was publicly praised by the president. A year later, Tauzin switched offices—and became president and CEO and general all-around promoter of PhRMA, the trade association that heavily lobbied him while he was in office (and along with other drug companies gave him $91,000 in 2002 alone).[9] Changing jobs wasn't a bitter pill to swallow: his annual salary is rumored to be some $2 million. Americans pay more for drugs than anyone else, thanks to laws, such as Tauzin's Medicare bill that bars any government control of prices. In 2003, PhRMA was nearly frantic over a bill that would have allowed reimportation of drugs from Canada, where they are far cheaper. Any drugs brought in would probably be counterfeit, PhRMA loudly warned, while hissing at Canada for passing on its government-controlled discount prices. Along with individual drugmakers such as Eli Lilly, PhRMA turned to lobbyists, tossing $720,000 at Alexander Strategy Group alone.[10] One of ASG's lobbyists, former DeLay aide Tony Rudy, lured the Traditional Values Coalition (sometimes called Rent-a-God) into joining the war to fight over-the-border drugs. Using a letter penned by Rudy—and relying on mysterious funding—the Traditional Values Coalition worked the pro-life crowd into a tither fretting that abortion-inducing drugs could be smuggled in from the Great White North.[11]

CORPORATE GUILDS

In a more romantic era, they'd have been called guilds, but modern trade associations do oh so much more these days than build fancy headquarters. They run lobbying operations, they host political fundraisers, they network, they work inside connections—and whether about taxes, profit-shrinking regulations, or class action suits, when these high economic achievers collectively roar they get heard; lately all it takes is a mew. A few to note:

- **Pharmaceutical Research and Manufacturers of America (PhRMA):** Formerly aggressive to the point of mean-spiritedness—the PhRMA website skewered authors who dared suggest that the cost of developing new drugs was a penny less than the $800 million figure that PhRMA touted—this well-moneyed association of drugmakers is trying to "consumer-friendlify" its image, which is part of Tauzin's vision; the group is also working with the U.S. Chamber of Commerce to try to get more workers to take antidepressants, which can enhance productivity, says PhRMA. The wallet behind the smile is tossing out major bucks: PhRMA alone sent out 136 paid persuaders and spent more than $16 million on lobbying to ensure passage of the 2003 Medicare bill (using fake grassroots groups such as United Seniors to confuse people).[12] All together the drug industry wound up paying more than 820 hired hands, spending over $108 million to ensure billions in spending on drugs, to prevent any price controls, and to effectively slam the door on importing drugs from Canada.[13]

- **U.S. Telecom Association (USTA):** Throwing gazillions into the Net neutrality debate, this group wants the Internet to be "tiered," requiring that we pay for "premium access" that today is free. With Ted Stevens' bill stymied in Congress, this trade association is unleashing its force on state legislatures and will be certain to reappear back on Capitol Hill.

- **Edison Electric Institute (EEI):** Headed by Thomas Kuhn, this association of electricity producers zings with lightning rod ideas like dropping most regulations and allowing utilities to voluntarily comply with requests to cut greenhouse gases. These days, they're getting what they want—including government funding to help them return to nuclear. Works closely with Nuclear Energy Institute (see chapter 4).

- **American Petroleum Institute (API):** Headed by Vice President Cheney's good pal Red Cavaney, API should be pumped up by all the favors recently bestowed upon it: the feds dropped the royalties companies pay on oil they take from federal lands, forgot to collect royalties that were due, lowered air quality standards at refineries, and this government just wouldn't dream of imposing price ceilings or a windfall tax on the industry's multibillion-dollar profits. But thus far it hasn't been able to crack open the Arctic National Wildlife Refuge in Alaska or the coastal waters in the Gulf of Mexico. Just as disappointing for them: not getting an item into the 2005 Energy Policy Act would shield them from damages associated with gasoline additive MTBE, a toxin that has leaked into drinking water systems. Not to worry: this association hasn't given up trying, and in 2006 lobbyists were helping lawmakers write up bills for the remainder of API's wish list.

- **American Medical Association (AMA):** The original fretters about smoking, AMA is now pained over the high cost of insurance—which they blame on malpractice suits from trial lawyers, though some studies say the insurance system itself is more to blame.[14]

- **Motion Picture Association of America (MPAA):** Piracy, copyright infringement, and file-sharing sites are its enemies; it is scoring new successes in shutting down some Internet download sites. Once headed by flashy Jack Valenti, the association is now led by Daniel Glickman, secretary of agriculture under Clinton. That the group dared choose a Democrat as its head brought a storm of threats from DeLay and others trying to give the GOP control of K Street. The words weren't empty: within months, DeLay and his House cronies deleted a tax credit for the movie biz worth $1.5 billion. Ouch.

Heading south, past the curving bar of singles hot spot DC Coast (where the fare is Cajun), beyond the gigantic glass wine cube storing three thousand bottles of vino at Charlie Palmer Steak (where customers order drinks from an oversized PalmPilot), but not quite as far as the Peasant Restaurant (which took over Signatures, the glam "grilled cheese and foie gras sandwich" dining establishment run by Jack Abramoff)—you might find Thomas Kuhn digging into the caviar at the restaurant called 701 Pennsylvania Avenue: his office in the trade association Edison Electric Institute sits right above it in a striking edifice that is a crescent of columns.

> One way to advertise power and wealth in DC is to open a chic restaurant. Abramoff, who ran swanky Signatures, where steaks rang up at $74, wasn't alone. Haley Barbour—of Barbour Griffith & Rogers—cooked up the snazzy Caucus Room with Tommy Boggs of Patton Boggs. The colors dazzle: red velvet chairs, blue velvet curtains, and yellow walls—and it's filled with the lunchtime back-slapping of hired guns.

Boyish, low-key Kuhn, who has a dash of Tom Cruise in his appearance, is the most powerful guy in DC—electricity-wise at least. A buddy of George W. Bush's since they were classmates at Yale, Kuhn is a cash magnet and proved himself a financial heavy lifter early in the Bush campaign—devising the idea of creating an elite "Pioneer Club" for those who raised contributions in the six figures. Shooting out memos to utility heads nationwide soliciting Bush campaign donations, Kuhn and Edison Electric Institute rated high on the political chit-o-meter when they charged in with nearly $200,000 for the presidential race.

Plucked as an energy advisor for the Bush transition team, Kuhn also found the door open when Cheney started up an Energy Task Force in January 2001; the veep even swung by the ultramodern digs of the Edison Electric Institute, personally asking members what they wanted written into the national energy bill—and pretty much every little old wish was addressed in the resultant energy policy.

Between the connections and the cash—EEI also contributed $200,000 to congressional candidates in 2004—it's paid off. Kuhn has been able to softly convince lawmakers and officials to lower standards for emissions of mercury, to loosen standards for assorted pollutants, and to simplify the process of firing up new nuclear plants. Sometimes all it took was a phone call to the White House to get his mission accomplished—as when in early 2001, Kuhn advised the still-fresh-from-Texas president that he'd better ditch a certain campaign promise about climate change. Bush's vow to limit carbon dioxide emissions—linked to global warming—wasn't playing at all well with Edison Electric's members, Kuhn warned.[15] And shortly thereafter, when Haley Barbour—a Bush Pioneer himself—made a follow-up call, that promise to voters to make a dent in emissions of greenhouse gases had pretty much gone up in smoke.

SHINY, HAPPY K-STREET STARS

- **Kenneth Kies** (Clark Consulting Federal Policy Group and others): Corporations, such as General Electric, just love him: GE alone paid the lobbyist more than $5.3 million[16] to help ram a corporate tax cut bill through Congress in 2004—which will save corporations some $170 billion over the next decade—but Kies ain't no pal of the common man. One of his star achievements was persuading Congress to pass a synthetic fuel bill that sucks up more than $1 billion and up to $4 billion out of the Treasury every year.[17] The problem isn't the idea—it's how Kies convinced Congress to hand out huge tax credits to companies doing pretty much zip to develop alternative fuels, except pouring diesel on coal and calling the result synthetic.[18] According to *Time*, the scam is so popular that Marriott Hotels shoveled out $46 million to buy four such "synfuel" plants—for which the company receives an annual tax deduction of $159 million.[19] Predictably, Kies is a big roller in the contributions department, raising millions for the GOP over the years and slapping down over $100,000 on the Bush-Cheney horse in 2004. He's also Mr. Moneybags to Congress, standing at the number five spot on the list of most generous lobbyists; with his wife, also a lobbyist, he's plunked nearly $300,000 into election piggy banks since 2000—92 percent to Republicans.[20]

- **Dan Mattoon** (Podesta Mattoon): A major GOP player (he's a close friend of ex-House speaker Dennis Hastert and advisor to Rep. Roy Blunt), Mattoon represents Lockheed Martin, Altria (Philip Morris Tobacco and Kraft Foods), and the Science Coalition—a group of five dozen universities reliant on earmarks. Mattoon, a generous contributor to congressional Republicans, was among the high-octane lobbyists who met with Tom DeLay in 2004, when DeLay demanded that K Street's paid persuaders cough up far more to the GOP election kitty. Well, DeLay couldn't point a finger at Mattoon: he's kicked more than $300,000 to campaigns of Congress members between 1998 and 2005, making him K Street's second highest individual giver.[21] And 96 percent of that amount went to Republicans.[22]

- **Stewart Van Scoyoc** (Van Scoyoc Associates): He's the King of Earmarks, snatching them for universities, small towns, and security companies, and of course that entails sweetening relations with legislators by showering them with campaign contributions. He leads in that department, too, being the lobbyist who has steered most to legislators' campaigns—a whopping $339,000 between 1998 and 2005, of which three-quarters went to Republicans.[23]

- **Denny Miller** (Denny Miller Association): Defense is his bag—he represents pretty much everybody, but Boeing is his main squeeze. His lobbying nearly resulted in a taxpayer boondoggle: he convinced Congress to lease Boeing refueling planes for $30 billion, which would have cost far more than buying them—and it nearly went through. We've got to wonder if Miller, who served on the staff of Sen. Henry Jackson from Washington along with Richard Perle and other neocons, had anything to do with Perle's editorial in the *Wall Street Journal* endorsing that iffy Boeing deal. Speculation aside, Miller and his lobbyist wife, Susan, shot more than $293,000 to congressional candidates' coffers from 1998 to 2005, more than half of which went to Democrats.[24]

But a few of K Street's most famous mugs don't show up around here much anymore. Haley Barbour—the silver–haired heavy-drawlin' powerhouse of a lawyer who brought riches to the GOP when he headed the Republican National Committee (1993–97)—was among those who rode the first big wave of the paid persuader craze. After leaving the GOP's fundraising arm in 1996, he returned to his law firm, this time heavily lobbying for the tobacco and booze companies that had given so much to the Grand Old Party. His clout and his successes made his house so famous—he was called Washington's "most powerful lobbyist"—that he sold off the firm for $20 million in stock to the Interpublic Group, a giant PR conglomerate that illustrates the new trend of pulling lobbying contributions and PR makeovers under one roof. He then headed down to Mississippi, to sit in the governor's chair. Some say he may return to DC: he's rumored to be considering a run for the 2008 presidential race.

Some former fixtures haven't met with such a happy ending. At least half a dozen former millionaires are glaring in the direction of Louisiana, no doubt cursing the day in May 2003 when David Sickey, a quiet, somber twenty-something, won a seat on the governing board of the Coushatta tribe.

THE GNARLY ABRAMOFF AFFAIR

First, the principal cast of characters:

- **David Sickey:** The Coushatta tribal member cried foul, not knowing that he was about to unwrap a scandal that would show us the cancer in DC.

David Sickey, the man who exposed Abramoff's racket, says "ordinary citizens need to be more involved with government."

- **Lovelin Poncho:** Head of Coushatta tribal council, he authorized enormous payments to lobbyists, PACs, and politicians' charities often without tribal OK.

- **Jack Abramoff:** Working with Reps. Tom DeLay and Bob Ney, among others, the superlobbyist was more of a con man and a gangster, laundering money, ripping off clients, and ultimately, inadvertently exposing how corrupt DC can be. (See "If I Were a Rich Man," page 61.)

- **Michael Scanlon:** DeLay's former press secretary, pretty boy Scanlon left Capitol Hill to start Capitol Ventures, a PR consulting firm that ripped off tribes for tens of millions.

- **Ralph Reed:** Executive director of the Christian Coalition from 1989, he left it in debt in 1997, then worked with college buddy Abramoff and brought in Christian leaders as pawns in Abramoff's schemes to nix casino plans of tribes that weren't Abramoff clients.

- **Grover Norquist:** President of Americans for Tax Reform, Norquist received millions from Abramoff's tribes, sometimes moving the money to Reed, Abramoff, or other cohorts. However, Norquist runs a fairly clean house, as evidenced by the fact that he didn't fall with the rest.

- **Gale Norton:** Head of the Department of the Interior (2001–06), former oil lobbyist Norton worked with mighty antitax guru Grover Norquist to set up an antienvironmental advocacy group, the Council of Republicans for Environmental Advocacy, which received hundreds of thousands in donations from Abramoff's tribes; whether she received any of that money is unclear. Working with Abramoff during the winter of 2000 when the lobbyist was part of Bush's transition team, she had a big say in tribal affairs, but at least once ignored Abramoff's wishes. Decided it was time to step down in spring 2006, right around the time the Senate Committee on Indian Affairs was releasing its report on the Abramoff scandal. Under Norton's reign, the Interior Department was so lax that it often did not collect the money oil companies owed to the government. Four comptrollers for the department filed a suit against the department because nobody would follow up on their findings that hundreds of millions of dollars' worth of oil royalties hadn't been paid.[25]

- **Department of the Interior:** Controls the federal lands that oil companies want to rip open further and also oversees Indian affairs.

- **Sen. John McCain (R-Arizona):** Led the Senate investigation into Abramoff's dealings with tribes, has tried to reform election finances, worked to steer Republican senators back to bipartisanship, and cosponsored 2006 legislation demanding transparency of the appropriation committee's earmark. Likely 2008 presidential candidate.

Sen. Barack Obama (D-IL): The great young hope of the Democrats is tidying up DC.

• **Sen. Barack Obama (D-Illinois):** Shining star of Congress, the freshman senator is a needed gust of fresh air that sweetens the stench of the Capitol's viper pit. Perhaps not yet knowing any better, he keeps introducing legislation that demands accountability of Congress, certainly a novel concept these days. Often working with centrist Republicans, including Sens. Tom Coburn and John McCain, he's cosponsored bills calling for new ethics committees to oversee Congress, and helped push through legislation, passed into law September 2006, that allows citizens to see the details of budget bills, including what earmarks are being handed to whom. Another bill that we like: one that would require that citizens are actually notified when nuclear plants release radioactive gases.

With warm brown eyes under a fringe of black hair, David Sickey is a slow-talking, soft-drawling Native American who epitomizes the term "low-key," but what he saw that day in early June 2003 made his stomach twist and sent his blood shooting up the temperature charts. "It was a shock," he says now. "None of the tribe knew we'd been making those sorts of huge expenditures."[26] Like the other 850 members of the Coushatta tribe of southwestern Louisiana, who live along the marshlands, catfish ponds, and cattle farms near Elton, he'd heard rumors. Some whispered that their tribal leader, Lovelin Poncho, was paying out lots of money to DC lobbyists, and something *was* fishy: the tribe's casino was making more than ever, but for the past few years, when profits were divvied up among the tribe members—giving each some $40,000 a year—the amounts weren't going up. In fact, Sickey, then a twenty-five-year-old office manager at the Coushatta mill, had that spring decided to run for a seat on the five-person tribal council with the promise that he'd try to figure out what was going on; some were skeptical that someone of his age could make a difference, but others saw his determination, and he won in a landslide. But though tribal councilman Sickey had suspected something had gone afoul, when he looked at the three pieces of paper before him he couldn't quite believe the news they bore—and he had to read them again and again, his eyes locking on certain figures in this memo reluctantly put together by the tribe's comptroller, who had announced he was leaving his post.

For "professional services," $940,000 was paid out on October 5, 2001. Three weeks later, two checks on the same day: one for $700,000, the other for $2.17 million, again with no explanation except "professional services." His eyes dropped farther down on the long list of multi-zeroed figures: on January 18, a trio of checks had gone out—totaling over $4 million. February 14, a check for $5 million; another for $1.3 million a few weeks after.[27]

All in all, the tribe had paid more than $32 million over two years—to Jack Abramoff and his sidekick consultant Michael Scanlon. And that money—which didn't reflect the additional checks made to political campaigns and charities—had gone through odd channels, noted the comptroller, with checks going to "different companies and/or flow-through Entities";[28] he couldn't even track or document it all. But wherever the money had ended up exactly, one thing was clear: payments to Abramoff and Scanlon had eaten into the budget for the tribe's education, housing, and health care; the chief had secretly authorized the tribe to borrow $10 million.

Memo in hand, Sickey rounded the corner to the office of council member Harold John, who was looking at a copy of the same clandestine memo, which had been slipped to them by an outgoing council member who'd been at odds with the tempestuous tribal leader Poncho. Wondering what to do, the two reasoned there was no point in confronting Poncho, whom they feared would bury the truth and impede their efforts to uncover what was happening. Instead they made a pact to document all they could and do something about it.

In September 2003, the *Town Talk* of Alexandria, Louisiana, ran an article about the Coushatta, the tribe that had in 1995 built the state's largest casino—a deluxe gambler's delight boasting two hotels, six restaurants, and an eighteen-hole golf course—which typically brought in $300 million a year. And that's why it was curious, the article noted, that the tribe's accounts were running in the red. Several sideline tribal businesses had faltered and, unbeknownst to the tribe, the chairman had recently bought a ranch as well as a twin-engine corporate jet. But the most mysterious of the tribal expenses were ones related to lobbying: records showed that the Coushatta had paid over $4 million to the firm of Greenberg Traurig, which employed Jack Abramoff. But another $28 million had gone to less well-known companies—where the phone was disconnected and the address was a mail stop. "Tribal Councilmen David Sickey and Harold John are questioning millions in expenditures made by tribal Chairman Lovelin Poncho and Councilman William Worfel," *Casino* added. "The Coushatta people," Sickey told a reporter, "have a right to know" what happened to the money. "It's not the chairman's money, not the council's money. It's the tribe's money."[29]

Between 2001 and 2004, six tribes paid over $82 million to Abramoff and Scanlon. The duo overcharged and bilked all the tribes—but the Coushatta took the worst hit. By way of comparison, General Electric had paid about $31 million to lobbyists between 2001 and 2004. Thanks to Abramoff, the Coushatta outspent the world's biggest corporation by about $5 million.[30]

Many Coushatta were livid, not only at the news—but that Sickey and John had blabbed private Indian affairs to the press. It didn't look good for the tribe, which had to apply for a new casino license every seven years; it didn't look good for the Indian people, just furthering the notion that they were incapable of handling money. But most of all, it didn't look good for Poncho: the article was greeted with calls for Poncho's resignation. But the chairman stayed in his seat and he kept paying Abramoff and Scanlon— $4 million more over the following months, says Sickey.[31] The DC duo even showed up in January 2004 to hit up the tribe for more money as a down payment for a new marketing plan, no doubt worried when they walked away empty-handed. The demands that the chairman step down grew louder and at a high-decibel meeting of the tribe in February 2004, Poncho finally resigned. The next day he called Abramoff, who put in calls to the Department of the Interior. There, the number two, Stephen Griles—whom Abramoff had been pals with since 2000, when the lobbyist was on the Interior Department transition team—reinstated the chief.[32]

And that's when David Sickey called the *Washington Post*. By fall 2003, the FBI had begun a secret investigation into the irregular state of affairs, and by the end of 2003 the Department of Justice was secretly on the trail of Abramoff. But Sickey's call to the *Post* yanked the rug that caused Jack Abramoff to nosedive.

GAMBLING WITH THE COUSHATTA

Jack Abramoff, whom some called "Casino Jack" for his penchant of drawing in gambling clients—among them five other casino-owning tribes—first met with the Coushatta in March 2001, when the tribe was renewing its contract with the state of Louisiana regarding the operation of its casino. Hired at $125,000 a month—plus expenses— Abramoff, who bragged that he was close to Rep. Tom DeLay and "had people" in the White House and Department of the Interior (which oversees Indian affairs), took care of that matter promptly, although he went wildly over budget, billing the tribe $4.25 million over six months. And having shaken that amount free, he wasn't going to let go. Bringing in Michael Scanlon—former communications director for DeLay—Abramoff suggested that the tribe work with Scanlon's consulting company for the projects—neglecting to mention he was splitting the dough Scanlon made. The two helped Lovelin Poncho see danger around every bend: Texas was going to legalize gambling, they informed Poncho; another tribe was planning to open a casino in Mississippi; some on the ruling council were trying to oust the chief, they whispered; without them there to fight for it, the tribe would be devastated, Abramoff assured Poncho. The DC hotshots formulated elaborate plans, giving them names like "Operation Orange," to battle threats to the casino, and unveiled project after pricey project, some involving surveillance, some involving PR campaigns, some involving religious leaders. To help snuff out plans for a new casino in Mississippi—which they assured Poncho would kill all his casino's business, Abramoff called in Ralph Reed, the former head of the Christian Coalition—instructing the tribe to funnel $400,000 of the casino's proceeds through a front company to pay Reed, since the holy roller was officially anti-gambling. Reed then worked with Pat Robertson, James Dobson, and Jerry Falwell to bring a loud evangelical shriek against proposed casinos that were deemed a threat to the Coushatta. Of course these programs didn't come cheap, and on top of the fees, Abramoff directed Poncho to throw millions into Republican politicians' campaigns or their nonprofit organizations and charities, to garner the votes and pushes they needed for success. In 2002 alone, the Coushatta shot over $283,000 into congressional war chests and charities, including $30,000 to Tom DeLay's political action committees.[33]

In September 2001, Jack Abramoff suggested that tribal leader Lovelin Poncho donate $25,000 to the Council of Republicans for Environmental Advocacy (a front group that attacks environmentalists) for a fundraiser dinner, where the chief met the Department of the Interior's secretary, Gale Norton. It was a bit of a price hike: four months earlier Abramoff had recommended that he make a different $25,000 donation, that time for Americans for Tax Reform, which was holding a meeting with President George W. Bush. Having paid his dues, Poncho was invited to the White House, where he met and shook hands with the president, certainly a much better value than hanging out with Gale.

IF I WERE A RICH MAN

There was always something Promethean about Jack Abramoff, who lived a life that fell out of *Vanity Fair* long before the magazine

profiled him. The swaggering son of a Diner's Club executive, Abramoff grew up amid the glitz of Beverly Hills, where his father was pals with golfer Arnold Palmer and Governor Ronald Reagan. A handsome jock—football player and weight lifter—known for his comical stories and hilarious imitations, the coal-eyed and long-nosed Abramoff possessed an almost manic drive and an intensity that made him stand out: profoundly moved as a teenager watching the musi-

Jack Abramoff in happier days.

cal *Fiddler on the Roof*, which exalted traditional Jewish ritu-

als, he shocked his family by announcing he would become orthodox. Shortly after graduating from Brandeis University, he made a vow of loyalty to the Republican Party that was as deep as his commitment to religion. And fueled by his Cold War spirit, which didn't go away even after the Cold War melted, he became a passionate GOP warrior.

While campaigning for Ronald Reagan in 1980, he befriended political activist and intellectual Grover Norquist, who was already pounding the anti-tax drum. The two instantly bonded in their deep hatred of Communism, liberals, Democrats, and big government. Norquist became the plotting brains of the duo and the one with insider connections; Abramoff had the bravado and could muster bucks—as became evident the next year, when Norquist ran Abramoff's successful campaign as national chair of the College Republicans (see page 111); Abramoff hired Norquist as executive director and Ralph Reed became intern. Under the umbrella of the organization, their Reagan worship and war against Communism was dramatized: the College Republicans sponsored mock "Knock Down the Berlin Wall" events and held a two-day celebration in honor of the one-year anniversary of Reagan's attack on Grenada. But their commie hating spurred them to much greater heights and distant parts of the world.

In 1985, Abramoff convinced wealthy conservative Lewis Lehrman to back him in Citizens for Americans, a Reagan-idolizing group that worked with Oliver North, raising funds for contra fighters in Nicaragua. Pulling in Norquist as consultant, Abramoff traveled to Afghanistan, where the two worked with Soviet-fighting mujahideen fighters to set up a clinic; they traveled to Angola to meet with UNITA rebel leader Jonas Savimbi, who was fighting the Cuba-controlled government. And as part of their plan to take down Communism, they organized the world's first conference of freedom fighters battling pinko commies.

Bankrolled by Citizens for Americans, they flew Nicaraguan contras, Afghan rebels, and Laotian fighters into the heart of the Angolan jungle; many of the scraggly fighters were detained at airports, but those who made it met with North and Savimbi and assorted reporters, including one from *Time*. Somebody read a letter from President Reagan, they decided they would all share intelligence, and the food soon ran out—with Abramoff selling the kosher food items he'd bought to the highest bidder.[34] Lehrman soon canned Abramoff and Norquist, furious that they'd blown through the group's $3 million budget in record time. Abramoff morphed the project into the International Freedom Foundation theoretically to promote free market economies and democratic thought worldwide, although the South African apartheid commission later reported that it was funded (to the tune of $1.5 million a year) by the apartheid government to besmirch Nelson Mandela.[35]

Even if he was out of a job, and the "freedom fighter convention" had been an expensive flop, the Angola trip launched Abramoff on his next venture—to make an action film based on Jonas Savimbi. The resulting "Rambo versus the commies" flick, *Red October*, was laughed off the screen, and his next venture didn't even get there. Abramoff's next career move came from the temple: a friend mentioned that a Seattle-based law firm, Preston Gates & Ellis, was desperately searching for Republican lobbyists. The year was 1994, and the GOP, led by Newt Gingrich, had taken Congress. And Abramoff had found a new calling.

His first client was the government of Pakistan, inquiring about buying fighter planes. Then Abramoff signed up his first Indian tribe, the Choctaw of Mississippi. Five others followed, unaware that he was referring to them as "morons," "monkeys," and "troglodytes." And Abramoff played tribes against one another. Take, for instance, how he worked the Tigua of Texas. Abramoff pulled off an elaborate scheme to shut down their casino (believed a threat by the other tribes): working with Ralph Reed, Abramoff had televangelists thumping the anti-gambling idea so heavily that the Interior Department's switchboard jammed up with irate callers—and the casino was indeed closed down. So Abramoff swung around to the Tigua, who didn't know what had hit them: portraying Ralph Reed and his televangelists as his enemies too, Abramoff hit the tribe for some $5 million to try to get the casino reopened.

Around 1995, Abramoff met Tom DeLay. The orthodox Jew and the evangelical Christian became instant friends—they talked about the Old Testament, about history, about sports and, of course, golf. And they shared a battle plan to keep the GOP in power: steer the big money of corporate clients to the Republican coffers.

Funding excursions through his new client, the government of the Northern Mariana Islands, Abramoff flew DeLay, staffers, and journalists for a getaway in the Pacific isles—a factor that would appear to play a part in DeLay's later killing of labor laws on the islands, where workers are reportedly imprisoned in guarded shacks without running water. The lobbyist and the lawmaker were forever finding artful ways of moving around the money Abramoff's clients paid for legislative favors, and Abramoff brought DeLay staff—including Tony Rudy and Michael Scanlon—to his lobbying team, to which he added more chiefs of staff from assorted lawmakers, including Neil Volz, who'd worked with Bob Ney. And while Abramoff collected chits through Congress, Grover Norquist helped with the executive branch, whisking him toward Bush's circle: Norquist helped ensure that Abramoff (a Pioneer) served on the 2000 transition team, and worked to set up meetings between the lobbyists and Karl Rove. As lobbyists are barred from directly paying for lawmakers' trips (they are free to arrange them, however), Abramoff often used nonprofit groups—including Norquist's Americans for Tax Reform as well as the National Center for Public Policy Research—as fronts since they didn't have to report where money came. For instance, he'd instruct Indian clients to make donations to the groups (implying they'd help the Indian causes), but then (after letting the group take a cut) he'd tap that money to fund ooh-la-la vacations such as his famous golf trips to St. Andrews in Scotland, where he took DeLay (and the gang) in 2000 and Ney (and the gang) two years later.

Before long, Jack Abramoff was bringing in over $10 million in business to his new firm, Greenberg Traurig. The lobbyist was spinning wheels in the House and pulling strings in the Senate, he had access inside the White House and Department of the Interior, he could plant the words coming out of televangelists' mouths, and his likeness was splashed across the covers of the *Wall Street Journal* and *New York Times*. Cash and checks were flapping around everywhere: he could raise hundreds of thousands holding fundraisers at his chichi restaurant, Signatures, he controlled the destinations of tens of millions every year, and was becoming a hugely valuable part of the GOP money machine. He'd bought a fleet of casino boats in Florida (fraudulently, it turned out), he was jetting all over the world, pulling capers wherever he landed, and while the fees paid by Greenberg Traurig (where he'd moved in 2001) made him wealthy, thanks to the tens of millions he was getting splitting the kitty with Scanlon, Abramoff was getting very, very rich and flying "at 30,000 feet," he told *Vanity Fair* in 2006.[36] Whether fueled by ego, powered by greed, or perhaps driven in his need to make the Republican Party the country's most unquestionably dominant, Abramoff flew too high, worked too many tricks, was too blatant in showing that Washington could be had for a price. On January 3, 2006, he fell back to earth with a painful crash, caught in the one word he would say that day in federal court three times and repeat the next day in Florida federal court twice more: "guilty."

Politicians who'd accepted hundreds of thousands from Abramoff and his clients began sending checks back and tossing the hot potatoes into charities. And as the name Abramoff was deleted from computers and BlackBerries, suddenly few could recall Abramoff or being chummy with the lobbyist. DeLay broke contact, as did Scanlon and

Reed. Sen. Conrad Burns (R-Montana), who'd collected over $150,000 from Abramoff and his clients, denounced him, saying he wished Abramoff "had never been born." And to top it all off, Abramoff says that Newt Gingrich "sneered" at him. Now, says Abramoff, who's heard friends and acquaintances by the dozens claim no recollection of ever meeting him, "You're really nobody in this town, unless you haven't met me."[37]

A few more weighted down in Abramoff's fall:
Bob Ney is soon to be on his way to prison for a stay of up to ten years; his chief of staff Neil Volz pleaded guilty to one charge of conspiracy for influencing his former boss and may get up to five. White House head of procurement David Safavian (and former lobbyist on the Abramoff team) took a dive and was convicted on four counts of lying and obstruction (he's asked for a new trial), after going on an Abramoff-sponsored golf trip to Scotland. DeLay aide Tony Rudy pleaded guilty to one charge of conspiracy (related to swinging a vote on Internet gambling), and is looking at a two-to five-year vacation in prison. Ralph "I hate gambling, but I get paid with gambling money" Reed lost his 2006 run for Georgia's lieutenant governor (perhaps he'll have better luck at the slots). Michael Scanlon pleaded guilty to conspiracy to bribe public officials and a member of Congress, and is now facing five years in prison, $250,000 in fines, and payback of $19.7 million to tribes— and his former fiancée helped to get him that verdict. (Emily Miller, reports the Wall Street Journal, *was so livid when Scanlon flicked her off and married a twenty-four-year-old waitress that she went to the FBI and spilled a few more beans.)* [38]

When Senator John McCain picked up the February 22, 2004, edition of the *Washington Post*, he zeroed in on a headline: "Jackpot from Indian Gaming Tribes: Lobbying, PR Firms Paid $45 Million Over 3 Years."[39]

"A powerful Washington lobbyist and a former aide to House Majority Leader Tom DeLay (R-Texas) persuaded four newly wealthy Indian gaming tribes to pay their firms more than $45 million over the past three years for lobbying and public affairs work, a sum that rivals spending to influence public policy by some of the nation's biggest corporate interests," the article by Susan Schmidt began. "Touting his ties to conservatives in Congress and the White House, lobbyist Jack Abramoff persuaded the tribes to hire him and public relations executive Michael Scanlon to block powerful forces both at home and in Washington . . ."[40] McCain kept reading.

At the behest of Abramoff, the article said, the tribes had become huge political donors, shucking out $2.9 million—mostly to Republicans, even though they traditionally supported Democrats. They'd also tossed out more than $15 million to Abramoff and his lobbying firm Greenberg Traurig—twenty times more than they usually paid lobbyists. But, the article added, that was tiddledywinks compared to what consultant Scanlon was taking in. Splitting the take with Abramoff it was later revealed, Scanlon had pulled down a cool $31 million, said the article—although ultimately the figure was closer to double that.

The following weeks were not happy for Jack Abramoff. Senator McCain's office called to notify Abramoff that they had a few questions, so many that they were starting an investigation. And Greenberg Traurig gave Abramoff a nudge out the door, and he started his own firm.

The Center for Responsive Politics had supplied the figures,[41] and watchdog groups from Public Citizen to the Center for Public Integrity had shot flares for years, but outside of Jeffrey Birnbaum of the Washington Post, few in mainstream media tried to unwind the twisty lobbying trail until Abramoff fell and the stench became impossible to ignore.

On September 29, 2004, Jack Abramoff—wearing a pinstriped suit and looking worried—appeared before the Senate Committee on Indian Affairs, where David Sickey and other tribe members were in attendance. Even though he pleaded the fifth throughout, by the end of the first hearing, his career was pretty much washed up—and criminal charges were just starting to hit. By January 2006, when Abramoff pleaded guilty to separate criminal charges of corruption, fraud, attempts to bribe, and tax evasion, heads were rolling all over the place. And there are still more to roll—because Abramoff and his gang of lobbyist con men were only one small part of the serpent of corruption slithering through DC.

The world of lobbying and earmarks is difficult to trace. Much of it takes place in e-mails and at lunches and casual meetings. But as the intricate details of the Abramoff case—and that of Cunningham (see page 28)—slowly unwound, the media finally woke up and focused on the wheelings and dealings of K Street. Suddenly names like Letitia White and Bill Lowery were bouncing through the rumor mills. Because in the splattering scandal of Abramoff, a lot of what had until recently passed under the guise of ethical, normal work relations suddenly looked very dodgy.

Letitia, Bill, Jerry, and the Gang's Very Tangled Web

Who would have guessed that a young receptionist holding a degree in fashion design would turn into such a mover for defense—but Letitia White's hard work, charisma, and eventual understanding of defense contracts would help her soar from secretary to "queen of earmarks." As secretary-turned-aide to Rep. Jerry Lewis (R-California), who then chaired the House Defense Appropriations Subcommittee, White was ushered into the world of unscrutinized earmarks, handing out a million perhaps for a high-security computer program or maybe $20 million to develop new monitoring equipment for high-profile sites.[42] In 2002, after almost two decades of working for

Rep. Jerry Lewis (R-CA): head of House Appropriations Committee is under the gun for defense giveaways.

Lewis, it was obvious that Letitia White had made a decision to move to K Street, because she accepted an $11,000 pay cut, which brought her salary to about $112,420 a year.[43] That's significant for one reason: congressional employees who make more than $112,500 have to wait a year—the so-called cooldown period—before lobbying their former colleagues. But since she fell under that ceiling, when Letitia White walked out of the House in January 2003 to take a job as lobbyist with the law firm of former congressman Bill Lowery, Jerry Lewis' good buddy, she could come back the next day to hit up her boss for grants and contracts for her clients. She immediately attracted over a dozen defense contractors—winning General Atomics a $15 million earmark to draw up plans for unmanned aerial vehicles—and for others she snagged millions more for everything from security contracts to software. And by 2005, she was pulling down a cool $3.5 million a year.[44]

That a congressman's former aide returned as a lobbyist and made hundreds of millions for her defense clients was business as usual, but White's problems arose when investigators realized that her employer, Lowery's firm, was the biggest single source of contributions to Jerry Lewis' political action committee and campaign fund: Lowery's firm had thrown in more than $480,000 between 2000 and 2005, more than one-third of the takings.[45] And not only did quite a few of the Lewis earmarks worth hundreds of millions go to the clients of this generous firm, but investigators pondered whether Lewis was indeed directing those who wanted earmarks to go through Lowery, forming an incestuous triangle: Lowery's firm made millions, Lewis' election coffers were filled, and the defense contractors won their coveted earmarks.[46]

The situation grew even more complicated as the revolving door kept whirling: another Lewis aide, Jeff Shockey, had also gone to work for Lowery's firm in 1999, representing a number of defense clients. But in 2005 he returned to Lewis' staff, in a move some worried smacked of milking the teat from the inside, particularly since Shockey made a handsome bundle in severance pay—nearly $2 million—and Shockey's wife was then hired by Lowery's firm. (However, the House ethics committee cleared Shockey of any ethical breach.) And then to top it all off, Letitia White bought a townhouse valued at more than $1 million with one of her clients, Nick Karangelen, owner of the defense company Trident Systems.[47] And Karangelen used the townhouse as base for his own political action committee—Small Biz Tech PAC—which employed Jerry Lewis' stepdaughter.[48]

Now Lewis' office and Lowery's firm are being subpoenaed right and left—and the brouhaha caused the firm to split up. Letitia White's defenders say she acted aboveboard throughout her lobbying career; detractors say it's just another show of how cronyism and money power the DC system. And when the *New York Times* profiled Brent Wilkes—who'd worked with Randy Cunningham, Bill Lowery, and Rep. Jerry Lewis in securing earmarks—the article was damning:

"Mr. Wilkes described the appropriations process as little more than a shakedown," noted the piece. "He said that lobbyists close to the committee members unceasingly demanded campaign contributions," said the *Times*. Wilkes and his associates had contributed more than $706,000 to federal campaigns since 1997, according to public records, and he had kicked in even more as a fundraiser. "Since 2000, Mr. Wilkes' principal company has received about $100 million in federal contracts."[49] The article set more teeth a-chattering.

The Neocon Influence

The fact is, alas, that the staffer-turned-lobbyist phenomenon is commonplace, although the appearance of questionable behavior seems to worsen in the case of defense. There's a reason: the Bush administration is pumping more than $532 billion into defense for 2007,[50] making it the second biggest outlay of the government, just after Social Security. And when the budget pie is divvied up by Congress, the biggest piece of this discretionary spending goes to defense.

That isn't how it was supposed to be. When the Cold War ended in the early 1990s with the fall of the Soviet Union, analysts predicted our budget for matters military would vastly shrink.

There's a reason it didn't—a reason that goes beyond September 11 and the war in Iraq. And that reason is called the neocons, a group of professional alarmists who had been itching to revolutionize defense and vastly increase the war budget since long before Osama bin Laden was a household name.

THE MYSTERY-FILLED NEOCONS

By now, the term "neocons" has a familiar, sickening ring: many realize that these ideological "America must militarily dominate the world" warmongers—whose ranks include Paul Wolfowitz, Douglas Feith, I. Lewis "Scooter" Libby, Richard Perle, and Michael Ledeen—are the bunch who teamed up with Cheney and Rumsfeld to lead us into an ill-fated mission in Iraq, spouting hot-aired assertions and wheeling out Iraqi storyteller Ahmed Chalabi to tell us tales about Uncle Saddam's weapons of mass destruction. It's not news that these American Enterprise Institute–affiliated intellectuals—many of whom were lobbyists and consultants for arms makers—coined the corny but dangerous concept of an "Axis of Evil" and held high positions in the Defense Department (from the Reagan administration onward and most prominently under George W. Bush). Nor is it news that their vehicle for imposing their blueprint for the United States to reign as global "rules don't apply to us" bully was the Project for the New American Century (PNAC), a report-issuing group that Cheney and Rumsfeld belonged to; big surprise that Cheney and Rumsfeld adopted PNAC's "arm to the hilt, stomp those who defy" recommendations as U.S. foreign policy. (PNAC, while still maintaining a website, appears to be in remission, having been silent since 2005.)

Yet mystery surrounds the neocons. Despite their happiness to park themselves in front of the TV camera and blather on about the latest looming danger worthy of American military intervention and to spout their "enemies are lurking everywhere" ideas in columns and think tank reports, they operate as an almost shadowy group. Their links to Israel's hawkish Likud Party are obvious—several neocons (including Douglas Feith and Richard Perle) have publicly spoken out for the party, and they've written ferocious reports for a Likud-linked think tank[51]—but their real relationship to that country is hard to discern. An FBI wiretap caught Richard Perle blabbing state secrets to Israelis in 1970,[52] and as assistant secretary of defense for international security, he was chastised in 1983 for recommending that the

Defense Department buy arms from a dealer who'd paid him $50,000. Even sweet-smiling Paul Wolfowitz was reportedly investigated for passing on classified info about an impending arms deal to Israelis in 1978,[53] as was Douglas Feith, for leaking state docs to the Israeli embassy while on the National Security Council in 1982.[54] Eyebrows raised again at that duo when their DoD policy analyst Larry Franklin was caught passing on secret government documents meant for Israel,[55] through "America's pro-Israel lobby," the American Israel Public Affairs Committee (AIPAC), a powerful lobby that U.S. politicians from the president on down actively court and that is believed capable of spelling defeat for those that don't support its views. Franklin was sentenced to thirteen years in January 2006 for espionage charges, and two other AIPAC members were indicted. While Wolfowitz walked away without a scratch—Bush appointed the former number two of Defense as president of the World Bank—Feith stepped down from his post as DoD's number three in 2005, although perhaps that was due more to his fantasy-fogged Iraq War planning.

The biggest mystery about these guys, however, is why the heck anybody would listen to them, much less give them positions of power. The paranoid neocons, since they first showed up in the 1970s, have *always* been wrong—starting with their Reagan-era hugely expensive "What if?" war game called Plan B: they conjured up weapons the Soviet Union *might* have, dreaming up wild weapons to fight them, and boosting military spending up to a trillion dollars for arms that weren't needed since the Soviets didn't actually have the weapons they imagined.[56] And one more perplexing element in this tale: why the name of neocon Bruce Jackson hasn't been plastered across headlines. After all, Jackson—until recently a vice president of Lockheed Martin—wedded the arms industry to the neocons and government policy.

AIPAC was instrumental in the 1978 decision to give Israel an annual $3 billion or so in aid; about $2 billion of that is essentially an arms credit to go shopping at Lockheed and Boeing (with American taxpayers picking up the bill). The ongoing grant was a requisite to convince Israel to sign the 1979 Israel-Egypt Peace Treaty, which also tosses about $2 billion a year in grants to Egypt, most of which goes toward arms purchases from U.S. companies.

Shunted off the main playing field during the Clinton administration, the neocons did not go away. They headed to think tanks such as the American Enterprise Institute, they took gigs as lobbyists for defense contractors, they wrote articles. And in 1997, they gathered together—with Dick Cheney (then CEO of Halliburton) and Donald Rumsfeld (then CEO of G. D. Searle)—to form a new think tank, one that would have dire effects for the world: the Project for the New American Century (PNAC). And the number one obsession of this group was Saddam Hussein, whose country the PNAC-ers insisted the United States should attack.

BRUCE JACKSON: ARMS AMBASSADOR

Was he a lobbyist or vice president of the world's biggest arms maker? Was he a quasi-government representative shaping foreign policy or a concerned citizen whose actions forged new military alignments across the globe and shot bundles of cash into American defense companies? Was he setting up future U.S. military incursions while working for the company that had most to benefit from those actions? Gee, things sure get blurry when Bruce Jackson—a bespectacled, mousy-looking former army intelligence man—slips into the picture. But one thing is for sure: his many "volunteer" efforts added up to a loud ka-ching for Lockheed Martin, bringing the defense company billions upon billions upon billions in orders. Funny thing, as vice president of strategy and development at Lockheed Martin, he just happened to be the guy in charge of boosting arms sales worldwide. How brilliant (if oh so slightly conflicted) that Jackson seized upon the idea of expanding NATO—the U.S.-dominated arms club originally created to fight any future Soviet expansion into Europe—by bringing in ten ex-Soviet republics and satellites that wanted more arms.

Founding the influential U.S. Committee on NATO in 1996, Jackson—who was regarded by foreign governments as a U.S. government official—helped former Soviet republics and satellite countries from the Czech Republic to Poland, Latvia to Lithuania, Slovakia to Slovenia climb on board the NATO roster—which many were keen to do as protection against Russia. Granted, admission comes with a price. NATO countries must commit to spending at least 2 percent of their GDP on arms sales, but not to worry: the U.S. government (or rather, the American taxpayer) helps governments acquire the needed war toys. Thanks to Jackson's machinations, Poland alone put in a $3.5 billion order for fighter plans, from Lockheed, of course. According to *The American Prospect*, Jackson also strong-armed those countries that hoped to be part of the NATO club into joining the "Coalition of the Willing" and signing a letter saying that they supported taking down Saddam—he implied that their John Hancocks would elicit a nod from Congress, which (sure enough) voted to let them join NATO;[57] according to *The American Prospect*, some Eastern European governments, including Slovenia, publicly regretted being coerced into signing the letter. Actually, by then (2003) Jackson had stepped down from Lockheed and was heading up a new powerful group, the Committee to Liberate Iraq, which lobbied long and hard for that misguided invasion of Saddam's homeland. In fact, Jackson—a PNAC board member, founder of the Project on Transitional Democracies and the International Committee on the Balkans and more—had even hinted at that invasion in the 2000 Republican platform, which Mr. "I Love Committees" helped pen, actually boasting, "I wrote the Republican Party's foreign policy platform."[58] Heading the GOP's foreign policy subcommittee, Jackson foreshadowed exactly what lay ahead if Bush was elected: the 2000 platform formally embraced "a comprehensive plan for the removal of Saddam Hussein." And that war made billions for Lockheed Martin.

Long shrugged off by intelligence agencies as extremists, this group scored big when President George W. Bush came to power—because his vice president handed most of the PNAC members top jobs. It was Cheney who chose Rumsfeld for defense, with Paul Wolfowitz just under him, and Douglas Feith under *him*; and assorted other neocons, PNAC members, and general hawks, including Newt Gingrich and the loudest promoter of the Iraq War—Richard Perle—were given chairs on the Defense Policy Board. In addition to pushing the invasion of Iraq to the government, this advisory group went out to sell it to the public.

Between the neocon-pushed wars that the Bush administration led us into, the modernizing vision that Secretary Rumsfeld had for defense, and the reintroduction of National Missile Defense, the defense budget has soared to nearly $532 billion—and those are only the expenses we can trace, since billions more are spent on classified, off-budget "black projects." But one thing is out in the open and plain to see. Nobody has benefited more from defense increases, our frequent wars, and our vast plans to seal off our nation than Lockheed Martin, the defense contractor that has married the government.

OH, SAY, CAN YOU SEE . . . WHO'S RUNNING THE COUNTRY?

With the merging and melding between corporations and our government, perhaps it's time for a country name change that reflects who's really running the show—forget the US of A, we're becoming the United States of Lockheed Martin. Nobody pulls more change out of the national wallet—the leading government contractor, Lockheed Martin, walked off with some $27 billion in 2005. And what with border fences, new fingerprint ID programs, IT systems that are redesigning the post office and Social Security Administration, transport planes that Congress orders (and the Department of Defense doesn't want), fancy fighter planes, nuclear missiles, and new spaceships (Lockheed shoved Boeing out for the $4 billion project to dream up a new passenger vehicle, the Orion), Lockheed is making upward of $65 million *a day*—from the United States alone.[59] Another 20 percent of its revenue comes from selling those fighter planes and missiles abroad, which is why the company, based in Bethesda, Maryland, is plenty happy that new countries are joining NATO and that the United States is now chummy with India and lifting decades-old sanctions; between the "War on Terror" and post-9/11 angst, Lockheed sales have soared by more than a third. Predictably, the revolving door spins rapidly here: National Security Advisor Stephen Hadley is but one Bush insider who was a former Lockheed lobbyist—Cheney's wife, Lynne, sat on the board until her hubby plopped down in the VP chair—while a dozen former government bigwigs are now formally working as Lockheed employees (including CEO Robert Stevens, a former DoD man, and director Pete Aldridge, formerly undersecretary of defense in charge of acquisitions). Dozens more fight for the defense firm from K

Street; Lockheed Martin's lobbying costs often wing toward $10 million a year.[60] And the firm's PACs drop plenty of ammo on the campaign contributions front, shooting most at those sitting on appropriations and armed services committees. But Lockheed Martin boasts another crucial weapon in its persuasion arsenal: its plants, located all over the country, put tens of thousands to work. As a result, Congress keeps ordering up unneeded planes or, worse, ones with designs that haven't been proven to work, such as the fancy Joint Strike Fighter—aka F-35—which is still mostly in the theoretical stage despite the very tangible $200 billion that the Defense Department plunked down for that theory, thanks to pressure from lawmakers.[61] From computer systems to satellites, missiles to fighter planes, social security to space defense, Lockheed Martin is shoving all the others aside as it conquers more and more companies and more and more government contracts.[62] The only thing left for this giant to do is to hand us a new national anthem.[63]

[What You Can Do]

Entertain new ideas. Public Citizen is but one group that suggests revamping how campaign finance works. The watchdog recommends that:

- Lobbyists should be taken out of the fundraising system.

- The national voting system should be reformed à la Connecticut and Maine, which have banned all private contributions to candidates. That would put the burden of campaign expenses on the public—at a cost of around $2 billion a year. Might be a small price to clean up this mess.

Another novel idea: Take the budget out of Congress. Send the appropriations back to the departments that request the money. And change the budget process so it's tackled every other year, instead of annually.

Track who's influencing your elected representatives: the Center for Responsive Politics (www.opensecrets.org) lists both those who give campaign contributions and those who receive them, as well as listing corporate lobbying expenditures.

Check out the investigative reports on lobbying and Congress from the Center for Public Integrity (www.publicintegrity.org).

Arms-wise, there may be little we can do to affect the world's biggest industry (and one that the United States leads in both sales and purchases) except to follow it—a daunting task unto itself. A few sites that do a fine job unraveling this gnarly ball:

- **Arms Trade Resource Center** (www.worldpolicy.org/projects/arms/reports.html). Headed by defense and weapons guru William D. Hartung, this research center churns out comprehensive and enlightening reports that offer a clear view into the shadowy world of arms dealing.

- **Federation of American Scientists** (www.fas.org). Arms sales monitoring, foreign military assistance, budget requests—and congressional reports that are hard to find—they've got it all.

- **Center for Defense Information** (www.cdi.org). Founded by former military brass, this independent center is a treasure trove of information on topics from global arms sales to missile defense to military plans for outer space that the media typically forget to cover. Free newsletters keep the public up to date with what's really happening in the world of defense and security.

- **GlobalSecurity.org** (www.globalsecurity.org). Founded by esteemed scientist John Pike, a leading weapons experts, this site covers areas from intelligence to homeland security—and like the Center for Defense Information, gives the public a look at what's happening in outer space, and the U.S. plans to control it.

- **Project for the New American Century** (www.newamerican century.org). If you want to know exactly where the United States went awry in foreign policy and security, be sure to check out this site. Responsible for many of the worst decisions to come out of the White House in the history of the United States, this "think tank" of powerful, intellectual, and utterly misguided ideologues appears to be hibernating, and we really hope it's a permanent nap. Although it would be fitting for them to be in hiding under a rock, individual members still hold power positions and are still making noise defending their strategy to invade Iraq, and other such grievous errors, although their rationale grows more feeble by the hour. For a blow-by-blow understanding of contemporary U.S. foreign policy, be sure to download their September 2000 report *Rebuilding America's Defenses* (http://newamericancentury .org/RebuildingAmericasDefenses.pdf), which reads like a checklist of Bush administration "accomplishments."

CHAPTER 3

Party Matters

"'Americans agree on core values!' is not a headline that editors expect to sell newspapers. 'Citizens describe themselves as moderates!' is not a good lead for the evening news."

—Morris Fiorina, author of *What Culture War?: The Myth of a Polarized America*[1]

"Even as Liberals continue their war against traditional American culture, it serves their purpose to deny the true scope and nature of the battle . . . the truth is that since the Sixties, Liberals, aided by the Democratic Party, of which they have taken de facto control, have been conducting a war against virtually all of traditional American culture, a fact that defines the Culture War as a real, all-encompassing war between the 17 percent of the population who call themselves Liberals and the rest of Americans."

—Columnist A. J. DiCintio in September 2006, apparently gearing up for the November midterm battle at the polls[2]

The subtleties are apparently lost on those foreigners who lump us all together as one loud, rich, gun-happy, Bible-thumping, flag-waving, bomb-dropping, nonsmoking, cola-swilling, burger-chomping bunch, with a vocabulary that consists of "anyway," "whatever," and "fill 'er up." Those who aren't familiar with Main Street America—or Fox News—may miss the loudly hyped cultural and political rift splitting our country. We may shop at the same chain stores, buy the same mass-produced items, drive similar cars, rally around the Super Bowl, and aspire to the same personal happiness—and lots of us are leaning on our credit cards lately, racking up debts averaging around $8,000—but we Americans know that we are not all the same, because that's what we've been told.

> *"Conservatives saw the savagery of 9/11 and the attacks and prepared for war; liberals saw the savagery of the 9/11 attacks and wanted to prepare indictments and offer therapy and understanding for our attackers. In the wake of 9/11, conservatives believed it was time to unleash the might and power of the United States military against the Taliban; in the wake of 9/11, liberals believed it was time to submit a petition."*
> —*Bush advisor Karl Rove in June 2005,[3] forgetting that Democrats (a term often used synonymously with "liberal" by Rove) backed President Bush when he called for invasions of Afghanistan—and Iraq*

We're Republican or Democrat, conservative or liberal, evangelical or secular, fierce ally or hateful foe. And as the media shows us in colorful maps, our country has been tearing apart in a loud, painful rip—with a bloodred heartland edged by two ribbons of blue—the latest indication of our culture wars that pundits liken to the rancorous nineteenth-century division between Rebels and Yanks.

"It may not be with bullets, but [we're fighting] a war nevertheless. It is a war of ideology, it's a war of ideas, it's a war about our way of life."
—Paul Weyrich on the conservative battle[4]

HOT BUTTONS

A few issues dividing the parties:

- **Global warming:** Three-quarters of Americans favor signing the Kyoto Protocol—the international treaty to cut carbon dioxide— and 43 percent believe that President Bush is all for it as well.[5] Guess they missed the 2004 Republican platform that states, "Our President and our Party strongly oppose the Kyoto Protocol and similar mandatory carbon emissions controls that harm economic growth and destroy American jobs."[6] True to promise, Republicans have mostly clouded the climate change issue, doing nothing to address the problem. Curiously, Democrats apparently cooled on the global warming arena: in the 2004 Democratic platform it didn't rate a mention. Fresh from their 2006 congressional victories, however, Democratic leaders promised to make global warming a priority in the 110th Congress.

- **Court changes (tort reform):** Handcuff the trial lawyer, demands the GOP's wealthy business core that's sick of being hit with class action suits: the Republican Party platform wants to limit punitive damages handed out to the wronged and to halt legal practices that "hinder our country's competitiveness in the world market." Quit shielding corporations and businesses from liability and stop stripping our rights, say the Democrat-leaning lawyers, whose many millions are the backbone of Democratic Party funding—the reasons, some pundits say, that the Republican Party kicked off its "court reform" attack. (See chapter 7.)

- **Abortion:** The Republican platform opposes abortion and endorses appointment of pro-life judges and "a human life amendment" legislation to protect unborn fetuses.[7] The 2004 Democratic platform regards a woman's ability to choose abortion as a constitutional right. American sentiment reflects the split: 51 percent of Americans think abortion should remain legal in all or most cases, and 42 percent say it should be illegal in all or most cases.[8]

- **Stem cell research:** The Democratic Party supports research into this groundbreaking area, which uses frozen embryos and blood from umbilical cords, but the Religious Right—mostly Republicans—loudly opposes it; President Bush vetoed a recent bill calling for additional research, ticking off those Republicans (including Nancy Reagan) who see it as holding the solutions to many illnesses, including the Alzheimer's that plagued her husband. Voterwise, 48 percent support using federal funds for stem cell research and 40 percent oppose it.[9]

- **Firearms:** The GOP now embraces the National Rifle Association, which is now loudly Republican and funds the meetings of college Republicans. According to Democratic Party chairman Howard Dean, the Republican National Committee is sponsoring "Fun with Guns" events, where young Republicans take fire at cutouts of Hillary Clinton and John Kerry with BB guns. Democrats aren't amused; they want to renew the assault weapons ban and to require more background checks and a gun safety test for handgun purchases.

- **Immigration:** The issue of workers from abroad—legal and illegal—is splitting the Republican core, as Big Business wants guest workers and eased immigration, while social conservatives are loudly calling to shove out undocumented Latinos. Racist remarks flying out of some Republicans' mouths frighten GOP strategists, who warn that Hispanics already lean toward the Democrats, who favor a guest worker program.

- **Taxes and tax cuts:** Cutting taxes for corporations and citizens and eliminating the inheritance tax, which brings in billions from the wealthy class, are part of the GOP platform. The Democratic platform endorses reversing corporate tax cuts.

• **Military and security:** Beefing up the military was on the Republican agenda long before 9/11, but the ballooning expenses and money-draining situations in Iraq and Afghanistan are eliciting calls from both parties to deflate defense spending. Democrats, however, are calling the loudest.

For the parties' platforms, politicians' voting records, and the sizzling topics of the DC day, check out www.ontheissues.org.

America is crumbling and should cleave, or so pundits suggest: the "red" states should gather together as the United States of Jesus, and the "blue" can go form the United States of Canada. From headlines in the *New York Times* to the insults hurled from talk radio, we're told that the United States is a hissing, schizophrenic nation where conservative nationalists frantically wave flags while liberal wildmen insist we have the right to burn them.

THIS IS A DIVIDE?

Regardless of their affiliation to the two dominant parties, on many key issues Americans don't stand all that far apart, as witnessed in recent polls of Americans.

	Republican	Democrat
Support abortion being available[10]	70%	78%
Support outlawing abortion[11]	28%	21%
Oppose Congress' actions in Schiavo case[12]	72%	89%
Believe war in Iraq made United States safer[13]	13%	19%
Support death penalty[14]	80%	58%
Feel government should require more efficient cars[15]	85%	86%

Feel government should boost spending on solar, wind, and hydrogen energy research[16]	82%	77%
Feel government should do more to cut CO_2 gases[17]	64%	78%
Support minimum wage of $7.15[18]	72%	91%
Pray every day[19]	67%	61%
Believe in life after death[20]	94%	92%

Despite all the blather about a right-left, Republican-Democrat schism rocking the country, the fastest-growing political designation is Independent and the breakdown of registered voters leading up to the 2004 election showed party affiliation cut roughly in thirds: 33 percent were Republicans, 34 percent were Democrats, and 33 percent were Independents or others.[21] And the intensity of our state color coding gets watered down by those 95 million of the 200 million eligible who aren't sufficiently stirred by any party to vote.

In fact, the biggest problem with our country's blue and red battleground is that it doesn't exist. That's the finding of Morris Fiorina of the Hoover Institute—Stanford's respected think tank—as well as other academics and researchers who probed the widely swallowed "America's new civil war" assumption.

"The mass polarization that we've been told is there simply isn't there," he says. "The idea of a war or a great divide is a huge exaggeration."[22] In fact, most Americans are purple: the academic and his team were shocked at how much agreement there was on most issues, even when comparing red and blue states. Gun control is perhaps the area where Democrats and Republicans most disagree. While overall 55 percent of Americans favor stricter controls, views divide by party: 71 percent of Democrats want more restrictions on firearms purchases (11 percent want less) while only 35 percent of Republicans are for gun control (35 percent also want less).[23] It's now become a party issue. The Democratic Party traditionally supports more controls on firearm sales, although its calls for it are growing fainter; the Republican Party favors streamlining gun sales—and protecting firearm manufacturers from court cases that target them in violent crimes. And while Hurricane Katrina boosted gun sales, as many came to believe that the government couldn't protect them no matter where they lived or the situation, the recent spate of gun attacks in schools has made weapon ownership all the more controversial.

FRIEND OF THE REPUBLICAN: THE NATIONAL RIFLE ASSOCIATION

Along with the Christian Right, which turned dominantly Republican over the past decade, the NRA began throwing its arsenal—3 million members, millions in contributions, and millions more in lobbying— behind the GOP in the 1990s, targeting Democrats and anyone else who supported a 1994 assault weapons ban (the Brady Bill) pushed and signed into law by President Bill Clinton.

Two Union generals created the gun group in 1871 to protect the Second Amendment—the right to own firearms. Nobody is seriously trying to strip away that right, but the NRA blasts gun control advocates even for suggesting background checks, longer waiting periods, and attempts to bar sales of military-style assault weapons, an issue that's reemerged since the Brady Bill ban expired in 2004.

Lately any impediments to quick, easy gun sales have been blocked by the Republican-controlled Congress. In fact, some Democrats are wondering if their party's gun control stance is a liability: the NRA claims responsibility for ejecting nearly 90 percent of legislators on its "enemy list," and Bill Clinton, for one, has lashed out at how effectively the NRA political machine shot down—i.e., voted out—its foes.

Meanwhile, the Republican Party is entwined with the gun lobby and in October 2005, President Bush signed the Protection of Lawful Commerce in Arms Act—which shields gun makers from liability when their weapons are used in homicide, manslaughter, holdups, and other violent acts.

In 1994, over a third of American households held some 192 million firearms; by 2000, the figure exceeded 259 million[24] and 46 percent of men and 22 percent of women owned one or more handguns.[25] Having pretty much saturated the U.S. market, American gun manufacturers want to repeal restrictive gun laws in other countries: the NRA is financially backing gun advocates around the world and trying to dilute UN efforts to control small arms. Ex–UN ambassador John Bolton loudly sang the NRA's tune, refusing to endorse the UN programs.

> The United States leads the West in homicides with 14,263 in 2002. Of those, 9,528 involved firearms.[26]

Even if it's not really there, America's "great divide" is nevertheless hammered home by those who benefit by keeping us worried, divided, revved up, and hateful—namely, talk show hosts, headline writers, venomous authors, and, most important, politicians and strategists who lure us to the polls by portraying a clearly defined black-and-white world with the opposing party painted in the darkest shades of sinister, weak-kneed wussiness or incomprehensible stupidity.

Iraq—and one's opinion about the 2003 invasion—was one way to know if you were red or blue, although that's certainly changing. Seventy-two percent of Americans waved the flag behind the attack on the way in; as of fall 2006, some 60 percent of Americans oppose the war and most want to pull out. In fact, Iraq is now a uniting issue, whatever our party. As of September 2006, only 15 percent of Americans believed initiating the Iraq War was the right thing to do; 76 percent agreed that it wasn't.[27]

ALL TOGETHER NOW

Although they've effectively united in occasional filibusters, Democrats clearly have not mastered the mass message machine: they throw out the occasional lonely outraged remark—rarely echoed by other Dems—in contrast to the Republican sound bite generator, which tosses out gross generalizations in unison. When several high-ranking Senate Republicans (including John McCain) briefly rebelled against President Bush in September 2006, questioning the government's aggressive interrogation techniques—i.e., torture—the loudly trumpeted responses from leading Republicans were identical if illogical: the real problem was, they announced, Democrats are peacenik wussies.

House Majority Leader John Boehner (R-Ohio) speculated that Democrats are "more interested in protecting terrorists than in protecting the American people"[28]—a sentiment previously voiced by President Bush, who dissed Senate Democrats as "not interested in the security of the American people,"[29] and further echoed by Sen. Rick Santorum (R-Pennsylvania), who says Dems "can't face the reality that we have a dangerous enemy out there, an enemy that wants to destroy everything we hold dear."[30] Any criticism of that overseas mistake—such as when decorated and twice-wounded former Marine and hawkish Democrat John Murtha (D-Pennsylvania) opined that the Iraq War "is not going as advertised" and that we should bring the boys home[31]—is answered back with glib attacks on patriotism: the White House speared Murtha as "endorsing the policy positions of Michael Moore and the extreme liberal wing of the Democratic party."[32]

The same "Democrats are limp-wristed flower children" excuse is wheeled out for just about any occasion these days. When asked to comment on the Connecticut primary defeat of Joe Lieberman—the Democratic senator who often sided with Republicans—Vice President Dick Cheney pondered aloud if "the dominant view of the Democratic Party" is the "notion that somehow we can retreat behind our oceans and not be actively engaged in this conflict and be safe here at home."[33]

The most volatile issues—the issues believed to bring us out to vote and that make for the best sound bites—have been selected to define the parties, or at least the GOP, where the core is becoming dogmatic about who and what should and shouldn't define it. Both in platform and in actions the party is drawing a sharp line, and in shock to many moderate Republicans, the GOP leadership is now extremely extreme: fervently pro-gun, anti-gay, and anti-abortion—and wildly supportive of a "hands-off" approach to business. In fact, the Republican core is working to shrink the government to little more than a war machine. And whether intentional or not, running big government into the ground—

with money-draining wars and stomach-turning corruption—is one way to break it.

STRATEGIZING: A GOP STRENGTH

The area where Republicans and Democrats have become most defined lately is strategy. The Republican leaders have one, and the Democrats apparently don't. Dems found victory in the anti-corruption sweeps in Congress—which played with Democrats taking Senate and House—but the "2006 midterm comeback" mostly seemed like victory by default. The strongly right-wing power group at the GOP wheel still has its program in place. Elements of that agenda include:

- Deflating government control—erasing departments from education to labor
- Ending the government's role in federal programs that smack of socialism, such as Social Security, Medicare, and even education, by turning those duties over to business and/or religious groups
- Reducing government to mostly a security machine
- Increasing the military arsenal and international presence
- Minimizing environmental regulation for corporations and industry
- Shrinking the power of the courts
- Speaking in a unified voice
- Repeating the same market-tested phrases again and again
- Knocking out the Democratic Party, using the same means used to try to strangle al-Qaeda: by cutting off its money
- Slamming Dems' main funding sources—trial lawyers and organized labor—and simultaneously steering more money to the GOP through lobbyist-controlled contributions

Meanwhile, the GOP continues to hone and refine its plans, and the Democratic Party appears to be lost, divided, and able to define itself by only one thing: being the "Not-Republican Party."

Most Americans are more or less moderates, but the problem is that our elected leaders and lawmakers are often intolerant bigots—as are our leading media personalities and pundits who divide and enrage the country. This is not by happenstance. That well-fiddled idea that the United States is experiencing a "culture war" fits very neatly into a program developed by the architects of the New Republican revival, who are redrawing the game board while Democrats are having a shrugfest trying to decide what they are. And certain right-wing strategists and elected officials use the public as pawns—in a showdown that is mostly of their making. Declaring a war—as figures such as Pat Robertson, Newt Gingrich, Paul Weyrich, and Ralph Reed have on any number of matters—is often simply a "tactic to wind up the troops to attack," says Morris Fiorina.[34] And winding them up they are. And in so doing they're changing the shape of the party.

> *"You're fighting a war. It is a war for power."*
> —*Newt Gingrich to College Republicans in 1978 speech*[35]

> *"Yes, Virginia, there is a war on Christmas. It's the secularization of America's favorite holiday and the ever-stronger push toward a neutered 'holiday' season so that non-Christians won't be even the slightest bit offended. . . . [It's] the liberal activists, lawyers, politicians, educators, and media people who are leading the war on Christmas. . . . [T]he situation is worse than you can imagine. Millions of Americans are starting to fight back against the secularist forces."*
> —*Heritage Foundation announcement of author/Fox anchor John Gibson's appearance in December 2005*

> *"Activist Judges are undermining democracy, devastating families, and assaulting Judeo-Christian morality. If you agree that enough is enough, if you're ready to fight back, come to 'Confronting the Judicial War on Faith,' April 7–8, 2005, Washington Marriott, Washington, DC. Speakers include Senator Sam Brownback, former Alabama Chief Justice Roy Moore, Alan Keyes, former Vatican Ambassador Ray Flynn, Rep. Steve Chabot, Rep. Todd Akin, Phyllis Schlafly and Tony Perkins of the Family Research Council. Congressman Lamar Smith will speak in place of Tom DeLay."*
> —*Announcement from the Judeo-Christian Council for Constitutional Restoration*

MEET THE MODERN REPUBLICAN

The Grand Old Party traditionally stood for wealthy northeastern industrialists and upper-middle-class Protestants, and many still belong. But the bus has been filling up as it stops to pick up new members, including:

- **Southerners:** Until 1964, when President Lyndon Johnson—a Democrat—signed the Civil Rights Act banning discrimination, the "solid South" lined up under the Democratic flag. After that year, most white southerners switched to the GOP—and now most of the southern blue states have turned red.

- **Religious Right and social conservatives:** First rallying around abortion when it was legalized in 1973, the Religious Right—and the related social conservatives who may not be as religious but hold many of the same views—has gone through plenty of shepherds, from the PTL's Jim and Tammy Faye Bakker to the Christian Coalition's Pat Robertson. Even though his show is actually about raising a family, radio host James Dobson has turned his millions of listeners into a quasi-religious/social conservative army—via the virtual organization Focus on the Family, which jams phone circuits and clogs e-mail accounts when he rails about anything from gambling to teaching evolution in schools. The political arm of the group is the loudly pro-life and powerful Family Research Council.

- **Big Business and small business, libertarians, gun rights activists, and many of the superwealthy:** They all want to minimize government interference in their lives.

- **Neoconservatives and defense contractors:** Walk loudly, carry the biggest stick, and spend trillions on security, treasure troves of cool war toys—and on weaponizing outer space. In some ways, these heavyweights are the odd men out—their treasury-draining agenda depends on tax dollars—but they've aligned with security-conscious conservatives on issues from immigration to Iraq.

"The core of the modern Republican party and the modern conservative movement—and there's a lot of overlap between the

two—is made up of everybody who voted for Ronald Reagan or
should have."
　　—Grover Norquist,[36] who says that the New Republicans come
　　together under the GOP banner for one reason: they want to
　　shrink the size and influence of government, including the amount
　　of money needed to feed it

The "our way or the highway" commandos who've yanked the GOP
wheel are harsh about branding their image, and they mandate con-
formity. Republican lawmakers who don't toe the line and who lean toward moderate are getting a shove. Stamped as "RINOs"—Republicans
in Name Only—they are being hunted down by members of their own
party: the GOP's wealthy Club for Growth, a group of East Coast conservatives, has poured millions into defeating these middle-ground Republicans in primaries.

"We have branded the Republican Party at the national level as the
party that will not raise your taxes. . . . You can walk into the voting
booths in any state in the nation, dead drunk, and vote for the
Republican for Congress and Senate, and he or she will not raise
your taxes. . . . The reason this is important is the same reason that
Coca-Cola has been so successful. . . . You just grab it off the shelf
because you know what's inside. . . . Republican elected officials
who vote for tax increases are rat heads in a Coke bottle. They
damage the Republican brand."
　　—Grover Norquist in October 2005 speech [37]

RINO HUNTING

Democrats have taken a beating recently from an aggressive GOP,
but so have some middle-of-the-road Republicans. The Club for
Growth (whose founder, right-wing power monger Stephen Moore,
coined the term "RINO") and the archconservative magazine *Human
Events* are among those targeting some Republican legislators who
are not fervently enough echoing the party line on matters from tax
cuts to abortion. A few on the dartboard:

- **Sen. Lincoln Chafee** (R-Rhode Island): He's pro-choice and backs strict environmental regulation, government-funded health care, and an increase in minimum wage. That he didn't endorse Bush in the 2004 election, wanted to trim the president's tax cuts, and opposes drilling in the Arctic National Wildlife Refuge only increases the hard-core Right's ire. Losing in the 2006 midterm election, Chafee is now toying with the idea of switching parties.
- **Sen. Olympia Snowe** (R-Maine): Pro-choice Snowe is a self-described "centrist"—and that alone is cause for RINO hunting. Snowe, along with Chafee and Maine's other senator, Susan Collins, were among the few Republican senators not to earn a 100 percent score from the Christian Coalition—adding more fuel to the fire.
- **Sen. Arlen Specter** (R-Pennsylvania): Being against abortion is not enough: conservatives say the powerful Specter warned President Bush not to appoint judges who would toss out *Roe v. Wade*, and he has voted for the Comprehensive Test Ban Treaty, for overtime pay for workers, and with Democrats opposing school vouchers. Hiss.
- **Rep. Jim Leach** (R-Iowa): He dared to vote against the president on invading Iraq, and he also didn't back the 2003 tax cuts. Add to that his fights for environmental causes and the right to abortion, and, well, you can see why hard-core Republicans get hot under the collar.
- **Rep. Christopher Shays** (R-Connecticut): Supports environmental regs, abortion rights, and has backed gun control. Eject!

Even though he's a hot contender for the Republican presidential nomination, Sen. John McCain has strayed a bit too close to the middle for some Republicans. Distinctly bipartisan, he was one of the Gang of 14—senators from both parties who worked in May 2005 to prevent the Senate from "going nuclear" over Bush's judicial nominees—and, with Lindsey Graham, he wouldn't support the Bush move to ignore the Geneva Conventions for war prisoners.

The new core of the GOP that emerged behind Newt Gingrich in the 1994 takeover has done more than embrace the most contentious issues as they've reworked the party and the values it stands for. They've also brought a distinctly Cold War feel to the country. The Red Scare—when Americans were called upon to look at their fellow countrymen and coworkers as commies—has been wound up and brought back to life. Fittingly, many of those who've rewhittled the Republican Party grew up during the Cold War, and its stark realities obviously made an impression. After decades of being shoved to the power sidelines, these Republicans spit the word "bipartisanship" out of their mouths: to them it's nearly the same as cozying up with Communists. The words "I disagree" or "Let's talk" are not part of their vocabulary: those who don't see eye to eye with those making "With us or with the terrorists" ultimatums are simply discarded as liberals, radicals, and Democrats—all of which they see as pretty much synonymous with Satanists.

> *"Back then, we had the House Un-American Activities Committee [HUAC] and the Senate Internal Security Subcommittee of the Judiciary Committee . . . [Oh] how liberal Members of Congress and the left-wing media hated these committees. [But now] we need a revival of internal security committees in both the House and the Senate."*
> —Paul Weyrich, in a September 2006, online column[38]

> *"There is a religious war going on in our country for the soul of America. It is a cultural war, as critical to the kind of nation we will one day be as was the Cold War itself."*
> —Pat Buchanan, in his 1992 speech to the Republican National Convention

> *Reporter: Grover, don't you think you're probably monitored by intelligence agencies?*
> *Grover Norquist: Our guys or the Soviets?*[39]

And as in the McCarthy era, the enemy is said to be lurking everywhere, and in higher numbers than ever. In all corners, New Republicans see their foes—the ones who ruined America by ushering in big government, environmental regulations, and loosened morals. The Enemy banned prayer in school and welcomed the era of *Roe v. Wade* while shrugging off gay marriage as acceptable. The Enemy tried to cut defense after the Soviet Union fell. The Enemy is embedded among us: the liberals, the Greens, and above all, the Democrats.

Yet, while the strident GOP core keeps declaring wars—figuratively and literally—in many ways, it really all boils down to an all-American Red v. Blue football game. And the reason the Reds want to win it so bad is that they were sitting on the sidelines for forty years.

> *"I think we're winning. I think their team is losing. And I think if we do our job right over the next ten years, we're going to have ten years or more where we have a lot of fun and they have a rather unpleasant time of it. It's only going to get more fun for us and less fun for them."*
> —Grover Norquist, in a September 1995 speech to the Council for National Policy[40]

What we're seeing today is decades' worth of bottled-up resentment that has been honed, strategically combed, and market-tested into a multipronged Republican battle plan to kick the Democrats' booty—and we mean that in every sense of the word.

Beyond simple character assaults and trying to brand the GOP, the party movers are ruthlessly smashing the Democratic treasure chest—trying to steer more contributions their way by forcing lobbyists (and their deep-pocketed clientele) to donate exclusively to the Republican election war chests, and they're even trying to systematically squeeze the main funders of the Democratic Party—trial lawyers and organized labor. And why are they doing it? What's forgotten about today's ruthless climate is the dramatic history leading up to it—and how today's headlines, the crafted accusations sung out in chorus, and the changes in leadership are the culmination of years of being dealt out of the game.

> *"When you have tort reform [limiting liabilities for damages awarded in courts], step by step, a little tort reform here and a little there, in each of the fifty states, every time you do that you puncture a hole in the fundraising efforts of the Democratic Party. Every time you have a new start-up company that's non-union—and jobs are created in new companies—you reduce the flow of cash to the Democratic Party."*
> —Grover Norquist in a September 1995 speech[41]

REASONS TO BICKER, THEN AND NOW

Roots of the Democratic Party shoot back to the 1790s, and the Republican Party—whose first president was Abraham Lincoln—was formed in a schoolhouse in 1854, but what best defined the early versions of the two parties was the Civil War. Simply put, Republicans (representing northeastern industrialists) were against slavery, particularly its expansion in the North; most Democrats (representing the plantation-covered South) were for it.[42] Other defining eras:

- **1896–1932:** Republicans led the country, dominating Congress and the White House, except for eight years starting in 1912, when Teddy Roosevelt campaigned on a third-party ticket, splitting the vote and allowing Democrat Woodrow Wilson to sneak in; the Republican-dominated Congress screwed Wilson, famously refusing to ratify his call after World War I for a UN-like League of Nations. Prohibition (1920–1933) was among the most fiery issues of that day, with the "wet" Democrats losing the debate to the "dry" Republicans, who wrote the Eighteenth Amendment that banned booze (and boosted bootlegging).

- **1933–37 (The New Deal):** Picking up the country after the Great Depression had knocked it flat, Democratic President Franklin D. Roosevelt repealed Prohibition and then went on to create big government: his socialist-influenced "New Deal" programs extended government's role in Americans' lives—creating new jobs through electrifying rural areas and building dams, regulating prices of farm products, assisting the poor, providing Social Security to the elderly, creating the forty-hour workweek, encouraging labor unions, reforming the banking system, and establishing the role of federal government as regulator of industry and commerce.

- **1964–65:** Following John Kennedy's lead, Lyndon Johnson banned discrimination with his 1964 Civil Rights Act, and the next year ensured voting rights to blacks long barred from voting in the South— causing a shake-up in the Democratic profile: many southerners ditched the party, and many blacks signed on.

- **1980–88 (Reagan years):** While boosting military spending to new highs, he appealed to friends of "small government" and to the Religious Right, first bringing the fervent to the polls in large numbers, and even attracting "Reagan Democrats" to temporarily jump their usual party's ship. The brightest star in recent Republican history.

- **1994 (The Republican Revolution):** Personified by Newt Gingrich, the Republicans in the House make a "Contract with America," vowing to vote on issues from welfare reform to term limits. Their success at the polls flooded both the House and Senate with Republicans, ushering in the first Republican-dominated Congress in forty years.

Roosevelt's post-Depression New Deal set the backdrop for much of today's partisan fighting and it gave birth to two words often hurled today: a "liberal" was one who supported the big government policies, a "conservative" didn't. Although New Deal policies were initially embraced by some in the GOP— the moderate "Rockefeller Republicans" among them— many Republicans ultimately fell into the latter category, and most have New Deal "big gov" policies in their sights today.

With the GOP punted to the far field since the mid-1950s, the country rolled along driven by Democrats. Even when Republicans (Eisenhower, Nixon, and Ford) took the White House, the New Deal ideal of regulation-heavy big government, social welfare programs, and farm subsidies became the accepted image

Roosevelt's New Deal programs boosted America out of the Great Depression, but laid the ground for today's conservative/liberal rift.

of government. Meanwhile, Republicans, particularly the conservative variety, plotted revenge. And their moment arrived in 1980, when rosy-

cheeked Ronald Reagan tottered in as the symbol they were waiting for—
and one they still cling to as though divine and whose likeness they want to
enshrine on the fifty-dollar bill.

> *"Under the Reagan Doctrine, one by one, the communist dominoes
> began to fall. First, Grenada was liberated, by U.S. troops. Then, the
> Red Army was run out of Afghanistan, by U.S. weapons. In
> Nicaragua, the Marxist regime was forced to hold free elections—by
> Ronald Reagan's contra army—and the communists were thrown out
> of power. . . . It was under our party that the Berlin Wall came down,
> and Europe was reunited. It was under our party that the Soviet
> Empire collapsed, and the captive nations broke free. . . . Ronald
> Reagan won the Cold War. . . . Most of all, Ronald Reagan made us
> proud to be Americans again. We never felt better about our country;
> and we never stood taller in the eyes of the world."*
> —Pat Buchanan in 1992 speech at the Republican National
>   Convention [43]

RONALD REAGAN: DEFINING
THE NEW REPUBLICAN

To part of the country, he appeared nearly comical: a daft, jelly
bean–chomping actor prone to dozing off in meetings—his claims under oath that he didn't remember certain key details about the Iran-
Contra scandal, such as his orders to Ollie North, were apparently
truthful since he was already suffering from Alzheimer's disease. To
another part of the country, he was a star—a Communist-loathing
hardballer who used everything he could to take down the Soviet
Union—including setting up Osama bin Laden and friends in
Afghanistan to fight the Russian invaders.

The Gipper supported democracy and freedom fighters and unlike
Jimmy Carter's, his administration—thanks to veep George H. W.
Bush—got the hostages out of Iran, even if he and his cohorts repeatedly worked iffy deals on the side and ignored the will of the Democrat-
dominated Congress. He boosted our military to new heights—in
addition to "Star Wars," Reagan's government spent a trillion funding
new weapons to battle what neoconservatives, including young Paul

Wolfowitz, only imagined the Soviets might possess. He was embroiled in the convoluted Iran-Contra scandal, in which national security advisor Oliver North illegally sold caches of arms to Iranians to covertly fund the anti-Sandinista "contra" fighters working to overthrow the Socialist government in Nicaragua, a plot that was so complicated that few could fully follow it. Later, George H. W. Bush pardoned the guilty— many of whom would become officials in his son's administration.

Loved and loathed, Reagan was the biggest enrollment booster the party had seen since Democrat LBJ inadvertently shooed much of the South to the GOP. Reagan was the first president to beckon to the Religious Right with his anti-abortion stance, and he embraced those who wanted government small by shredding regulations and slashing taxes by 25 percent. A lifelong NRA member, Reagan didn't back down to calls for gun control even after John Hinckley Jr. shot him (and press secretary James Brady) in March 1981.

He called the Soviet Union "the evil empire" and—standing before Berlin's Brandenburg Gate, the literal embodiment of the "Iron Curtain"—he demanded that Mikhail Gorbachev "tear down this wall!" He tried to launch a Strategic Defense Initiative ("Star Wars") and he fought Moscow via a proxy war in Afghanistan (1979–89), where the United States covertly funded mujahideen guerrillas. Reaganites credit the president for bringing an end to the Cold War and the Soviet Union, which crumbled in 1991. And non-Reaganites point out that the U.S. backing of the mujahideen in that war is precisely what led to the rise of al-Qaeda and Osama bin Laden and many of our troubles today.

The Kennedy years were known as Camelot—at least for Democrats. But the Reagan years were when Republicans bloomed—and when many of today's power mongers began planting their seeds for an all-new and improved GOP. And having tasted power under Reagan, they weren't giving it up, even if George H. W. Bush screwed up the succession. Bush Senior's first-term blunder: he dared raise taxes after famously declaring during his campaign, "Read my lips: No new taxes." His defeat allowed Democrat Bill Clinton to sneak in for two terms, during which conservatives did everything they could, including getting him impeached, to undermine him.

> Grover Norquist's Wednesday meetings were born when Newt
> Gingrich, Norquist, and other Republican leaders gathered over cof-
> fee to strategize how to kill Hillary Clinton's health-care plan. The plan
> would have not only increased the role and cost of government—an
> idea that was anathema to fiscal conservatives such as Norquist—it
> smacked of Socialist ideals, equally abhorrent to the right.

The eight years of Clinton allowed the GOP to gear up: once President George W. Bush walked in, the pieces were already in place, and
Republicans had a solidarity never before witnessed in their party. They
had their identity: right-wing, pro-gun, anti-taxes, anti-abortion. They had
party unity and a team of strong leaders built up in Congress who
worked as a bloc. They had branding experts who gave them certain key
phrases to utter—and they do so in unison (see page 114). Republicans
had made a "PAC" with themselves—to fund other Republicans in difficult elections; those who didn't help out the team would be blocked from
committees. And they had the so-called K Street Project, an attempt to
shove Democrats out of the lucrative lobbying biz.

K STREET PROJECT

The story goes that in the 1980s, an ad appeared in the DC paper
Roll Call. From a Fortune 500 company, the advertisement sought an
in-house lobbyist—specifying the position should be filled by a Democrat. That's what supposedly gave Republicans the idea to turn the tables. After Republicans took both sides of Congress in 1994, the plan
was fully hatched by, among others, Rep. Tom DeLay and Sen. Rick
Santorum. The Project would pressure lobbying firms and trade associations to hire Republicans—guaranteeing only Republican lobbyists access to top legislators, who since the 1994 victory were almost
exclusively from the GOP. Not only would such a strategy close the
Republican inside circle even tighter, it would also deplete Democratic Party funds, since many lobbyist-lawyers become wealthy, and
quite a few donated to that party. Some say it worked—but the movie

industry flipped off the movement by replacing showy Jack Valenti as head of the powerful Motion Picture Association of America with Clinton's secretary of agriculture, Dan Glickman. The move wasn't well received. Norquist for one regarded it as "a mistake" and "a studied insult"—and shortly thereafter, the House deleted a $1.5 billion tax credit for the movie industry.[44] Some say lobbyist hiring has heavily favored Republicans ever since. And Sen. Rick Santorum, along with Rep. Tom Delay—now both departed—squeezed firms to contribute Republican as well. It remains to be seen how "the Project" fares given the overthrow of GOP tyranny.

As recently as October 2006, Rep. Tom Reynolds (R-New York), who also heads the Republican Congressional Committee, issued a warning to lobbying firms. Even though it looked like Democrats might take the House, he warned them to continue pouring money—and their clients' millions—almost exclusively into the GOP coffers. If they didn't, he reportedly threatened, "We will have no choice but to report to the Republican Conference any changes in your pattern of giving," reported respected DC publication *Roll Call*.[45]

Even if the party took "a thumpin'"—as President Bush summed up the 2006 overthrow—the GOP's muscle and organization continues to be formidable. Over the past twelve years, Republicans steamrolled Washington like a well-oiled machine—and a lot of people say Grover Norquist was driving it. They point to a drab building on L Street, where Norquist runs his nonprofit Americans for Tax Reform, saying that here is the nexus of power—at least right-wing power—in the United States.

[Forces at Work]

- **Paul Weyrich:** He organized the social conservative movement that helped bring social conservatives and the Christian Right to the GOP. (www.freecongress.org)

- **Grover Norquist:** His childhood vision turned into the guiding theme of the Republican Party: no new taxes. Networking giant Norquist has proven his strength and genius in the party, and his Americans for Tax Reform remains incredibly powerful. (www.atr.org)

- **James Dobson:** The Christian-valued radio talk show host put together Focus on the Family with more than 2 million members, whom he unleashes on government agencies and individuals who strike his ire. He shepherded Christians toward the GOP in previous elections, but in 2006 apparently led them away. (www.family.org)

- **Family Research Council:** Originally the lobbying arm of Focus on the Family, this force of the hard-core Religious Right is led by Tony Perkins, who persuaded the Bush administration to stop funding any organization that Perkins believed to be involved in abortion referrals. Perkins has also explained the torture committed at Abu Ghraib as a result of MTV and pornography.[46] (www.frc.org)

- **Heritage Foundation:** Headed up by Ed Feulner, the original right-wing think tank still exerts tremendous clout. (www.heritage.org)

- **Newt Gingrich:** Leader of the Republican Revolution of 1994, Gingrich's ego brought him down, although a police radio scanner and an elderly couple in Florida helped.

- **Karl Rove:** The master strategist of the GOP, he's embraced Christian voters and homophobes, key groups in George W. Bush's reelection, when gay marriage on state ballots brought out many to vote. Can't say "pass the sugar, please" without mentioning 9/11—a strategy formalized by lingo meister Frank Luntz.

Close-up

He was looking out the window as the school bus rolled down Church Road in Weston, Massachusetts, when it hit him. How to save the Grand Old Party. At age fourteen, round-faced and bespectacled Grover Norquist was already a Republican and an avowed anti-Communist, who'd long before traded in his Hardy Boys for Red Scare books by FBI head J. Edgar Hoover and about Alger Hiss.

The year was 1971 and President Richard M. Nixon was pulling troops out of Vietnam, a humiliating retreat with no victory against Communism, the symbol of evil itself. Alarmingly, Nixon was warming up to Communist China, negotiating détente with the Soviet Union, and talking about slashing the number of nuclear missiles; on the home front, the president was launching programs for the poor and signing landmark laws protecting the environment and workers—the sort of behavior one would expect from bleeding-heart, big government–lovin' Democrats, Norquist thought, regarding such expenditures as a waste of tax-payer dollars.

To the fourteen-year-old, the Republican Party of that era appeared utterly doomed. Until, that is, the school bus turned onto Church Road and he was struck with a plan to save the GOP.

"What I realized was that people usually had no idea who they were voting for or what the parties even stood for," says Norquist, now fifty. "And I thought if we could just brand the Republican party as the 'no tax party' then people would know that whomever they voted for—president, congressman or dog catcher—as long

Grover Norquist transformed the GOP into the "Won't Raise Your Taxes" party.

as they were Republican, they would not raise taxes. And I knew if we did that, we could get at least half of the vote."[47]

That very "no taxes" idea has made Norquist the reigning behind-the-scenes power monger in DC today. "Grover Norquist is running the country," says Public Citizen's Taylor Lincoln, not particularly happily.[48] As president of Americans for Tax Reform, a nonprofit advocacy group, Norquist, who with reddish hair and beard framing owlish features looks like a heady 1950s RAND thinker, is frequently summoned to 1600 Pennsylvania Avenue for parties and private consultations: Norquist met with White House officials, including the president and top advisor Karl Rove, an astounding ninety-eight times since the Bush administration walked in—only one show of his access and muscle. Reportedly, Karl Rove's assistant, Susan Ralston (who'd previously worked for Jack Abramoff, and in October 2006 resigned her post with Rove because she'd accepted a number of gifts from the dishonored lobbyist), would call Norquist for a green light before letting calls through to Rove.[49] But Norquist's prowess extends beyond the executive branch: he's often found on Capitol Hill, where he advises powerful heads of committees—telling them what points are on his agenda and asking how he can help out with their plans.[50] Regularly strategizing with the GOP's congressional chiefs of staff—who often usher in Norquist for private meetings—he's the man that big-name Republicans come to with their plans, knowing that if anybody can make an idea fly, Norquist can—or at least he'll have the right number to call. Presidential hopefuls are calling up constantly these days, soliciting Norquist's endorsement, which many Republicans now regard as essential: plenty believe Grover Norquist struck George H. W. Bush down in the 1992 presidential election, and that Norquist ushered George W. Bush in. The capital's king of networking and ground-level strategizing, Norquist has ascended to the top rung, and his success is all about taxes, all about branding, and all about the Wednesday meetings, which have helped glue the diverse pieces of the Republican Party together. And it's all about "the Pledge," a piece of paper that he's turned into a political weapon.

Taxpayer Protection Pledge

I, _____, pledge to the taxpayers of the district of _____ in the state of _____, and to the American people that I will:

ONE, oppose any and all efforts to increase the marginal income tax rates for individuals and/or businesses; and
TWO, oppose any net reduction or elimination of deductions and credits, unless matched dollar for dollar by further reducing tax rates.

GROVER'S WORLD

Some paint him as a monster, but Grover Norquist is wonderfully charming in person: articulate, cordial, bright, and not at all pretentious, he's perhaps the most helpful man in DC, at least if you fall right of center. And he blanches when people describe him as ruthless. "I don't know what they mean by that," he says, his jaw clenching. "I never criticize anybody in public for something I haven't warned them about in private. But if they raise taxes, after I only told them a hundred times not to cross that line . . ."[51]

Take, for instance, what happened in 1988, the year that President Reagan tottered off and Republicans were determined to keep their White House hold. Sen. Bob Dole initially was running ahead in the primaries. But when approached to sign the Pledge, Dole declined—"which is why he lost," says Norquist. Reagan's vice president, George H. W. Bush, was floundering. However, Bush signed the Pledge that year—"when he was 17 points behind. And he won."[52]

Apparently the elder Bush didn't attribute his victory to the vow he had taken not to raise taxes or the support of Norquist's Americans for Tax Reform; his evangelical son George W. was out stumping to lasso the religious vote, and the candidate himself published a book that year trumpeting his born-again experience to the Christian crowd. Perhaps Bush attributed his election miracle—shoving aside Dole and holier-than-thou Pat Robertson in the primaries—as the will of God, not Grover Norquist. Whatever Bush was thinking, two years later Norquist got word that President George H. W. Bush wanted to raise taxes. "We warned him," says Norquist, his lizard green eyes darkening. "We told him for months what a disaster it was going to be. But he threw away his presidency. He raised taxes in 1990 and lost two years later."[53]

George W. personally discovered Norquist's ire when as governor of Texas, he made a move to boost taxes. Norquist's organization sponsored a wide anti–tax hike campaign, and by the end, Bush had dropped the idea and Norquist had made his point: in 1998, about the moment the younger Bush decided to run for president, Grover Norquist was flown down to Texas. In his briefcase, he carried the Pledge.

"We became allies," says Norquist, who also advised him on issues from expanding free trade to privatizing Social Security, and suggesting numerous ideas that Bush immediately embraced.[54] The anti-tax man was soon strategizing alongside Karl Rove, who, like Norquist, had been a College Republican. Norquist says he never formally endorsed George W. Bush in the 2000 election, but Bush's people soon began showing up at the invitation-only Wednesday meetings and many Republicans in DC fell in line behind the Texan once Norquist gave Bush an informal nod. And Bush opened the White House door to help out Norquist with fundraisers, happy to meet with Jack Abramoff's tribal clients who made out $25,000 checks to Norquist's nonprofit, ATR.

It's debatable whether Americans for Tax Reform (or rather the president's tax hike) took President George H. W. Bush down in 1992, when some of the typical GOP vote went to Ross Perot, who ran on the Reform Party ticket and promised tax cuts. Enough people, however, believed that Norquist—who did not support Bush in the 1992 election—had something to do with the defeat that his crossed-armed stance also whipped the Republican Party into shape—tattooing "No Tax Hikes" onto the elephant. Now most Republicans are quick to scribble their names on the document: currently 222 House members and 46 senators—all Republican—have taken the Pledge. And when President Bush sends in a request to cut taxes—which he's done every year since he took office—Republican congressmen are quick to push it through.

Around the same time that fourteen-year-old Grover Norquist was figuring out how to save the GOP, a Wisconsin radio broadcaster found himself in a Democratic planning meeting for a proposed low-income housing project. Whoever mistakenly invited Paul Weyrich, a pale blond Christian "traditionalist" who was then a press officer for senator Gordon Allott (R-Colorado), inadvertently altered the future of the Democratic Party. After he'd heard guarantees for endorsements from the *Washington Post*'s editorial board and promises for favorable reports from the Brookings Institute, a DC think tank, Weyrich walked out both sickened and inspired: he'd never before realized the extent of the Democrats' formidable opinion-influence racket. But he quickly surmised how to adopt their strategy to his cause—beginning by creating a right-wing, Christian-valued think tank that would attack Democrats, liberals, and feminists—and speak out on issues from abortion to how best to slay Communists.

And within short months, after tapping the beer fortune of Joseph Coors for a quarter million in seed money, he put together the Heritage Foundation—a think tank that would become the first line of an assault from the social conservative movement that Paul Weyrich would not only help create but would link to the Republican Party.

"We are different from previous generations of conservatives . . . We are radicals, working to overturn the present power structure of this country."
    —Paul Weyrich in 1973[55] around the time Roe v. Wade *passed, which he deeply opposed*

HERITAGE FOUNDATION

At first, people thought it was a joke. When Paul Weyrich and Ed Feulner, who, like Weyrich, fashioned himself a conservative intellectual, opened with a staff that could have fit into a phone booth, most rolled their eyes at the right-wing nuts calling themselves a think tank. They didn't have PhDs; most didn't have a master's; some of them—including Weyrich—didn't even have a bachelor's degree. But they had money, drive, and a religious zeal to fight the conservative war.

And they kept churning out reports and position papers, keeping faith in the abstract chance that someday somebody would listen. And when Ronald Reagan walked into their lives, they hit the mother lode. The Heritage Foundation greeted the California governor turned president with a 1,100-page twenty-volume book of demands—a "Mandate for Leadership"—which, among its far-fetched notions, first inserted the idea of "Star Wars" in Reagan's brain, and hammered home the need to boost the military (by $1.5 trillion) and vanquish Communism once and for all; the president fulfilled almost two-thirds of the "mandate's" demands.

With Reagan immediately granting them the legitimacy their architects craved, the Heritage Foundation did more than simply support his "wars of liberation" against Communism and Socialism— be they in the jungles of Nicaragua or the beleaguered countries of Africa such as Angola, where the think tank advocated arming tyrant Jonas Savimbi simply because he wasn't Red; the Heritage Foundation actually devised many of Reagan's guiding foreign strategies—some called the think tank Reagan's shadow government—and at least some connected with the group created organizations to help fund those guerrilla wars. Like the Reagan government itself, they were accused of making some under-the-table deals: the South Korean government reported that Korean intelligence had donated $2.2 million to the foundation, which Heritage denied.[56]

Littering Congress with slick, concise, and figure-laden "position papers" (so what if the numbers were sometimes very wrong?—see page 201), they kept up the momentum even when Reagan stepped down. Newt Gingrich worked with Heritage in devising his 1994 Contract with America that brought the GOP rolling into Congress, and he also embraced one of their pet projects, which had been dropped by President Clinton: Star Wars, which Gingrich helped bring back to life. Working with the Republican power base ever since—and handsomely funded now by a half dozen conservative foundations—Heritage now boasts a $36 million annual budget, and their thinkers are invited to the most exclusive meetings on Capitol Hill. The unlikely right-wing think tank that Paul Weyrich dreamed up is now regarded by some to be the most powerful think tank in the world.

> Predictably, in this era when (as Jack Abramoff and public relations firms have aptly illustrated) at least some "expert" opinions might be bought for a decent price,[57] the Heritage Foundation—now without Weyrich at the helm—is all tangled up with K Street, and according to the Washington Post that involvement has proved capable of swaying the think tank's official opinion.[58] President Ed Feulner, reports the Post, started up a separate "for profit" lobbying/consulting firm Belle Haven (employing Feulner's wife) and although the Heritage Foundation had previously slammed the dictatorial Mahathir government in Malaysia, once Feulner's firm was hired by that Asian government, well, wouldn't you know, Heritage suddenly had a change of heart. The foundation, which subcontracted work to Alexander Strategy Group (the ballsy firm headed by DeLay's ex–chief of staff), was suddenly flying in congressmen, among them Tom DeLay, to discover Malaysia's charms, and even writing up briefings—"Malaysia: Standing Up for Democracy."[59] Perhaps North Korea's Kim Jong-il should put in a call.

Weyrich wasn't alone in wanting conservative Christians to amplify their voice: Baptist minister Robert Grant, whom some regard as the true father of the Christian Right movement, cobbled together a religious advocacy group in California in 1974; two years later, after meeting Weyrich, he launched a national lobby, Christian Voice. And Paul Weyrich couldn't have been more pleased: he invited Christian Voice to set up in the Heritage Foundation headquarters—and helped to bring in new religious members, including direct-mail king Richard Viguerie and Howard Phillips, a former government official in the Nixon White House, who led conservative crusades to "defund the Left."

The Christian Voice ultimately led to the rise of a far mightier religious forum—one that began in anger. In 1978, Christian Voice leader Robert Grant lashed out at what had happened to his lobby. Christian Voice was "a sham," he announced at a press conference: it was "controlled by three Catholics and a Jew."[60] Weyrich and Viguerie, two of the Catholics, and Howard Phillips, the (converted evangelical) Jew, put in a call to a rising televangelist, Jerry Falwell, urging him to form a new Christian noisemaking group. Weyrich himself christened Falwell's

organization "the Moral Majority," and it soon gave voice to the disen-
chantment of millions of conservative Christians, who wrote millions
upon millions of letters to TV programmers, government officials, and
judges—and anybody else who offended their anti-abortion and anti-
gay views.

Wheels were already turning when Grover Norquist, freshly gradu-
ated with a BA in political science from Harvard, showed up in Washington, DC, to take a seat as executive director of the National Taxpayers
Union, a nonprofit that lobbied for tax cuts and became the first vehicle
to make the articulate reformer a well-known personality on Capitol Hill
and in the conservative circles that were shooting roots in DC. Democrat
Jimmy Carter was in the White House, the Democrats dominated
Congress—holding two-thirds of the House and nearly as much of the
Senate—and conservative circles were small: Norquist met Paul Weyrich,

who had started a lobbying group (the
Committee for a Free Congress, which,
like Falwell's and Grant's groups, was
throwing money and efforts into recruiting
conservative lawmakers) that was helping
to bring in a dozen right-leaning legislators to DC in the election of 1978, among
them freshman representative Dick Cheney. Even though few were taking note,
the Heritage Foundation was already
showering Capitol Hill with reports, and it
was writing a long wish list for the next
Republican president to step up to the
plate. Norquist met Howard Phillips, who
shared his zeal for tax reform. And he
quickly hit it off with an energetic former
professor, now a freshman representative

Manic, militaristic Newt Gingrich: guided Republicans to
victory in Congress; now he
wants the White House.

from Georgia, by the name of Newt Gingrich—who, after two failed runs,
finally nabbed a House seat. "He was the only other person I knew who
could say, here's where I want to be in twenty-five years and work back-
wards," says Norquist.[61]

The two shared a vision and a goal: to yank Congress from the Democrats. It would take them sixteen years—and yet a few more wheels—to do it. And what helped them to accomplish the goal was a group known for dodgy deals and nastiness: the College Republicans. The next year, when Norquist returned to Harvard in the MBA program, he signed up with the group. And that's how he became part of the troika—with Jack Abramoff and Ralph Reed—that would change the face of Washington, DC, the Republican Party, and the country.

THE COLLEGE REPUBLICANS

The oldest student organization in the country—and the best funded, with a multimillion-dollar yearly budget—the College Republicans have never been nominated for any "Most Congenial" or "Most Clean-Nosed" awards.[62] Their deceptive fundraising schemes, using "Republican Headquarters" letterhead in their direct mail solications, for instance, are only one reason they've gotten in hot water. The kids' political tactics are alarmingly brutal and cutthroat: candidates for the national chair (a position held in 1973 by Karl Rove) pull capers and the campaigns are so dirty that the FBI has sometimes come in for criminal investigations, including of College Republican Rove. But the competitive spirit ratcheted up to new heights when a somewhat handsome, bright, scheming, and egotistical football star by the name of Jack Abramoff decided to run for the presidential ticket. With the help of the brainy Grover Norquist, a new friend whom he'd met while campaigning for Reagan, Abramoff won the campaign—Salon.com reports that his father heavily outfinanced all campaign opponents, further ensuring victory.[63] Upon becoming College Republican chairman in 1981, he appointed Norquist as the group's executive director, and around then a wide-eyed Georgian with choirboy looks asked Abramoff for a job. Ralph Reed was hired as intern, working closely as assistant to Norquist. And the boys quickly launched a vicious war against Democrats and the Left. So loathed were Dems, that the trio reportedly forced recruits to demonstrate their fealty by, among other things, memorizing passages from the movie *Patton* and replacing the word "Democrats" for "Nazis."[64] As chairman of the College Republicans, Abramoff summed up the enemy in the organization's 1983 annual report noting, "It is not our job to seek peaceful coexistence with the Left. Our job is to remove them from power permanently."[65] While blowing through its treasury, the triumvirate was so zealous in its conservative mission—burning Soviet effigies in Lafayette Park, for instance—that it managed to attract not only local newspaper write-ups, but even Newt Gingrich took to hanging out with the collegiates. The trio was so impressed by Gingrich's vision for a Republican-dominated DC that it soon embraced Gingrich's goal—to become Speaker of the House—as its own. And it wasn't post-adolescent dreaming: when the trio marched on Washington a decade later, its mission—to destroy Democrats and liberals—was nearly accomplished.

The effect of the Norquist-Reed-Abramoff triumvirate can't be overestimated. Through the 1980s and 1990s, Norquist would redefine the Republican Party as the tax-cutting party, an idea that appealed to the wealthy, Big Business, and libertarians. Ralph Reed would be crucial in linking the Religious Right to the GOP. And Jack Abramoff would finance it, not only dumping hundreds of thousands of his own money into the Republican machine, but redirecting hundreds of millions of the money of his clients, many of whom originally leaned toward Democrats, into the GOP machine.

The Washington, DC, that Norquist returned to in 1981, was a whole different world: Ronald Reagan was in power, the military budget was soaring, and the Heritage Foundation was suddenly prestigious. Norquist, who worked as head speechwriter for the U.S. Chamber of Commerce, was in the thick of it: the twenty-something was featured in *Washington Post* articles about the new Reagan conservatism. He helped Abramoff make the College Republicans a veritable force and he spent hours upon hours plotting with Rep. Newt Gingrich about exactly how the GOP could conquer Congress—an idea that Gingrich as much as Norquist was obsessed with. Pretty much nobody else—except Abramoff and Reed—thought such an outrageous notion was possible.

"When all other political analysts and even party officials were writing off the chance to win a majority in the House of Representatives, Newt Gingrich was there, telling them, 'No, it can be done.'"
    —Paul Weyrich in 1996[66]

Gingrich was developing new tools for the Republican Party takeover, among them cable TV, a medium that other politicians hadn't yet exploited. Nobody more adored C-SPAN than loudmouth Newt, who had learned early on that the way to snag ink and airtime was to say the outrageous. In 1984, he pulled the stunt that first made him infamous. Standing on the floor of the House, he viciously laid into the Democrats, lashing out at them for being soft on Communism and being defeatists and losers. As the camera held tight on Gingrich, he bellowed and he roared at the party that held both the House majority and the Senate, shaking his finger and making searing accusations about their weaknesses and how they were degrading the country. And the Democrats did not utter one word back. There was nobody but the cleaning crew in the room. The move so infuriated House Speaker Tip O'Neill that he attempted to excoriate Gingrich on the floor—but Gingrich held up, winning both party admiration and the interest of the media who henceforth turned to Newt to shoot out pithy quotes.

And in the mid-1980s, Gingrich found yet another vehicle—the GOP's political action committee (GOPAC). But Gingrich didn't use it as merely a means to raise money, although that it did—bringing in millions. The congressman exploited a different angle: leadership tapes, which he peppered with a mix of morale building and propaganda, recording thousands of tapes for wannabe politicians, or those just launching their careers.

"You favor a political revolution. You want to replace the welfare state with an opportunity society. You favor workfare over welfare. You want to lock prisoners up. . . . If you fly with us, work with us, fight with us, we are going to create a real revolution, we are going to replace the Welfare State."
    —Newt Gingrich in GOPAC tape[67]

Gingrich also highlighted a skill that has since become the GOP trademark: selective forceful words to bang home the point. GOPAC handed out textbooks of power words for freshman Republicans to use when describing party members—"truth," "moral," "reform," "pioneer," "opportunity"—alongside another list of words to use when describing the opponents: "betray," "endanger," "corruption," "taxes," "liberal," "cheat," "hypocrisy." The repeat-a-thon had begun.

TALKING YOUR WAY INTO POWER:
BLURRING, BRANDING, AND BURYING THE TRUTH

It's not the message. It's the words upon which ideas glide that decide whether they're embraced or rejected. That's what politicians are learning—from master of messaging Frank Luntz, a hulking GOP pollster and linguistic wizard, who sculpts words, lifting and plumping them to entice and delight, regardless of substance.

In laboratories and conference rooms, Luntz is listening to America—trying to assess how we think, what we want, and, most of all, what we want to hear. His goal: to discover which words hit our brain's pleasure center and enhance the chance that messages are happily swallowed or, conversely, which terms disturb or alarm—and are thus handy for knocking down opponents. Gathering small groups in his laboratory, Luntz prods them on preferences—do they favor "21st-century technology" over "21st-century approach" and "integrity" or "reliability"? The greatest

Pollster and strategist Luntz helped the GOP prettify controversial statements and say nothing with style.

insights are derived when he hands out small dials—essentially "like-o-meters" that individuals turn to rate how strongly they warm to certain words while watching taped speeches. PBS's *Frontline* showed Luntz monitoring the "like-o-meter" responses in his laboratory, studying a screen where a green line peaked and dipped as it reflected dialed "votes." The people in the focus group, watching a speech by an energy exec, predictably weren't wowed by much—until they heard the term "changing fuels" and the green line suddenly surged. Another chart-topper: "phasing out older plants."

Based on his studies into what resonates and what doesn't, Luntz penned a dictionary of massaged messages for the Republican Party. It's brimming with political slogans that may not mean much, but bring a warm feeling to our hearts.

To enhance Republicans' "sell-ability" to American voters, Luntz recommends a revamped lexicon:[68]

- Cool down the furor over "global warming": call it "climate change."
- Kill the "estate tax": call it the "death tax"; promise "tax relief" not "tax cuts."
- Republicans want "goals and results"; those darn Democrats are obsessed with "partisanship and politics."
- Call those stalking trial lawyers "predatory."
- Liberally season speeches with terms such as "common sense," "balance," and "safe and healthy."
- Frequently refer to the United States as "the greatest economic power in the world" and in trade discussions remind Americans that "we will remain the greatest economic power in the world only so long as we continue to do business with other nations."[69]
- Spangle messages with symbols such as the bald eagle or the American flag that "inkblot upon which Americans project their ideals."[70]
- "Appeal to America's greatness. Americans love being told we're the best, that we're number one. We will do *anything—ANYTHING*—to remain number one, and will oppose anything that undermines that superiority."[71]
- And always pull in 9/11—the attack that changed everything—as the backdrop when being criticized over anything from the budget deficit to the war in Iraq. (Too bad it doesn't work in the case of Katrina.)

Pollster Luntz—who in the 1990s got Newt Gingrich jazzed up on the idea that language matters, helping him come up with the phrase "Contract with America"—is the leading guru at selling GOP ideas in snappy matchbox-sized messages: Bush's speeches, for one, are brimming with pretested phrases that make us feel all gushy inside. And the snappy messages Luntz devises—be they "tax relief" or "death tax"—have been honed to fit on a bumper sticker and stamp a strong impression. In short, it's just another way we're being manipulated by politicians, and another area where Democrats have been left in the dust. "Republicans now have semantic hegemony," says Taylor Lincoln, head researcher of government watchdog Public Citizen. "They put a lot of money into studying focus groups and developing sound bites—basically, creating propaganda."[72] Meanwhile, progressives and Democrats haven't "articulated their message in a bumper sticker way."[73]

Meanwhile, more and more Republicans were talking about how to reform taxes. In 1982, Reagan and Congress had made a fumbled attempt to reduce them—slashing the amount of income tax, but also reducing deductions—and some conservatives demanded more. In 1985, Secretary of Commerce Donald Regan pulled in Norquist, who was then not even thirty. President Reagan wanted to pass a sweeping tax cut, but was afraid the move would be shot down by the Democrat-held Congress. Regan asked Norquist to form a nonprofit advocacy group to help sell the idea to Congress and the public. Launching Americans for Tax Reform, Norquist devised a tool to ensure that what went down did not come back up: he came up with the idea for the Pledge—a pledge not to raise taxes. And President Reagan was the first to sign it. The next year, the president's tax cut made it through Congress. And Norquist, the anti-tax star, soared up the power and influence charts.

The foundation was being laid for something quite spectacular, particularly once Ralph Reed showed up in DC in 1988. Because the schemer with the innocent little-boy looks would put together a powerful mechanism for hitching the cross to the elephant. And the meeting that would spark it was the inauguration of George H. W. Bush.

THE BUSH YEARS

Reagan was a hard act for anybody to follow. But it was particularly hard for George H. W. Bush; his words—"a thousand points of light" and "a kinder, gentler nation"—seemed hollow, his persona stiff, compared to the actor who preceded him, and this ticked off the Reaganites, who'd been hoping for a GOP king Part II and instead ended up with Reagan Side B. Bush went after Saddam, but merely chased him off and hadn't come back with his head—a matter that infuriated many, including Newt Gingrich. He puked on the Japanese prime minister—a faux pas worse than Gerald Ford's frequent falls. Despite his claims of being born again, he did little for the Religious Right. He had a political tussle with the powerful American Israel Public Affairs Committee over funding for Israel, and he'd inherited Reagan's huge "voodoo economics" deficit. And when he raised taxes, Gingrich—at Norquist's insistence—loudly balked and the duo organized a power coup: hours after the news circulated through Congress, more than ninety Republicans sent a strongly worded rebuke to the president, vowing to fight the hike. It went through, but Bush had put his head in the noose and pulled tight. And Gingrich had once again emerged as a hero.

For all the problems that befell George H. W. Bush, he did one thing right for the GOP, even if it was inadvertent: he introduced Ralph Reed to Pat Robertson, an early contender in the presidential primaries, who had shown the promise of the religious vote—buoyed by evangelicals, he'd taken Iowa—but had dropped out, and endorsed George H. W. Bush. Reed and Robertson were seated together at Bush's inauguration dinner, and from the start something clicked. Robertson was taken by Reed's wholesome looks, Reed was taken by Robertson's mailing list. And before long, the Christian Coalition was born.

Ralph Reed had a plan: to bring "family values" back to government. And in 1989, when he first sent out mailers to Christians, inviting them to get involved with government and grassroots activism, some thirty thousand signed on, sending in checks and asking for the newsletter, which helped pinpoint the issues that God wanted rectified, Reed asserted, from abortion (Reed was a proponent of dramatic demonstrations at clinics, and had previously held "baby funerals" outside of them) to schools that taught liberal values. Advocating "stealth campaigns," he helped Christians win posts on school boards, where they could more easily monitor books and curricula. The Christian Coalition not only urged members to vote, it told them exactly how to—mailing out more than a million voter guides. The coalition put out a congressional report card, and actively encouraged Christians to run for government positions, be they on city councils or in the House of Representatives. Within three years he'd pumped up membership through his coalition to over a million and he'd moved the headquarters of his Christian movement to DC, not far from Capitol Hill, and unleashed a dozen lobbyists to sway legislators—and identify which were unswayable. And all the while he was strategizing with Grover Norquist and Newt Gingrich on how to bring the Republican army to Congress. Hillary Clinton would play a starring role.

THE CLINTON YEARS

When the governor from Arkansas took control of the White House in 1992, he was scarcely greeted with loud cheers. He'd won with only 48 percent of the vote (a fact the GOP didn't let him forget) and his first move as president was a huge gaffe: he tried to make good on a campaign promise—to allow gays in the military, where they already were anyway, albeit under the unwritten "don't ask, don't tell" rule. Clearly, Clinton didn't understand his constituency. While 10 percent of the population was gay, much of the other 90 percent, particularly the men, were downright homophobic, and Clinton from the start was branded a flaming liberal. Second, his inexperienced staff alienated the press, and reporters' initial impressions of a haughty, closed-off president created a resentment evident in their reports.

And third, there was the Hillary factor: strong, opinionated, and feisty, Hillary was disliked by many men, particularly among the baby boomer crowd and retirees, because, according to GOP pollster Frank Luntz, she "reminds them of their first wife." And many thought it a farce when the president appointed the First Lady—whose job is typically not more demanding than redecorating the White House and meeting with charities—to develop a socialized health-care plan. From the minute Hillary's health-care plan was announced in 1993, conservative Republicans vowed to shoot it down as yet another outrageous expense brought to the American people by the Democrats.

In fact, sheer loathing of the health-care plan brought together a new group that vastly strengthened the GOP: those who met at Grover Norquist's Wednesday meetings (see page 122). What began as an informal get-together with Norquist, Gingrich, and other Republican leaders turned into a strategizing vehicle and a networking nexus that has been meeting every Wednesday for fourteen years.

In 1994, it all came together: only half of the country approved of the performance of President Bill Clinton, 34 percent approved of Congress, and 32 percent believed the country was headed in the right direction. Hillary's health bill had been sent to the shredder, with even dominant Democrats refusing to back the program that now appeared to have been a big waste of money, ink, and time.

Meanwhile, Newt Gingrich had been toiling away, working not only the Heritage Foundation but GOP pollsters who'd help identify what Americans thought: the research showed they were worried about crime, ticked about "welfare mothers," and wanted lower taxes. And most said that in the midterm elections they would vote for candidates who didn't support Clinton.

Along with Rep. Dick Armey (R-Texas) Gingrich had an idea—to draw up something like Norquist's Pledge, except in reverse. He needed a pledge, a promise—a Contract with America! Armey drew up a draft of it, borrowing ideas and words from Ronald Reagan's 1985 State of the Union speech, and Newt took over the publicity wheel.

The Contract promised to make reforms—social, economic, and political. There was the Take Back Our Street Act promising to battle crime, and the Fiscal Responsibility Act to help prevent any tax increase, along with promises to slash them. There were pledges to bring the former Communist countries of Eastern Europe into the guiding forces of NATO, and to clean up Congress, starting with an audit that would cut waste.

And most of all there was accountability built right in: if the public voted Republicans into Congress, and they didn't live up to their promises, then Gingrich told the public that they should kick them right out.

Norquist lined up support of fiscal conservatives. Reed brought in the Christian Right. Weyrich brought in the social conservatives, who financially backed right-leaning Republicans to run. The arms sellers signed on with the hopes of loading up Eastern European countries in NATO. Corporations backed the promises for corporate tax cuts. Gingrich, bright and charismatic, hit the heart of millions. And in November 2004, the Republicans won in state after state, district after district, from the governor's chairs to seats in Congress. The victory astounded even those who'd designed it: not a single incumbent Republican lost his or her seat, while the GOP won nine seats in the Senate and fifty-four seats in the House, giving Republicans the first majority in the House since the elections of 1952. The Revolution had begun.

NEWTIE'S NEW GOP-DOMINANT WORLD

Formerly a Georgia history professor, Newton Leroy Gingrich—or "Newtie" as he was called by his ma—married his high school teacher (and dumped her in 1981, while she was in the hospital for cancer), and shed his former leftie thinking to snag a House seat in 1978. The charismatic (if petulant) loudmouth rose as self-appointed GOP general—boosting spirits of the once-outsider party, showing how language could be a weapon, and unifying the GOP as an army quick to assault. His 1994 "Contract with America" (conceived by Dick

Armey) led to the GOP taking over the House and he soared as House Majority leader, his ego swelling dangerously—so much that Republicans tried to boot him in 1997. Informally slapped for questionable acts—his acceptance of more than $4 million as a book advance from a Rupert Murdoch house, while Murdoch was lobbying for changes in legislation, led to such an uproar that Gingrich returned it—he convinced the ethics committee to drop eighty-four charges leveled at him, if he paid $300,000 for being evasive during investigations. Soon thereafter, a retired couple overheard him (via scanner radio) plotting to change that agreement; they taped the conversation and the *New York Times* ran in, leading to more outrage. After boycotting Clinton's budget—which led to a government shutdown—he'd led the attack to impeach the president, which blew up in his face. In 1998, when the GOP lost thirty-four House seats, Gingrich resigned. Still active in advising the feds on space and defense, and a "thinker" at the American Enterprise Institute, he's penned a new book—*God in America*—which might come in real handy if he makes a rumored run for the White House in 2008.

Gingrich became Speaker of the House, Dick Armey was majority leader, and Tom DeLay came in number three as majority whip. Bob Dole led the Senate. And in between voting on a record number of items—including all those promised in the Contract—the GOP elite led by Gingrich began setting new rules. Rule 1: Powerful Republicans henceforth would be obligated to raise at least $500,000 for the party, to ensure that elections in all corners of the country would be well financed. Rule 2: The party had to stick together. And rule 3: Republicans were going to wring more money out of lobbyists and their clients, even forbidding them from contributing to Democrats. And handily, it was right about then that Jack Abramoff—who'd been traveling the world helping out anti-Communist forces from Afghanistan to Angola in between making an anti-Communist movie that was laughed out of the critics' viewing room—decided to make his *entre vous* in DC. And before long he was directing millions to Republicans, on checks made out by American Indian tribes.

WEDNESDAY AT GROVER'S

It's not much to look at—a conference room with a few antique maps on the wall, a table in the middle, and a plethora of conservative magazines and newsletters piled around everywhere. But this second-floor space in the back of the offices of Americans for Tax Reform has become the GOP's war room. Drinking coffee and chomping on bagels, over one hundred of DC's most influential right-of-center thinkers, politicians, lobbyists, and activists gather together every Wednesday to hear short speeches and updates and tackle the issues of the day. Under the fluorescent lights, alliances are formed and spears are sharpened and battle strategies are drawn. And it's all off the record: the roster of who was there and the specifics of what was discussed are not for public consumption, and the gentlemen's agreement holds, even though these days plenty of women are present.

From its casual beginning in 1993, the Wednesday meetings of what Norquist calls "the Leave Us Alone Coalition" have turned into the networking nexus of conservative DC. The basis is a simple idea that's as much libertarian in origins as Republican: reduce government and reduce the amount of taxes needed to feed it.

"What brings these people to politics," says Norquist, "the thing they want from central government, is to be left alone. So around the table are tax payers, saying, 'Don't raise my taxes,' and property owners saying, 'Don't tax my property,' and homeschoolers saying, 'I want to teach my kids, just go away,' and gun owners saying, 'Just leave me alone, let me hunt,' and the self-employed saying 'Just let me run my business, don't interfere.' And also around that table there are also people from various communities of faith—orthodox Jews, evangelical Protestants, conservative Catholics, Muslims, Mormons—who don't agree theologically. But they want to raise kids, practice faith, and be left alone. So people have different interests, but they agree they want government to leave them alone and that's why the coalition holds together."[74]

The ideology attracts many—from the NRA (where Norquist is board member, sitting between Ollie North and "Tarzan rocker" Ted Nugent at meetings) to the U.S. Chamber of Commerce, which represents millions of businesses. But what lures just as many to the Wednesday meetings, to which attendees must be formally invited, is the access to so many big-time players in one room. Karl Rove stops by every so often, as do Dick Cheney, Ralph Reed, and Newt Gingrich; and if congressional players aren't in attendance, their chiefs of staff are. Whether visiting dignitaries or corporate leaders, the up and coming or the already there, each participant is given a few minutes to talk about accomplishments and concerns, as plans are mapped out on how to further everything from the branding of the Republican image to how to tighten the grip of the K Street Project, while Norquist makes a point of teaming up strangers with a cordial "This is somebody you should know." And in the process of holding the city's most prestigious and productive meetings, Norquist has become the GOP's go-to guy, whose strategy, devised on the bus when he was fourteen, has now come to be the motto of the Republican Party. And since President George W. Bush has been in power, he's made good on the vow he signed for Norquist back in 1998. Bush hasn't raised taxes a penny; in fact, every year, he's sent a tax cut to Congress, which has given them the green light.

"The Democratic Party of lawyer and labor is on its way out. Oh we'll always have a two-party system, maybe the opposition party will be the tree huggers party or the weird sex party, but the Democratic Party of today won't be around much longer."
—Grover Norquist, September 2006[75]

During the past four years, when they had locked up both houses of Congress and the White House, the Republican Party had a profound effect. The positions written out as its platforms have manifested in striking ways. Indeed business has been promoted—corporate taxes have been slashed, handsome incentives given for investing in everything from ethanol to nuclear plants. Tort law and Medicare have been reformed. Yet it's rather ironic that the party that so despises big government has created a machine far more convoluted and invasive than the one in effect when it walked in. That while taxes have been decreased, government spending has soared to its highest level since the Reagan years. That the party that vowed in its Contract with America to be fiscally responsible brought the accounting sheet from no deficit to one that is soaring into the trillions. That the party of the Leave Us Alone Coalition has tolerated an administration that has ripped up privacy rights, bugged and tracked us, and defends snooping on its own citizens even when it has been declared illegal.

Then again, when historians look back at the lunatic extremism of George W. Bush, they'll be sure to point out he was neither Republican nor in many ways conservative, despite the fact that both groups voted him in.

And for all the strategizing that's gone into the rise of the Republican Party, for all the money that's been poured in and the creation of a unified machine, some of the core factions are now talking about leaving. "The Republican Party believes in absolutely nothing," chastises Paul Weyrich. "And with leadership which is for sale, we will never win."[76] The Christian Right and moralists are spitting mad that Bush and the Republicans in Congress didn't do more when they had the chance: *Roe v. Wade* still hasn't been overturned, gays can still be wed in some states, creationism-linked "intelligent design" hasn't replaced Darwin's theory of evolution in textbooks nationally, and the FDA has approved RU-486, an abortion-causing pill (even though few doctors prescribe it and some religious pharmacists refuse to hand it out). Congress stalled on bills that social conservatives want pushed through, including boosted fines for broadcasters deemed obscene and laws that outlaw the use of blood from umbilical cords, an area related to stem cell research.

> *"If they get disinterested in the values of the people who put them in office as they have done in the past, if that happens again, I believe the Republican Party will pay an enormous price in four years and maybe two."*
> —James Dobson, Focus on the Family[77]

The Republican Party appears at the moment to be shattering. Meanwhile the Democrats appear confused on what they stand for. And in the middle stand 300 million American people, red, blue, and purple, among whom we can only hope there are still a few candidates for honest leadership.

[What You Can Do]

Stress bipartisanship: Democrats point fingers and portray the GOP as corrupt, but Democrats have their foibles as well, and like Republicans they haven't yet figured out how to reform a very broken system that needs help. What we need at this point is bipartisanship. Encourage your representative to step over the red/blue divide.

- Check out the platforms. Many are surprised to see what the parties stand for.

- Get involved in primaries. Low voter turnout allows motivated extremists to secure the candidacy.

- Reconsider voting along strict party lines. Having both a Republican-controlled Congress and White House has spelled disaster—and the Democrats have been horrid as well. Vote for balance.

CHAPTER 4

Going Nuclear

His approval rating had nosedived to 42 percent, and gas had shot up to $2.23 a gallon, forcing SUV owners to shuck out some $400 a month for fuel. His vice president's chief of staff was tangled up in a sticky security leak scandal—and the ensuing federal investigation threatened to snare his top White House advisor, Karl Rove, or even the elusive vice president himself. The administration was at that moment under the gun for directing the National Security Agency to illegally snoop on U.S. citizens, and by then, the mere word "Iraq" caused Americans to flinch; high-profile thinkers publicly fretted that he was planning a nuclear attack on Iran. The messy fallout of the Abramoff affair was splattering very near his most ferocious Texan ally, House Majority Leader Tom DeLay, and, alarmingly, the fallen lobbyist Abramoff kept insisting he'd hung out with the president, who feigned having no recollection of the Pioneer who had been on Bush's transition team. Meanwhile, it was hard to forget that his good chum Enron's "Kenny Boy" Lay, whose requests were embedded in the administration's controversial energy plan, was in Houston that week testifying in court on eleven criminal charges of deception and fraud regarding his electricity biz.

It was definitely time for President George W. Bush to have a frank talk with his country.

Indeed, as he took to the podium that January evening, President George W. Bush looked Americans straight in the eye and blurted out the truth. Standing before expectant congressmen, Cabinet members, and Supreme Court justices, who assembled in the House Chamber's horseshoe of leather-seated power, President Bush gazed soulfully into the television camera. "We have a serious problem," he read from the teleprompter that spelled out his 2006 State of the Union speech. "America is addicted to oil."

FOGGING THE ISSUE

Few leaders are "yes," "no," and "the buck stops here" personas anymore. When problems arise they obscure the topic at hand rather than addressing it and placing or assuming blame outright. But the Bush administration systematically twists logic in mind-boggling fashion. Fears about global warming are answered by the administration's cheerful-sounding Clear Skies Initiative—which relaxes existing air pollution regulations and entirely ignores emissions from carbon dioxide, the gas most linked to climate change. Never mind that the culprits behind the California blackouts were energy wholesalers, such as Enron, which bought and sold utilities' electricity—and had manipulated prices, causing them to plummet so low that utilities didn't want to sell their juice; some electrical plant operators purposefully had shut down, thus causing the blackouts. But the Bush administration seized upon the outages as proof that we needed more electricity—the major component of its 2001 energy plan. When consumers complained about being crushed by debt and rocketing credit card interest rates, President Bush signed a revised bankruptcy law that squeezed consumers harder to ensure that debts were paid. When Americans said drug prices were too high, the Bush administration answered back by blocking drug imports from Canada—following up with a convoluted Medicare that made health care more expensive for many seniors. Inside the Department of Defense, the immediate response to 9/11 was "Go after Saddam"—even though Saddam had nothing to do with it; Defense Secretary Donald Rumsfeld, who'd walked in with a hard-to-sell plan to revamp the military, used the attack to revolutionize our battle machines and armed forces—nearly doubling the defense budget to more than $420 billion. In other words, when a problem arises it's usually turned on its ear and used to spur action that was on the "to-do" list from the start. And such was the case with the 2006 State of the Union speech when our addiction to oil became an excuse to pour billions into funding a controversial means to produce electricity, which has nothing to do with our cars.

Never mind that if Americans are oil junkies, it is because President Bush and kindred spirits headquartered in Texas are oil pushers who suckered us in. Never mind that America's "oil addiction" is actually a "car addiction" that results from living in the suburbs—a settlement pattern shaped by tire makers and car manufacturers who sometimes bought up, then destroyed, public transportation in cities, and who ran the country's urban planning schools and instructed city designers to settle us in the outskirts, requiring we drive to our workplace in their automobiles. Forget that Congress—besieged by thousands of lobbyists representing Big Oil and the Big Three automotive makers, and influenced by the millions in campaign contributions those industries kick in to the coffers—consistently slams the brakes on bills requiring that Detroit make cars that squeeze more miles out of every gallon, even though the technology is available. And overlook (for just one moment) that Bush's radical energy plan released in 2001 had been crafted by his vice president—himself an oil man—who'd pulled in other oil men (and electric utility bigwigs) to "co-write" an energy program that in the name of fighting our dependency on overseas oil in fact keeps us hooked on imported fuel. President Bush at least was ignoring such inconsistencies that night, as were many of the postspeech analysts.

On that Tuesday evening in January 2006, while rain plunked on the heads of a few hundred protesters gathered outside the Capitol Building, the president pulled a bunch of promising rabbits out of his hat. We could kick the foreign oil dependency problem easily: America has the makings for gobs of ethanol, he reminded us, and we have modern technology to guide us. The government, he pointed out, was helping car companies develop hybrid and electric cars, even "pollution-free cars that run on hydrogen." Good old American inventiveness would release us from the clutches of unstable foreign regimes that supplied our needed fix: the programs in his energy policies and initiatives, he promised us, would allow us to slash "more than 75 percent of our oil imports from the Middle East by 2025."

In fact, the Bush administration had done quite the opposite: instead of encouraging manufacturers to make electric cars, it had pressured California to drop the law mandating that electric cars make up 10 percent of the cars sold in California by 2010; instead of helping develop hybrid cars, the Department of Energy dropped funding and abandoned the Clinton administration's program with the Big Three that showed that Detroit is capable of making cars that get seventy miles per gallon. The Department of Energy did launch the Freedom Car Project—looking at hydrogen fuel cell power, although most experts say hydrogen cars won't be hitting the road for a decade. And while it's nice that they threw in a $3,400 tax credit for hybrid cars that run on either gasoline or battery, that's pretty piddly compared to the tax credit of up to $100,000 they gave to drivers buying SUVs.

What George Bush seemed not to recall on the night of his 2006 State of the Union address, as he looked out into the sea of faces, including sixteen-year-old Jeff Lyng, a symbol of tomorrow, who'd built an eight-hundred-square-foot completely solar-powered house, was that Americans had heard almost those exact words many times before—starting with President Nixon back in 1973, when the sudden oil shortage resulting from that year's oil embargo brought us our first taste of gas lines and was the first of several warnings that we needed to kick the foreign oil habit.

"Let this be our national goal: At the end of this decade, in the year 1980, the United States will not be dependent on any other country for the energy we need to provide our jobs, to heat our homes, and to keep our transportation moving."
    —*Richard Nixon, 1974 State of the Union address*

"[W]e must reduce oil imports by 1 million barrels per day by the end of this year and by 2 million barrels per day by the end of 1977 . . . to achieve the independence we want by 1985."
    —*Gerald Ford, 1975 State of the Union address*

"The crises in Iran and Afghanistan have dramatized a very important lesson: Our excessive dependence on foreign oil is a clear and present danger to our Nation's security. The need has never been

more urgent. At long last, we must have a clear, comprehensive energy policy for the United States."
—Jimmy Carter, 1980 State of the Union address

The energy pep talk that George Bush gave in 2006 was inspiring and hope-filled—radically different from the morose energy messages of previous leaders—especially that of President Jimmy Carter: he'd urged Americans to down their thermostats to sixty-eight degrees, an idea quickly binned once Carter was out. But President George W. Bush had a distinct advantage over presidents of yore. He had twenty-first-century spin doctors and focus groups' findings not available to Nixon, Ford, and Carter and he had speechwriters skilled at "branding" images and linking heartwarming words to ideas. And as though waving a magical energy wand before our very eyes, he conjured up rainbow-filled, leprechaun green pictures of "incredible advances" in our energy future. The government was developing "cutting-edge methods of producing ethanol, not just from corn, but from wood chips and stalks, or switch grass." Thanks to his all-new Advanced Energy Initiative that would soon be unveiled, his government was shoveling sacks of money into research for "zero-emission coal-fired plants" and "revolutionary solar and wind technologies," he promised, eyes sparkling.

And then he said something curious, which, had he dared to say it a decade or two before, would have gotten him laughed, or perhaps booed, out of the room. Among the "renewable" projects that his government would be spending billions to develop, he said without so much as a chortle or guffaw, was "clean, safe nuclear energy." The experts at Hill & Knowlton and Potomac Communications, two of the PR specialists called in to give nuclear's image new sheen, had ample reason to cheer. The president had done more in the four seconds it took to utter those words before 42 million viewers than the years' worth of editorials that they had placed in newspapers around the country: he had connected the two words "clean" and "safe" with "nuclear energy"—and in so doing he breathed new life into an industry that had pretty much died during the years between President Nixon's and President Carter's speeches. Or rather, he'd played the safe and clean card yet again.

TATTOOING OUR BRAINS

Along with the energy industry, the Bush administration is trying to delete the words typically associated with nuclear power—namely, "Three Mile Island," "Chernobyl," and "radioactive waste"—from our minds. Instead they're branding the nuclear image with two words that resonate with focus groups: "clean" and "safe," even if it's a stretch—some would say an outright lie—to tie those words to nuclear power. Spinmaster Frank Luntz recommends a heavy play of repetition and, indeed, these days it's nearly impossible to find a speech from anyone in the entire Bush administration that doesn't have the words "safe" and "clean" connected to nuclear power.

The day after President Bush's 2006 State of the Union speech, the stock of ADM, the country's largest maker of ethanol, spiked to its then highest point. That same day, when journalists called the Energy Department to uncover the details of how the president planned to cut our foreign oil dependence by 75 percent within twenty years and "make our dependence on Middle Eastern oil a thing of the past," Energy Secretary Samuel Bodman hemmed and hawed and said the president had been talking figuratively. "This was purely an example," said Bodman, admitting it would be nearly impossible to so drastically cut imports from the Middle East. Only a few months before, the Department of Energy had released a report saying that in fact by 2025 our demand for Middle Eastern oil would substantially rise. Editorials lamented that the president's energy programs merely prolonged our oil habit—since much of the technology, for such things as hydrogen-powered cars, wouldn't be available for decades. The president's commitment to renewable power looked entirely iffy when, days after his speech, he slashed the budget at the government's renewable energy laboratory, laying off thirty-two scientists.

And the president's commitment to developing new, alternative energies looks even more laughable when one reads the Advanced Energy Initiative that President Bush touted in his State of the Union address. His initiative, which outlines several energy projects, does indeed briefly mention solar energy and wind power—the nonpolluting energy typically associated with the terms "renewable" and "alternative energy." But buried within the pages is a controversial program, one that has scientists and congressmen alike shaking their heads. It's called Global Nuclear Energy Partnership—and it involves the hazardous and extremely pricey reprocessing of nuclear fuel, which the government has spent billions trying to achieve before, ending up with little more than a radioactive mess to show for it. And that program goes hand in hand with the energy plan drawn up by Vice President Cheney's task force back in 2001. In the warp-the-logic manner that is now a Bush trademark, we were getting duped once again. Under the guise of cutting our addiction to oil, the Bush administration was raising nuclear energy from the dead—along with all the bogeymen that come with it.

> Nuclear energy does nothing to offset our oil needs. In the United States, almost all of our oil is used for one thing: transportation, be it for cars, trucks, or planes. Nuclear energy, on the other hand, is used to generate electricity. So saying that the United States needs to add thousands of nuclear plants to cut down on our oil needs—as our officials have often told us—is akin to saying you're going to buy a new hat because there are holes in your shoes.

On September 11, only one thing prevented a nuclear meltdown, the death of tens of thousands, and the panicked exodus of hundreds of thousands fleeing from radioactive gases. And that one thing was a misunderstanding. Had the plot unfolded as originally envisioned, the events of that day could have included a radioactivity-spewing fireball. Mohammad Atta's initial targets included Indian Point, a nuclear reactor that sits barely thirty-five miles north of Manhattan; if he had indeed slammed into Indian Point on that Tuesday morning, the number of people that perished might have have been closer to forty-four thousand. And instead of causing a tower to crash, it could have triggered the reactor core to melt down and spew clouds of radioactive gas that would have drifted over Manhattan and beyond—affecting 7 percent of the U.S. population. The cost, says Dr. Edwin Lyman of the Union of Concerned Scientists, would probably have exceeded $1 trillion.[1] And the reason Mohammad Atta didn't fly United Flight 11 into Indian Point that day was bad information. Atta's fellow operatives—like the American people themselves—believed that nuclear plants are well guarded. The plot to run into at least two nuclear facilities was ditched simply because they believed that the plane would be shot down before it even neared the plant.

They were wrong: had the plane come barreling in, the chances were next to nil that it would have been stopped by any planes. For one thing, most were busy on emergency drills scheduled that day by Vice President Dick Cheney.[2] For another, they're usually not guarding our nuclear plants anyway—and certainly not before 9/11. What's scarier: security around plants still isn't high.[3] And the scariest: in its next attack, al-Qaeda *will* be aiming for nuclear plants—says the FBI.

"During debriefings of an al-Qaeda senior operative, he stated there would be a second airline attack in the U.S. . . . The plan was to fly a commercial aircraft into a nuclear power plant."
      —From an FBI memo sent to the Nuclear Regulatory Commission in January 2002[4]

Any terrorist hoping to make good on Atta's unfulfilled nuclear dreams will have plenty of targets: we already have 104 of these nuclear sitting ducks scattered around the country, supplying one-fifth of our electricity. And they've already created over fifty-five thousand tons of radioactive waste that's just lying around at the plants, waiting for somebody to figure out where to take it.

THE ACHILLES HEEL OF NUCLEAR: SPENT WASTE

Submerged in deep pools across America, not far from schools, suburban neighborhoods, and shopping malls, some fifty-five thousand tons of highly radioactive waste lie in cooling pools right next to nuclear plants, waiting for the federal government to come pick them up. At some nine hundred degrees, these "spent rods" require five years of continuous chilling to cool to a temperature that allows them to be stored in thick steel casks without risk of fire—and security experts and scientists warn these temporary storage pools are vulnerable to attack and radioactive fires.[5]

Electrical utilities were never supposed to be left holding the spent fuel bag. Back when they signed up for nuclear plants, in the 1960s and '70s, they were assured the government would take care of the waste. But despite attempts to open a national repository in Nevada, the country still doesn't have a federal storage unit for highly radioactive nuclear waste. Now the electric utilities are forced to pay hefty amounts for armed guards to watch over the spent fuel—and they are suing the feds. Thirty cases are pending[6] and the plaintiffs are winning: the Department of Energy is shucking out billions to utilities to guard the waste onsite until a national dump opens, if one ever does. The Department of Energy says storing the waste at plants, even for one hundred years, is perfectly safe. Nuclear Regulatory Commissioner Peter Lyons boasts that "Our civilian power plants are among the most secure sites in the entire world . . . no credible scenarios could result in radiological consequences from an attack."[7] They don't publicize the fact that sabotage is as much of an issue as attacks or that three plants have recently reported that several fuel rods of radioactive waste are missing.[8] And Congressman Ed Markey recently forced Nuclear Regulatory Commission officials to admit they don't even know exactly how much waste is being stored at nuclear plants.[9]

Given that we now know these sites are sitting ducks, do we want even one more nuclear plant—much less the nine hundred or more nuclear plants that the Bush administration is insisting we need?[10] That's just one of the many questions raised by the energy plan that Vice President Cheney and his mystery task force concocted in 2001. And here's another one: should we perhaps cock an eyebrow at an energy plan that was shaped and written by the energy industry itself alongside its hired guns—and that provides over $27 billion in subsidies and tax credits to energy companies, including Big Oil, that are already rich?

You've got to wonder if anybody who had a hand in putting together this policy wasn't a lobbyist, a former lobbyist, a future lobbyist, a CEO of a utility, or an oil man. We know that the Cheney task force met with industry heads and their paid persuaders more than seven hundred times during the four months the energy policy was being hammered together. But there were plenty of lobbyists on the inside too. Among them, Secretary of the Interior Gale Norton, who previously cajoled for Exxon, Chevron, and Marathon, and her number two, Steve Griles, who did the same for Shell and Texaco. Commerce Secretary Don Evans, like the president and his VP, is an oil man. And that's just the beginning.

NUCLEAR PROS AND CONS

Nuclear power is being song-and-danced around the planet as the savior of our energy future, but that message was broadcast high and low before, and it wasn't true back then either. The industry has spent millions to spiff up nuclear's tarnished image, even launching a fake grassroots group, called Clean and Safe Energy, to emphasize the picture it would like us to see. To be sure, using nuclear power to produce electricity does have its pluses, which number three:

- Nuclear plants don't directly produce dark clouds of sooty smoke, nor do they emit carbon dioxide.
- Nuclear plants don't directly use oil or natural gas.
- Uranium is relatively cheap compared to oil and natural gas.

The list of its drawbacks, however, is quite a bit longer. The short list:

- **Waste** (see "The Achilles Heel of Nuclear: Spent Waste," page 136)
- **Safety:** While not emitting anything we can smell or see, nuclear plants do sometimes emit radioactive gases; we're just not informed when they do. While safer than before, nuclear plants are still hazardous operations that hold the potential for meltdowns, explosions, radioactive fires, and toxic leaks. A plant in Ohio came millimeters away from a meltdown in 2002; a plant in Sweden came closer in 2006; and recent explosions at plants in Japan killed five workers.
- **Security:** Whether you are talking about a plane crashing into a plant or a car bomb explosion, or the much more easily accom-

plished act of sabotage, these sites are security risks and it's not as though they're surrounded with missile launchers.

- **Costs:** Start-up and close-down costs—that is, decommissioning— are astronomical, and the industry is tainted by so many financial nightmares it was kissed off by the 1980s as an iffy investment. Investors in the Washington Public Power Supply System—its acronym, WPPSS, is pronounced "Whoops"—were burned in the 1980s. Bond holders ate $2.25 billion in losses—history's biggest default.

In short, from its multibillion-dollar cradle to its multibillion-dollar grave, nuclear energy has proved to be a mountain-sized headache on all fronts, not even considering the billions that taxpayers are unknowingly shoveling out for insuring plants and guarding the waste.

Black storm clouds were rolling in that Tuesday in May 2001, but the mood was jolly at the Nuclear Energy Institute's annual convention, held that year in DC. Inside the Washington Monarch Hotel, the capital's white-marbled luxury lodge, the publicists handed out glow-in-the-dark Super Balls and yellow lightbulbs that declared "Nuclear—the Clean Air Energy," to reporters for the *Washington Post, New York Times*, even the *Cleveland Plain Dealer*, while wide-smiling executives in fine suits slipped on NEI's yellow "gyrating atom" ties, shook hands, and slapped backs.

NEI: A POWERFUL BUNCH

Many of the world's economic giants gather under the Nuclear Energy Institute's umbrella. Among the highfalutin players:

- **Reactor makers:** General Electric, Westinghouse, and French manufacturer Areva reactors sell for upward of $2 billion each.
- **Assemblymen:** Engineering firms, particularly Bechtel, put together the plants here or abroad—on at least one occasion assembling it backward. Bechtel wins huge contracts for decommissioning plants and is deeply involved in creating a nuclear repository at Yucca Mountain, a $60 billion–plus project.

- **Electric utilities:** All of the country's twenty-seven utilities running nuclear are NEI members, including the giants of recent mergers: Exelon, Dominion, Entergy, Duke, and Southern Company. Their concerns: saving billions by relicensing forty-year-old nuclear plants instead of decommissioning them, as well as cutting costs of regulations for new plants, and nabbing federal funding for new designs.
- **Nuclear arms labs:** The U.S. Department of Energy's premier nuclear weapons labs, Sandia and Los Alamos (University of California), also get billions for their work on reprocessing/transmutation of waste from nuclear plants.

The festive spirits at that year's leading nuclear convention marked a switch. Not that long ago it was hard to get members mildly charged up about the pricey two-day convention sponsored by the Nuclear Energy Institute, the trade association known for dogged lobbying, generous campaign contributions, and dropping millions to jet congressmen overseas on nuclear sightseeing trips. The convention was usually populated by bureaucrats who droned on about regulations and marketing gurus giving PowerPoint presentations about how to work pro-nuclear materials into grade school science books. Some wondered if the millions they paid in NEI membership were worth it.

WORTH HER WEIGHT IN URANIUM

The Nuclear Energy Institute has thrown heaps of money into market research. And the numbers marketing experts came back with were well worth the expense: it's amazing how many Americans support nuclear power when Bisconti Research is conducting the surveys. The company is headed by Dr. Ann Bisconti, a former vice president of the Nuclear Energy Institute, now paid to sit on its board—and to conduct surveys that generate numbers that are a dream come true. A whopping 70 percent or more of Americans favor the use of nuclear energy, she claims, broadcasting numbers far higher than anyone else's.[11] And an astonishing 85 percent of those who live near plants would love to see a new one go up, says Bisconti.[12] She enthuses that it's a case of "Yes, in my backyard!"[13]

Gallup numbers certainly don't mirror the trend: its polls show 56 percent approval for nuclear energy and for expanding its use, but 55 percent oppose a new plant near them. On the other extreme, surveys conducted by the Opinion Research Corporation indicate that 61 percent of Americans give nuclear the thumbs-down, saying the country can't afford to wait if "building more nuclear power plants will take a decade or more . . . and cost tens of billions of dollars."[14]

Besides being a numbers whiz, Bisconti is also NEI's resident branding expert. "Our research," she noted at a recent lecture, "finds that clean air, reliability, and affordability"[15] are top on the public's mind. That's why, as part of NEI's "nuclear energy branding campaign," the researcher implores "every company and every individual industry-wide"[16] to make it their personal duty to stamp three ideas into the public's mind. "Whenever you have a chance," she says, "remind your listeners of these three benefits of nuclear energy: Clean Air, Reliability, and Affordability."[17] And Dr. Bisconti didn't have to mention the payoffs if you get the magic words to flow out of the mouths of leaders, especially if they are connected with another booster word: "safe"—a word that the nuclear industry was recently forced to drop from its advertising campaigns.

For all the money the NEI had blown—the $7 million tossed to lobbying and millions more on "clean energy" advertising campaigns—there appeared to be little to show for it except happy slogans, a few paid-for newspaper op-eds, and the persistent optimism of Joe Colvin, the association's chubby-cheeked president. Some CEOs were growing impatient—like Exelon's John Rowe, who told shareholders, "Nuclear is not a cause—it is a business."[18] He wasn't alone in wanting simple yes or no answers. Was nuclear going to take off again or would it quietly slither off? Would the government make it easier to extend the lifetime of plants or wouldn't it? And, most important, was the nuclear waste graveyard at Nevada's Yucca Mountain—which had been in the works for twenty-four years—ever going to open? Because decisions needed to be made and the chances for disaster were piling up: for decades, power plants, never designed to be fortresses or storage centers for radioactive materials, have been forced to manage their deadly by-products.

But for all the rocky moments of the past, for all those who didn't have faith before, the "nuclear assembly" convention would be different this year, the first of the George W. Bush administration. This year, for once, Joe Colvin, NEI's pudgy president and CEO, wouldn't have to wheel out the same assurances about how a change was in the air and how some-day, soon, nuclear would be reborn. His thinning hair was a bit more tinged with gray than in the days when he'd first started trumpeting the cause, but this year the Nuclear Energy Institute's front man could have gloated, "Told you so!"

Throughout the hotel lobby, where oversized potted plants lazed under skylights, and amid the columns of conference rooms, over martinis and into microphones, one phrase kept ricocheting across the hotel: "I had no idea . . ."—interspersed with "wonderful," "unbelievable," and "very good news." Or as Rep. W. J. "Billy" Tauzin neatly summed up that special moment in nuclear history: "Who would have thunk?"[19]

Indeed, who woulda thunk that nuclear energy would be back on the agenda? It had died thirty years ago: long before Three Mile Island and Chernobyl hammered in what then seemed to be the final nails, utilities had already pulled nuclear's plug. The problems were seemingly endless: cost overruns in the billions, construction delays of five or more years, bond defaults that socked investors, and frequent near-accidents—not to mention the ruckus and scenes when protesters dramatically chained themselves to gates—had convinced most utilities to drop the nuclear hot potato in the mid-1970s.

The clock is about to strike midnight at the nuclear ball—and the ticking is excruciatingly loud for the twenty-seven utilities invested in nuclear: most plants will soon hit their fortieth birthdays, and initial licenses will expire. But they're not shutting down. Thanks to the Bush administration, old plants are being relicensed—and the process is speeded up, a move that some, such as Rep. Edward Markey, think is demented. He likens this generation of nuclear plants to middle-aged humans whose bodies are starting to fall apart. Not pretty.

Apparently nobody remembered to slam a stake in nuclear's heart—it's trying to crawl out of its crypt. And like a desperate emergency team, zapping stopped hearts with electric shocks, the Bush administration won't let nuclear go—jolting it with billions of dollars in tax credits and underwriting research projects just to keep it alive.

THE ENERGY TASK FORCE: PAY TO PLAY, PAY TO WIN?

It started ten days into the new regime, when still-fresh president George W. Bush signaled his first priority to the hungry media: energy. So crucial was altering our energy course—an issue hammered home by the California blackouts (that the manipulations of his pal Ken Lay had helped cause)—that his first major action was to call a Cabinet-level commission chaired by Vice President Cheney. Officially, the resulting National Energy Policy was authored by assorted Cabinet members, but it was custom-designed to light up Big Oil's and Big Electricity's boards.

Cheney in turn tapped an executive director to herd the process along: pale, tight-lipped, and fleshy-faced Andrew Lundquist, the lumbering former chief of staff to two Alaska senators, Frank Murkowski and Ted Stevens—the lawmaker most famous as sponsor of Alaska's Bridge to Nowhere.

Despite the many governmental "co-authors," the energy report that Lundquist pulled together drew heavily from the energy industry. Lundquist, by his own admission, met with energy execs and lobbyists hundreds of times—714 times at least, according to the Natural Resources Defense Council,[20] which filed a Freedom of Information request to glean at least some idea of whom the task force had met with; despite lawsuits from Judicial Watch and demands from Congress' Government Accountability Office, the vice president's office is shielding most information.

The wishes that Lundquist fielded on Cheney's behalf included:

- Cheney's good pal Red Cavaney and others from the American Petroleum Institute wanted to tap whatever hadn't been squeezed out of Alaska and to drop royalties from new oil found on federal lands.

- Enron, including Ken Lay, wanted a revamp of the national electricity grid and to gain more access to it.
- Another major Bush supporter, Forrest Hoglund, lobbied Lundquist to get behind his natural gas pipeline from Alaska.[21]
- Chicago-based electric utility Exelon (which contributed over $1.9 million to Republicans between 1999 and 2004)[22] discussed the designs for a new "pebble bed" reactor, requesting the government's financial help in developing novel nuclear technology.
- Bush's friend Tom Kuhn (whose Edison Electric Institute had brightened Republican campaigns with some $600,000 in recent elections) wanted pollution regulations lowered for new electric plants.[23]
- Task force members met with reps from at least five energy companies (some of which had each dropped in over $100,000 for the Bush-Cheney campaign hat[24]—and which were facing lawsuits and huge fines for ignoring environmental regs).
- Task force members met with the Nuclear Energy Institute (which kicked in over $438,000 to Republican coffers between 1999 and 2002). Most frequently met with NEI—nineteen times, according to the Natural Resources Defense Council. And NEI, predictably, wanted incentives for a nuclear rebirth.

The many meetings, the PowerPoint presentations, the graphs—and the repackaging of nuclear as clean and safe, cheap and reliable—sure seemed to pay off on that beautiful May day in 2001: even nuclear industry bigwigs claimed shock at the many enticing incentives that beckoned them in the Cheney energy report.

"In my wildest dreams," Christian Poindexter, chairman of Constellation Group, told the *New York Times*, "when I was over at the White House in March, I couldn't imagine them getting so behind us."[25] Andy White, head of GE Nuclear, was equally astounded. "We didn't think nuclear was going to come this hard and fast," he said, adding that GE Nuclear expects to double, maybe even triple sales by 2016.[26]

The task force had a major redesign of American electricity in mind: the energy policy recommended that a whopping thirteen hundred to nineteen hundred new power plants be up and running by 2025—a figure based on DOE estimates but that some believe is

excessively high. But those were the figures Energy Secretary
Spencer Abraham ran with, saying U.S. utilities needed to put up
sixty-five plants a year, which amounted to a new plant, on average,
going up every six days. And the energy task force loudly hinted in its
report that most of the new plants should be nuclear—a suggestion
later echoed even more loudly by President Bush, Vice President
Cheney, Energy Secretary Spencer Abraham, and congressional
reports.

Cheney and his task force's executive director, Andrew Lundquist,
were fairy godfathers to the entire energy industry, making its players'
almost every wish come true. Lobbyists for Red Cavaney's American
Petroleum Institute, for example, drafted an executive order—complete
with preferred legalese wording—that directs all government agencies
to issue statements when their policies adversely affected oil companies; two months later, a very similarly worded executive order was
signed by President George W. Bush. That was just the start.

- The task force waived many regulations for new plants, as
  Thomas Kuhn had requested, and pending lawsuits and fines for
  polluting utilities were dropped.[27]

- Forrest Hoglund got his natural gas pipeline from Alaska.

- The Bush administration offered royalty-free oil from federal lands,
  saving oil companies some $7 billion.[28]

- The concept of "protected areas" was shredded: the task force
  recommended opening the gulf waters to offshore drilling and encouraged oil exploration in the Arctic National Wildlife Refuge.

- Companies such as Peabody Energy (another huge contributor—
  which had plastered DC with issue ads pointing out how coal,
  too, could be clean) were showered with financial incentives to
  develop new types of products, and the government would help
  develop clean coal plants.

But nobody won more than the nuclear energy industry, which nabbed some $12 billion worth of goodies,[29] from tax credits to government-backed R&D, taxpayer dollars would defray the costs of getting the first six plants up. And the government would also toss in $2 billion of taxpayer money for insurance to cover any delays if the revamped one-stop licensing for nuclear plants ran too long. The Bush administration obviously understood the utilities' fears: they'd been burned before when nuclear plants ran billions over budget, and few wanted to touch nuclear power after Chernobyl, but the government was going to hold their hand and guide them right back to the atomic age.

By the time Tuesday, May 22, 2001, rolled around, the NEI convention was a publicity "mega-event" sure to put news of the rebirth of nuclear back on front steps and kitchen tables nationwide. The lineup of speakers was impressive: U.S. Chamber of Commerce head Thomas Donohue would take to the dais, as would Sen. Pete Domenici (chair of the Senate Committee on Energy and Natural Resources) and Rep. W. J. "Billy" Tauzin (then chair of the House Committee on Energy and Commerce). Former secretary of the interior Bruce Babbitt would give his thumbs-up to nuclear along with MIT economics professor Lester Thurow (who suggested that those living twenty miles from a plant should be paid $100 a month in exchange for dropping future claims of health woes from radioactivity). But the gleaming jewel in NEI's publicity crown was the upcoming speech by a big-name VIP whose very presence would officially rechristen the nuclear kingdom.

At 11 a.m., some four hundred of the world's most powerful business leaders, politicians, and academics—among them bigwigs from Goldman Sachs, GE, and Harvard—packed into the hotel's Imperial Conference Room 2, not far from the banners that colorfully proclaimed "A Flourishing Renaissance." Fifteen minutes later, flanked by bodyguards, the celebrity speaker scurried in. At his entrance, the room exploded in booming applause, peppered with hoots and cheers, and the execs rose to their feet in a standing ovation. As Vice President Dick Cheney took his place at the podium and welcomed the crowd, the jubilant heavyweights rose to their feet again in exaltation of the twenty-first century's most powerful nuclear hitter.

As head of the group that sculpted the country's just-released energy plan ("Reliable, Affordable, and Environmentally Sound Energy for America's Future"), Vice President Cheney had done more for the nuclear industry than anybody since President Dwight D. Eisenhower, who, eight years after the bombing of Hiroshima, ignited the idea of nuclear energy as a source of commercial electricity. A dozen near-meltdowns and more than fifty-five thousand tons of highly radioactive waste later, Vice President Cheney resold nuclear energy as a panacea—good for the environment, great for the economy, beneficial even for foreign relations. Eisenhower's feat had been impressive, but Cheney's accomplishment was amazing: he revived a dead horse.

[Forces at Work]

Lobbying:

- **Nuclear Energy Institute:** Advertising campaigns, lobbying, speeches, reports—and of course campaign contributions—all help NEI sell nuclear energy for its members, which range from utilities to universities. (See "NEI: A Powerful Bunch," page 139.) NEI spent over $10 million lobbying between 1998 and 2005.

- **U.S. Navy:** It's always been keen about splitting atoms—and was quick to put it to use for nuclear-powered subs—and many of nuclear's keenest advocates share a Navy background: Joe Colvin and Tom Kuhn, for instance, were both naval officers, as is Colvin's successor, Admiral Skip Bowman.

Officials and legislators:

- **Sen. Pete Domenici** (R-New Mexico). Congress' most devout fission fan—he's made a personal mission of leading us back to the atomic power path—just happens to head the weighty Senate energy committee. As chair, Domenici skillfully shepherded through the 2005 Energy Policy Act, a financial piñata of sweets for every energy industry—especially his fav. Assorted PACs and individuals from electrical utilities to national weapons laboratories, dropped over $3 million into his 2002 reelection kitty[30]—and he routinely tosses billions of taxpayer dollars to New Mexico's nuclear labs Sandia and Los Alamos. Pushed the atom to a flock of devoted staff—some call them "the family"—and the missionaries have done quite a sales job: former right-hand men Clay Sell and Alex Flint as well as scientific advisor Peter Lyons are orchestrating the nuclear "rebirth" from various very high posts.

- **Sen. Harry Reid** (D-Nevada): Minority leader since 2004, Reid vehemently opposes turning his state's Yucca Mountain into a national home for radioactive waste. Called President Bush a liar when Bush claimed that "sound science" determined the choice of Yucca as a nuclear dump.

- **Rep. Edward Markey** (D-Massachusetts): During 1986 House subcommittee investigations, fission foe Markey uncovered that the U.S. government and General Electric conducted nuclear experiments on hundreds of hospital patients and prisoners during the 1960s and purposefully released radioactivity in Washington state to monitor health effects.[31] He's now blasting the Nuclear Regulatory Commission about lax security at plants and raising Cain about reactor sales to India.

- **Vice President Dick Cheney:** The snoozy world of policy making actually becomes an intriguing whodunit when snaky-smiled Vice President Cheney is anywhere near. In crafting his business-snuggly energy plan, he drew down the shades on whose outside hands were massaging the policy—and his secretiveness created a hullabaloo that still hasn't been quieted. His energy policy, custom-designed to satiate Big Oil's and Big Electricity's wildest dreams, doesn't do diddly for lessening our dependence on oil. But the initial question was exactly who put their two cents into the task force's policy pot. Cheney isn't telling. When the Government Accountability

Office inquired about the specifics of who had attended energy task force meetings, the vice president's office shipped it a bag of nonsensical papers with scribbled numbers, and a crumpled pizza receipt. The Sierra Club and Judicial Watch sued for the exacts, and Cheney was hauled before the Supreme Court; the federal court said to turn the info over, but Cheney's office keeps blocking the move. (Curiously, the task force did hand over maps used in their meetings—maps of the oil fields, pipelines, and infrastructure of Iraq, Saudi Arabia, and the United Arab Emirates.)[32]

Industry:

- **Exelon:** The Chicago-based utility—created when Illinois utility Unicom merged with New Jersey's PECO—is now the country's largest utility, with over 5.2 million customers, $15.36 billion in 2005 revenue, and 17,000 employees. The company operates seventeen nuclear plants, but CEO John Rowe is on the fence about building new ones: he wants Yucca Mountain opened before he'll commit to firing up more.

[**Close-up**   ]

Despite the standing ovations at the Washington Monarch Hotel, despite the rousing speeches lauding nuclear power given by Bush, Cheney, and Energy Secretary Spencer Abraham, and despite the support of weighty congressional players, there was a small snag with the energy policy. Before many of the recommendations came into effect, Congress had to pass an energy bill embracing the report's action plan. And while Republicans dominated the House of Representatives, Democrats held the Senate, making passage of the policy less than guaranteed.

Andrew Lundquist, who'd been promoted to the White House's director of energy, became the energy policy's lobbyist, persuading legislators

Yucca Mountain: future home for radioactive nuclear waste.

to adopt the task force's report and helping them write the recommendations as law. He was indeed qualified for the position: his former boss
Sen. Frank Murkowski was then the Senate's number one energy
man—conveniently sitting as chair of its energy and natural resources
committee.

But given a number of distractions, including the 9/11 attack, the energy policy didn't become law in 2001. Growing panicked, the executive
branch launched programs designed to boost nuclear—independent of
the passage of a major energy bill. On February 14, 2002, Energy Secretary Spencer Abraham unveiled "Nuclear 2010," a new program to get
six fission plants up and running within eight years—with the Department of Energy footing much of the bill. The next day President Bush
pressured Congress to formally designate Yucca Mountain as the national repository for nuclear waste; Secretary Abraham urged Congress
to adopt a law as well, knowing that Yucca was the symbolic key to
restarting the atomic energy machine. The Nuclear Energy Institute
launched a mega-money advertising campaign—"Put Nuclear in Its

Place: Yucca Mountain." NEI's Joe Colvin and lobbyist John Kane—
along with hundreds of other nuclear industry lobbyists—swooped
through, distributing NEI reports and fact sheets and whipping open
their checkbooks, particularly in the Senate, which—unlike the House,
where a Yucca bill quickly passed—the legislators were dragging their
feet. The persuading finally paid off: the Senate finally passed the bill in
July 2002. It was promptly vetoed by Nevada governor Kenny Guinn, but
President Bush overrode the governor's veto and signed the resolution
on July 23, 2002, making Yucca Mountain the country's official nuclear
trashbin—on paper at least.

YUCCA MOUNTAIN

These days most Nevadans are none too fond of nuclear energy:
their state doesn't have any nuclear plants (most are east of the Mississippi), but there is plenty of radioactivity seeped into the ground—
thanks to the hundreds of atomic bomb tests at the Department of
Energy's Nevada Test Site (now managed by Lockheed Martin)
through the 1950s and 1960s. Nevadans once watched the mush-
room clouds from the tests as entertainment—the government had
assured them they were safe. Now Nevadans claim that their state is
the thyroid cancer capital of the world. Since 1986, when the Department of Energy zeroed in on Yucca Mountain, a bony ridge of mountains some hundred miles outside of Las Vegas, as a national
repository, many Nevadans, from grassroots groups to the governor's
office, have battled the government's plan. It would expose them, they
fear, to new dangers—this time from the seventy-seven thousand
tons of future radioactive waste the Department of Energy plans to
store at the still-to-be-opened Yucca dump. The state shut off water to
the site (forcing engineers at Yucca Mountain to construct a reser-
voir), the mayor of Las Vegas banned transport of hazardous material
through the city, the local Shoshone tribe sued the federal government over violation of the 1863 treaty that gave them the land, but
nothing permanently halted the project. For two decades now, the
Department of Energy has been working with Bechtel (and now
France's Areva) digging over fifty miles of tunnels to store nuclear

waste: the site and its sealed casks of radionuclides is supposed to hold up for a million years. Falsified hydrology reports and a legal battle over how long the radioactive waste needed to be kept secure—the courts said ten thousand years wasn't long enough for safe storage—are only the latest of many headaches that pushed back the scheduled opening from 1998 to 2010 to (most recently) 2017. The problem is the waste has to go somewhere—and nobody wants it. Most scientists concur we do need some sort of geologic underground storage to hold what we already have—the question is whether Yucca Mountain is the best site. And the more important question is: since, after sixty years of trying, we still don't have a solution for the fifty-five thousand tons of waste already sitting around, why do we want to build new plants and generate even more? Even by the time Yucca Mountain opens—if it does—in 2017, the nuclear waste generated by then will have exceeded what it's designed to hold.

The Department of Energy's deputy secretary, Clay Sell, predicts that (if the federal government has its way) we'll have over three hundred new nuke plants up by 2050.[33] His department says the amount of waste those plants will generate is so great that we'll need at least nine Yucca Mountain–sized repositories to hold it, and, given the problems in opening Yucca Mountain, that isn't a selling point.

The Union of Concerned Scientists says that one year's worth of waste from one plant generates enough plutonium that, if reprocessed, could make at least thirty nuclear weapons. So if Clay Sell's three-hundred-plant vision comes true, American plants alone would produce enough plutonium for nine thousand nuclear bombs—a year.

Even though Yucca Mountain had received the official government stamp, the Energy Bill didn't pass in 2002, despite the $170,000 NEI dropped taking lawmakers on vacations, and despite the $45 million showered on congressmen's reelection campaigns from assorted energy companies through their employees' PACs.[34] The next year the situation was getting more desperate: Congress was distracted by the invasion of Iraq and turning the energy policy into law was not a priority.

And that's where Sen. Pete Domenici entered the picture. A skilled bipartisan negotiator, in spring 2003 he suddenly moved from the Senate Budget Committee, which he had long chaired, to take over for Frank Murkowski as the chair of the Senate Committee on Energy and Natural Resources. And that was certainly fortunate for the nuclear industry.

MEET ST. PETE

There's a steely intensity in Sen. Pete Domenici's piercing eyes. New Mexico's rangy former math teacher (and farm team pitcher) runs his mighty committees with an efficiency, team spirit, and negotiating finesse rarely seen these days. In 1997, he negotiated a budget-balancing bill that had been so contentious it closed down the government for thirty days. Informed, concerned, and prone to overwork, Domenici is Mr. Energy on Capitol Hill. Chair of the Senate Committee on Energy and Natural Resources as well as chair of the Energy and Water Development Appropriations Subcommittee, he holds more power in the matter of electricity generation than pretty much any congressman ever. Moderate in most matters, Domenici is fanatical about at least one: nuclear energy. He loves it—he's even written a book on the matter (*A Brighter Tomorrow: Fulfilling the Promise of Nuclear Energy*, which handily came out in November 2004, while Congress again considered the energy bill). And even before the nuclear renaissance, which many credit the six-term senator for giving birth to, Domenici (previously chair of the Senate Budget Committee) doled out billions in taxpayer money to fund research into nuclear energy, nuclear recycling, and oversight of nuclear weapons—and threatened major hacks at the Nuclear Regulatory Commission's budget if they didn't ease regulations for nuclear plants. His state doesn't have any nuclear plants—most of it is powered by coal. In fact, the poor state doesn't have much—except the Los Alamos and Sandia Research Labs, where he steers so many billions of dollars annually, for assorted programs from giant accelerators to transmutation technologies for nuclear waste, that he's known as St. Pete.[35] That's why the labs' political action committees hand him a big bundle of checks every election, and even though he hasn't had a heated race for over twenty years, energy companies and trade associations from Bechtel to Westinghouse and their employees' PACs forked over $289,000 for his 2002 election to keep their man in the power seat, according to the Center for Responsive Politics.

Sen. Pete "I ♥ Nuclear Energy" Domenici (R-NM) keeps "peaceful atoms" alive and shoots billions to his state's nuclear labs, Sandia and Los Alamos.

At the news of his appointment as chair of the energy committee, Domenici quickly put in a call to Alex Flint's K Street office.[36] Not long before, youthful Flint was the senator's right-hand man—helping prioritize which projects should be funded by the Domenici-chaired Energy and Water Development Appropriations Subcommittee (which Domenici still heads). In late 1999 Clay Sell, another thirty-something whippersnapper, took over the job when Flint left Domenici's staff to lobby for the nuclear interests of Johnston & Associates. Predictably, in his role as a private persuader Flint frequently had the ear of Domenici and Sell, and Flint even wrote out checks for Domenici's reelection campaign.[37] Now, in the latest twist of their relationship, Domenici wanted lobbyist Flint to come back and work for him—as head of staff for the Domenici-chaired Senate energy committee.

With the return of Alex Flint—who, back in his role as Senate staffer, could help write policies that very much affected his former clients Areva, Exelon, and Duke—Senator Domenici had assembled a formidable team. Even if he looked like a frat boy gone wrong, thirty-five-year-old Clay Sell, still Domenici's main man at the powerful energy and water subcommittee, was knowledgeable, politically savvy, and popular with politicians and industry leaders. Not as energetic as the kids, Domenici's resident nuclear expert, Peter Lyons, always looked like he'd be more comfortable in a lab coat and had serious scientific clout (and the support of New Mexico's nuclear labs). Together Flint, Sell, Lyons, and Domenici were the atomic dream team. Whether due to financial investments, paychecks, contributions, or sheer ideology in the sci-fi dream of splitting atoms to power the world, they were such a fervent nuclear club that some inside Congress called them "the family"—as in "nuclear family." But they wouldn't stay together for long. In the chain reaction that fueled the nuclear "renaissance," Domenici helped them launch to more powerful roles that would cover all of the necessary bases.

Alex Flint—is he a Senate chief of staff or is he a lobbyist? Depends on the week; he twirls through revolving doors at dizzying pace.

Domenici's "family" wasn't the only high-powered bunch yukking up nuclear on the Senate floor. Andrew Lundquist came barreling back onto the scene—also wearing a different hat. The former White House energy director, who'd overseen the writing of the task force's energy policy, was now a registered lobbyist as head of the new Lundquist Group. He was uniquely positioned not only to push for projects for his clients, such as reactor maker Toshiba and North Carolina utility Duke Energy, but to simultaneously persuade congressmen to adopt the energy policy that he had drawn up.

Hundreds of other lobbyists for energy interests from Areva to Exxon descended on Capitol Hill in a zeal to get the energy policy back into motion. But Congress was distracted by the war in Iraq, the ongoing war on terrorism, and homeland security. Memories of the energy policy and the California blackouts that had been a driving force behind its creation were becoming hazy.

But just as it seemed that the national energy policy might spend eternity in the dark of a file drawer, the country was hit with another electricity catastrophe: the August 2003 blackout. By the time the lights came back on for 50 million people across the Northeast and Canada—after

tens of thousands had spent hours trapped in subways and elevators—
the energy policy was dusted off and put back on the table. A lot of
people must have heaved a big, if premature, sigh of relief because
plenty of dough was riding on that pile of suggestions. If it passed, the
bill could bring billions in orders for reactor manufacturers, and billions
of saved dollars for utilities. Not to mention billions in pipeline orders for
oil from offshore areas, and billions of savings for coal companies. And
millions upon millions were being spent on lobbying to get the bill passed
after that mysterious blackout brought it back from the dead.

A VERY HANDY BLACKOUT

How embarrassing: the culprit behind the blackout on August 14,
2003, was Akron-based electrical utility FirstEnergy, whose top executives raised over $600,000 in contributions for the Bush-Cheney
campaign and whose president had even served on the Energy Department's transition team.[38] The Canadian-American investigation
team headed by Canada's Natural Resources Minister Herb Dhaliwal
and U.S. Energy Secretary Spencer Abraham said that a sudden, un-
expected shutdown in one of the utility's plants—the exact cause of
which was never determined but was perhaps exacerbated by over-
grown trees along transmission lines—caused a section of the electrical network to go down, with effects that cascaded across the
northeastern electrical grid. Even before the blackout, FirstEnergy
had been in hot water: in March 2002, workers had discovered that
acid had bored a hole the size of a pineapple in a nuclear reactor's
cap—a rather serious problem with a mere three-eighths of an inch
of metal all that was preventing a meltdown, likely within several
months. The utility faced not only a huge fine; FirstEnergy heads
faced possible criminal prosecution. The Department of Justice,
working with the Department of Energy and the NRC, had been building a case against the company since August 2002, although even by
August 2003, when the blackout occurred, the specifics of the fines
weren't yet known nor was the status of any criminal prosecutions.
Eighteen months after the blackout, in April 2005, the Nuclear Regulatory Commission announced it would drop any criminal prosecu-

tion, but fined the company $5.4 million—a nuclear record. As the *Cleveland Plain Dealer* pointed out, though, that amount was but "a fraction of the $75.8 million in penalties the agency could have levied"[39] against FirstEnergy. As for causing the 2003 blackout, well, FirstEnergy wasn't fined a penny for causing the blackout that jolted the energy bill out of the dark—and would save utilities billions.

The energy bill became a daily obsession for Domenici's "family," who wheeled and dealed across the Senate floor. Andrew Lundquist, Joe Colvin, John Kane, and Tom Kuhn were among thousands working the "bring back nuclear" angle, and Energy Secretary Spencer Abraham testified before congressional committees on the need for nuclear energy.

The American Petroleum Institute and thousands of oil and gas lobbyists were angling for everything from making opening refineries easier to tapping the offshore riches along the off-limit Gulf—without paying royalties. The coal industry sent out its troops to secure billions for "clean coal" projects as Congress wrote up the energy bill.

But after months of fierce lobbying and debate, just as the energy policy was poised to become law, the Democrats killed it—with a filibuster—over opening up the Arctic National Wildlife Refuge and a clause that would have protected petroleum companies from liability in cases concerning MTBE, a gasoline additive that had contaminated water sources.

The following year all players were back in position. But despite the work of Domenici, Flint, and Lundquist, despite the charm of NEI's Joe Colvin and Edison Electric's Tom Kuhn, despite the connection of the American Petroleum Institute's Red Cavaney and the hundreds of lobbyists madly writing out campaign contribution checks, and all the fundraising dinners, the energy bill still didn't go through.

And that was why it became even more important that Republicans take back not only the White House but both sides of Congress in 2004. Which was why energy companies boosted contributions to $115 million to congressional campaigns that year, most to Republican candidates.

That November, President Bush was reelected and Republicans gained both chambers of Congress. Passage of the energy bill seemed guaranteed. NEI tossed out $100,000 for the inauguration ceremonies. "He's a big supporter," NEI's John Kane said of President Bush. "Our donation is just a small way of supporting him."[40] Indeed, they'd spent far more in contributions to the campaigns of the president and Republican congressmen.

In 2005, energy lobbyists were called back to duty again. Domenici was hell-bent on getting the bill passed. Along with Alex Flint, he wheedled and negotiated and cajoled to win the votes needed to finally pass the energy act. Among the terms they negotiated:[41]

- Tax credits for nuclear generators that could total $5.7 billion

- Taxpayer-financed insurance of $2 billion that would cover any delays in licensing the first six plants—making new construction more attractive to lending institutions and investors

- Incentives for new technology and R&D, including: $1.1 billion for a fusion demo plant, $1.25 billion (plus additional "sums as necessary") for an Idaho nuclear test plant to produce hydrogen (widely considered a ridiculous means of producing hydrogen), grants of $432 million for new technologies, and loan guarantees that could cost taxpayers as much as $6 billion

- Extension of the crucial Price-Anderson Act that caps utility liability in the case of disaster

- Ethanol production to increase by 8 billion gallons by 2012 (to win over farm state senators)

- Oil makers would not be shielded from liability in the oil additive MTBE water contamination cases (to garner more support from Democrats, including New Hampshire senator Judd Gregg; New Hampshire was one state where a big MTBE case was pending)

- The Arctic National Wildlife Refuge would stay closed to drilling (a controversial clause, included as another move to woo Democrats)

- No increase in fuel efficiency standards for cars (a nod to Michigan)

Finally, on July 28, 2005, the House passed the energy bill (275 to 156), and the Senate passed it the next day (74 to 26). The new law embraced nearly every recommendation of the Cheney task force's National Energy Policy. In fact, the energy bill drawn up by the energy industries doled out even more to nuclear, which walked away with $12 billion in subsidies alone. President Bush signed the bill into law on August 8, 2005, a swelteringly hot day in New Mexico when air conditioners were running full blast. Sen. Pete Domenici was at his side for the long-awaited inking, staged at Sandia National Labs, a laboratory that specialized in developing nuclear weapons.

GLOBAL NUCLEAR ENERGY PARTNERSHIP

The president wasn't yet done with nuclear, although the next piece of his energy plan wasn't mentioned until his State of the Union speech six months later—and even then it was only hinted at. That's when the president, in the course of discussing our addiction to oil, brought up his new Advanced Energy Initiative—which he framed as being all about renewable fuels. But the show stealer of that initiative was the Global Nuclear Energy Partnership—a plan to recycle nuclear fuel—putting it through another reactor process to concentrate the fuel. That may sound easy enough, but it's a technology that the United States hasn't mastered, although it's spent billions trying and even more billions trying to clean up the resultant messes, which still haven't been cleaned up.

Protests immediately rose up from nearly all corners. The Union of Concerned Scientists worried that the concentrated plutonium that resulted could easily make nuclear weapons—and they worried about an inside job. "It's too risky, especially when the prospect of corruption is so prevalent," says Dr. Edwin Lyman.[42] Groups from Public Citizen to the Natural Resources Defense Council advised Congress not to fund it, saying that it would cost over $100 billion, a cost borne by taxpayers, and would only increase the problems of dealing with nuclear waste and weapons. And congressmen didn't much like the idea. When new energy secretary Samuel Bodman presented reprocessing as vital to keep America's "clean and safe emissions-free" nuclear program afloat and requested $250 million to fund the repro-cessing program in the annual budget request to Congress, Rep. Ed-ward Markey damned the Global Nuclear Energy Partnership as a "reckless and dangerous boondoggle that will bust the budget, wreak havoc with U.S. nonproliferation policy, and only further facilitate the spread of nuclear materials around the world."[43]

The sneaky manner that the administration used to bring the United States back into reprocessing—with a program that would cost $6 bil-lion its first few years—enraged even Bush administration supporter Rep. Joe Barton (R-Texas), who, as chair of the House Committee on Energy and Commerce, had helped push through the energy bill. The whole recycling scheme was "premature," he announced, saying he didn't intend to support it.[44] But over on the other side of Congress, Sen. Pete Domenici gave the idea of GNEP a big nod. After all, the original idea had come from his favorite lab, Sandia, which stood to benefit from the program—to the tune of billions of dollars.

Having finally pushed through the energy bill, the cast was duly re-warded. Andrew Lundquist became a director for Areva—and former en-ergy secretary Spencer Abraham waddled in as Areva's chairman of the board. Domenici's former subcommittee director Clay Sell was pro-moted to number two in command at the Energy Department. The sen-ator's scientific advisor Peter Lyons was appointed as one of the five commissioners on the Nuclear Regulatory Commission. And as for Alex Flint, he went back to K Street again, this time as vice president—and head lobbyist—for the Nuclear Energy Institute.

[What You Can Do]

Act local:

- The legislatures of nineteen states have passed laws requiring more advancement of alternative energy—from solar to wind to biomass. Let your state congressman know what you'd like to support.

- Attend utilities' public meetings—and write individualized letters to their CEOs.

- Install a solar panel on your roof: cuts down on water heating bills.

Act national:

- Join a national organization, such as Public Citizen, Union of Concerned Scientists, Natural Resources Defense Council, or Common Cause.

- Public Citizen, which has an extensive section questioning nuclear energy, will advise citizens on how to form their own groups and how to talk with the media and write effective op-eds.

- Call and write to the Department of Energy and to members of the House and Senate Energy Committees requesting they stop funding projects you don't like.

CHAPTER 5

Quit Stalling

The Sad Affair of Our Cars and Oil

C hris Paine wanted his car back. It wasn't just any automobile that had been wrested away: this was his coolest set of wheels ever, a sleek silver compact car that went from zero to sixty in nine seconds and was extraordinarily quiet and so fast he could outrace sports cars. Everybody wanted to go for a spin, and to sit behind the wheel and take his baby for a whirl. But one day the keys to his favorite car were yanked out of his hands. The "carjacker" in this case wasn't a thug, but a corporation—General Motors—taking back the car that he'd leased. But he wanted to buy it, he'd protested. Not an option, they'd informed him. Because this car, the EV1, was an electric car, and GM, says Paine, wanted to destroy it—viewing the electric car as threatening competition, even though they had made it.[1]

ALTERNA-WHEELS

- **Electric:** Powered by battery, you just charge them up and go—well, for at least sixty miles or so, although newer models may go four times farther. The lack of an internal combustion engine makes them oh so quiet. Hard to get in the United States: check for the first car out of new California automaker Tesla Motors, who is producing small numbers of powerful electric cars.

- **Flex-fuel:** Powered by gasoline or different blends of ethanol.

- **Hybrid electric:** Another dual-fuel vehicle, which can run on gasoline or electricity.

- **Hydrogen:** The car of the future, it will run on hydrogen fuel cells and emit nothing but water.

That's what Paine concluded after researching the issue for his 2006 documentary, *Who Killed the Electric Car?*—an amusing, if damning and ultimately depressing whodunit that looks at how America's car companies, and GM in particular, have shot themselves in the foot by refusing to adopt alternative-fuel cars, and have screwed consumers in so doing. GM claimed that scanty demand for the car meant it had to stop producing and leasing the cars—"they said the technology wasn't ready"[2]—and, as Paine discovered, hauled them to the crushing works to destroy them. Paine's experience contradicted the car company's claims: the car was so adored by those who had tried them—including Hollywood celebs Tom Hanks and Mel Gibson—that people offered to buy them, and held demonstrations (complete with arrests) at the storage lot where the last seventy-eight were being held before heading to the crusher. In fact, says Paine, there were waiting lists for the EV1 electric cars—orders that never got filled because GM stopped making the model.

TAKING ON CALIFORNIA

Smog, the eye-smarting pollution that sometimes limits visibility to three blocks, first began hovering over Los Angeles in 1943. Since then, California has been adamant about curbing pollution, enacting several revolutionary laws that have been much stricter about emissions than national standards. The electric car first appeared on California highways in the mid-1990s when General Motors launched a trial run of about one thousand entirely electric battery-powered EV1s, leasing them for three years. The debut was in response to the state's 1990 law mandating that by 2003, 10 percent of cars sold in California had to be "emissions-free." When manufacturers protested in 2001 that they were having difficulties making enough electric cars, the California board also allowed them to sell hybrid electric vehicles—part electric, part gasoline powered—to meet the demand. Cutting the manufacturers a break turned out to be the demise of the law: in 2002, the White House—where former GM head lobbyist Andrew Card, who'd also been the president of the powerful automakers' trade association, was now chief of staff—jumped into a lawsuit with GM and DaimlerChrysler against the state of California, challenging the state's right to dictate what kinds of cars were sold. Avoiding the emissions issues, they attacked on fuel mileage. Even though the goal was to reduce emissions, the cars that did so got better miles per gallon of gas since they were also powered by electric. The court agreed that the state had no right to regulate fuel mileage and the state emissions board was forced to ditch that law. And in 2003, GM began taking back its electric cars—and destroying them. "There were a few people that it was perfect for, but a large company like General Motors has to make vehicles that appeal to a vast market," GM spokesman Dave Barthmuss explained.[3]

The California legislature also passed a 2003 law cutting the amount of carbon dioxide that could be released by cars—an emission that the Environmental Protection Agency, under pressure from the White House and industry, has decided not to regulate (see "Baby, It's Hot Outside," page 176). That California law is also being contested in the courts by automakers, using the same logic that killed the zero emissions law. Another factor: carmakers say that adding carbon dioxide controls would add $3,000 to the sticker price of their cars.

One might imagine that oil companies, more than carmakers, would try to pull the plug on the electric car since models like the EVI run free of gasoline—some getting 250 miles on batteries before needing a charge. And indeed Big Oil did try to steamroll the novel mobile. Among the tactics, says Paine, was forming a fake grassroots group—Californians Against Hidden Taxes—run by a PR company that speared electric car fans, such as Jay Leno, saying taxpayers were tossing in some $7,000 of subsidies for every car. And predictably Big Oil threw massive amounts into lobbying to crush "any government encouragement of the electric car, including charging stations," says Paine.[4]

But even GM, hiding behind front groups as well, ran "reverse advertising" campaigns, discouraging car buyers from going electric and assuring the state regulators that there was no demand for the car. Why would GM thwart its own efforts? Paine says it all stems back to the car industry's love for the internal combustion engine, a technology they know inside and out and the rights to which they own. And they even adore the engine for its flaws: "Forty percent of auto dealers' revenue comes from tune-ups, oil changes, and parts,"[5] he says. The electric car, on the other hand, ditched the internal combustion engine—and didn't need tune-ups. After some 250,000 miles, you just bought a new battery. "They make too much money from the internal combustion engine," says Paine. "And they were afraid consumers were beginning to move toward electric cars."[6]

Whatever GM's motivation, it's yet another chapter in a sordid tale about how car companies and oil companies—the very industries that made the United States great—are now holding us back, and how corporate finances dictate our ability to evolve. What his film underscores, says Paine, is "how difficult it is to change a situation, even when that situation is not working for society's benefit."[7]

—Melik Boudemagh

ADDICTED TO OIL OR ADDICTED TO CARS?

Nobody loves their wheels more than Americans, who drive farther, more often, and more frequently alone than residents of any other country. Given that 87 percent of the population over age sixteen holds a license, our roadways serve as playground for the 230-

million-strong national armada of cars and light trucks: 30 percent of the world's fleet is parked here. And when gas prices dropped during the 1990s, we put the pedal to the metal and drove unprecedented distances. The trend continued even as prices went back up. In 2004 alone, America's drivers logged in almost one thousand miles a month—almost one and a half times the global average. And since the promises of electric cars for the masses and engines that could run on pure ethanol have stalled—thanks to the oil and auto industries essentially pouring sugar in the tank—we're forced to fuel up with gasoline derived from oil, often with a tad of ethanol mixed in. Americans represent only 5 percent of the world's population (as the rest of the world is quick to point out), but we burn through a quarter of the world's oil—and about 60 percent is imported. Averaging twenty miles per gallon, our vehicles are actually less fuel efficient than they were in the 1980s. Our love affair with oil-gulping SUVs and pickups (which now represent 40 percent of U.S. vehicles) is part of the reason; Congress has also been handing out hefty tax credits to those who drive SUVs off the lot. But the trend may now be changing. With gas prices topping three dollars a gallon in summer 2006, there are now a few years' worth of back orders for hybrids from abroad, and some Americans are looking to buy Europe's favorite—the tiny Smart Car. SUVs, tanks like the Hummer, and big revving trucks, which were once roaring off lots, are now a liability: sales are down by some 25 percent, and both GM and Ford are losing billions, thanks to their own shortsighted stupidity.

[Forces at Work]

Lobbying:

- **American Petroleum Institute:** The petroleum trade association's finger-pointing ads, ferocious lobbying, and generous campaign contributions aim to a) prevent price caps, b) prevent laws to decrease greenhouse gases, and c) lessen viability of competition—ethanol.

- **American Automobile Manufacturers Association:** The mighty trade group of Detroit's Big Three—General Motors, Ford, and Chrysler—used lobbying, advertising, and contributions to stall any action to increase auto efficiency for decades. Folded in 1998, after German carmaker Daimler merged with Chrysler, deflating the domestic power of the Big Three. (See Andrew Card, page 171.)

- **Alliance of American Automakers:** Representing the Big Three, plus Honda, Toyota, BMW, Porsche, Mazda, and Mitsubishi, it's taken over the "upping fuel efficiency will kill us" chant in ads and lobbying.

- **Global Climate Coalition:** Created by PR megalith Burson-Marsteller, this group of oil companies, carmakers, and electric utilities tried to torch the news that the earth is warming up and that greenhouse gases from fossil fuels are responsible. Broke up in 2002, after most members decided global warming was real.

Think tanks and other outside forces:

- **Competitive Enterprise Institute:** An anti-regulation "think tank for hire," CEI cranks out reports questioning global warming and linking smaller, more fuel-efficient cars to increased deaths from crashes. And here's a surprise: ExxonMobil donated nearly $2 million between 2000 and 2005. CEI's Myron Ebell also headed up the Cooler Heads Coalition to debunk "myths of global warming." CEI launched an offensive against Al Gore's documentary, *An Inconvenient Truth*: one CEI ad on TV claimed the earth was cooling; another assured us that carbon dioxide was good, and both garnered CEI a raft of criticism.

- **National Academy of Sciences:** The venerable "honorific society of distinguished scholars" can be counted on for, ahem, moderate and business-respecting reports. Nevertheless, NAS announced there *is* global warming due to human activities and said that technology exists to upgrade auto fuel mileage without undue economic hardship to carmakers. Bush ignored them.

- **Union of Concerned Scientists:** An all-purpose expert resource on pretty much everything related to science—energy to genetically modified food—this laudable group lobbies and issues reports pointing out ways to reduce carbon dioxide levels, improve fuel efficiency, and reduce dependence on fossil fuels. (www. ucsusa.org.)

- **Public Citizen:** President Joan Claybrook created the country's fuel efficiency standards when she headed the National Highway Traffic Safety Administration in the 1970s; now she testifies before Congress and writes reports for this consumer group demanding that carmakers make more efficient autos. (www.citizen .org/autosafety.)

Officials and legislators:

- **Andrew Card:** The dapper and mighty former chief of staff for President George W. Bush (2001–06) was CEO and president of the American Automobile Manufacturers Association (1993–98) and head lobbyist for GM (1999–2000).

- **Secretary of Energy Spencer Abraham** (2001–05): As U.S. senator from Michigan (1994–2000), he received over $907,000 from the oil and auto industries, and was the all-time highest recipient of automaker contributions.[8] Avoided the issues of global warming and increasing standards for fuel efficient cars while energy secretary, and blocked the issues as senator.

- **Rep. Joe Barton** (R-Texas): Head of the House Energy and Commerce Committee since March 2004 and recipient of $2 million from energy industry players since 2000, Barton helped push through the 2005 energy bill and supports ongoing legislative efforts to open up oil drilling in the Arctic National Wildlife Refuge and the continental shelf off Florida.

- **Reps. John Dingell and Tom DeLay and Sen. Trent Lott:** John Dingell (D-Michigan) is Detroit's point man in Congress; DeLay

(R-Texas) and Lott (R-Mississippi) fanatically protected car and oil interests. (See "The Big Three's Anti-CAFE Society," page 178.)

Industry:

- **General Motors:** CEO Rick Wagoner is calling for early retirement of employees, and the company's early buyout deals have prompted thirty-five thousand workers to cash in. With losses of $8.6 billion in 2005, GM is cuddling up to French carmaker Renault and whispering about a partnership.

- **Ford:** Henry's environmentalist grandson Bill Ford stepped in as CEO with a vision of producing 250,000 hybrid cars by 2010, but dropped that idea and is now laying off forty thousand workers. He slunk off from the CEO's office in September 2006, handing the burden to Alan Mulally of Boeing. Like Daimler-Chrysler and GM, Ford opposed laws to boost car efficiency, but all three are now pushing flex-fuel cars that can use ethanol and gasoline.

- **Oil's "supermajors":** ExxonMobil, BP, and Royal Dutch Shell are cashing in: they made more than $931 billion between them in 2005—of which $78 billion was profit. Lobby to expand operations in the United States, avoid windfall profits taxes and price lids, escape litigation, minimize regulations in refining—and stifle use of ethanol by limiting availability at gas stations. Also push to avoid paying royalties on oil they obtain from federal lands—depriving the U.S. Treasury of billions a year.

[**Close-up**]

In March 2006, around the time President Bush returned from India, peddling his controversial plan that would open the door to GE and Westinghouse to sell beaucoup bucks' worth of nuclear plants across the subcontinent, the American public was shrieking about what was happening in their backyard. Specifically, they pointed to the gas station—and the wads of money forked over there as gas approached $2.30 a gallon—as a symbol of the American dream (liberty, justice, and cheap oil) gone very wrong. Nobody wanted to out-and-out ask, but an unspoken question hung in the air: "Wasn't this why we went to Iraq— to prevent prices like this?"

Well, you see, as President Bush explained in speech after speech, the reason gasoline prices had gotten a bit higher was demand had shot up in places like India, where his program to sell them nuclear technology would help keep them off our oil, he claimed with flawed logic.

By the end of March, gasoline had shot up to $2.54 a gallon. In mid-April it jumped to $2.92 a gallon. The expense that hammered Americans—69 percent said gas prices were causing financial hardship[9]—benefited at least a lucky few: headline after headline trumpeted the news that oil companies were pulling in buckets of gold, making revenues never dreamed of before and ringing in history-making profits. ExxonMobil led the pack, clearing $36.1 billion in 2005, making more than any other company in the world—ever. Nobody in the industry was hurting: the twelve U.S. oil companies netted over $96 billion in 2005.[10] But ExxonMobil, which reported profits of over $10 billion during the first quarter of 2006, stood out as the symbol of excessive corporate greed, all the more when the oil giant's multiple-chinned CEO, Lee Raymond, waddled into retirement with a sweet bundle: between stocks, consulting fees, salary, and options, the package weighed in at nearly $400 million.

As the public began glaring in the direction of ExxonMobil corporate headquarters and everyone from Bill O'Reilly to the *New York Times'* editorial board expressed outrage (O'Reilly hissed that Raymond was a "greedhead") and Congress began growling about "windfall profits tax" and "price caps," ExxonMobil took its trademark posture: it blurred the issue.

The petroleum behemoth started kicking sand in every direction. Exxon wasn't really as prosperous as it seemed, the company proclaimed in advertising campaigns and public relations calls to the press and Wall Street: if you wanted to see outrageously high returns, look at finance firms like Citigroup and drug companies, they said. Exxon-Mobil's profits, publicists explained, merely appeared to be so huge because, well, it was a big company, you see.

ExxonMobil looked positively bullyish when it began taking potshots at farmers: why was the government propping up ethanol, CEO Rex Tillerson asked in March 2006, demanding that subsidies be halted. "The fact that the subsidies exist," said Tillerson, "shows [that ethanol is] not a viable alternative."[11]

Then the oil supermajor took aim at Detroit's already bruised hiney. In cartoons depicting a monster SUV—and the diminutive driver climbing up on a ladder to feed its gas tank—ExxonMobil demanded to know why American cars had such voracious appetites. Subtly slammed in the process were the consumers who had been lured into buying them—with enticing tax credits of up to $100,000.

Even President Bush, who'd happily signed the bill that tipped the scales in favor of buying SUVs, jumped into the fray. The Big Three, he told the *Wall Street Journal*, should get up to speed and make "a product that's relevant."

EXXONMOBIL

In 1998, when Exxon—the company infamous for the *Exxon Valdez*, the oil tanker that spilled 35 million gallons of petrol-goo in Alaska in 1989—announced plans to merge with Mobil, eyebrows raised and words such as "antitrust" echoed across the globe. The relationship between the two, with a collective worth of $230 billion, was indeed incestuous: the two oil companies were the biggest that had emerged from the early-twentieth-century petroleum empire of John D. Rockefeller—Standard Oil—which the government had hacked into thirty-four pieces in 1911 due to concerns that it was far too powerful. Editorials denounced the move—the British newspaper the *Guardian* accurately predicted that "we will end up with three 'Super Sisters' that will monopolise global energy at the start of the next millennium."[12] The Federal Trade Commission, which had grown rather lax since John D. Rockefeller's day, approved the marriage—requiring only that the company sell off a California refinery and over three thousand gas stations. Even with the divestiture, ExxonMobil was hands down the planet's biggest oil outfit—stepping up as the world's largest refiner, and the world's largest oil seller—and drilling, refining, and selling over 4 million barrels of oil and natural gas in two hundred countries every day. Admitting that "by itself, ExxonMobil's downstream business [including shipping, refining, and gas sales] would be one of the world's largest companies,"[13] the company holds interests in forty-five refineries in twenty-five countries, operates a hefty fleet of thirty-two oil tankers, pumps petroleum products through twenty-five thousand miles of pipeline, and pumps it out at thirty-seven thousand gas stations in more than one hundred countries.[14]

The corporation, headquartered in Irving, Texas, is today considered the "world's most valuable company"—earning more than Fortune 500 chart-toppers General Electric and Wal-Mart—but it is also the sootiest of the petrol supermajors. While BP and Shell have spent billions on developing "renewable resources"—including investing in solar, wind, and "biofuels"—ExxonMobil makes no pretensions of being green. It is an oil company pure and simple and does all that the role requires—although the public never knows just what may be involved in getting that oil, whether Exxon or another company is getting it. In the murky world of oil deals, rumors run rife of bribes, government overthrows, and/or cuddling up with dictators, but just how dirty (or clean) the global petrol biz is has never been proven.

But the reason this company stands out as "a worse environmental villain than other big oil companies"[15] is for the millions upon millions ExxonMobil pours into clouding up the issue of global warming. Even after BP, then Shell, then Ford, GM, DaimlerChrysler, and Dow Chemical left the Global Climate Coalition—which dismissed global warming—Exxon hung fast to its position that the global warming jury is still out. And, under current CEO Rex Tillerson, it still holds by the story. Meanwhile, former CEO Raymond now heads the National Petroleum Council advising Bush on energy policy.

BABY, IT'S HOT OUTSIDE

It's the biggest disinformation campaign yet unleashed in this country, outside of the one to invade Iraq: the American campaign against global warming. It's not a campaign to prevent global warming from continuing—the U.S. government doesn't care about that; it's doing precisely zip, zilch, nada to cap the emissions that cause climate change. Rather, this campaign denies that global warming is happening and feigns confusion over whether humans have anything to do with it—even when government experts are saying that global warming is here, it's man-made, it's serious, and we have to do something now. The Bush administration has taken over for industry in the information cloud-a-thon, leading the shrugging "gosh, we still don't know what triggers climate change and therefore let's not do anything" parade.

A decade ago, it was the oil companies and carmakers—the industries whose fossil fuels and emissions are the major causes of climate change—who began strategizing about how to keep the blanket over our heads. Back then Exxon, Chevron, Shell, Texaco, the American Petroleum Institute, Ford, GM, and the U.S. Chamber of Commerce joined forces to form a bogus "grassroots" front group—the Global Climate Coalition—to run a multimillion-dollar ad campaign to try to fog up the science. The good news is that the group folded in 2002 when most of its members changed their minds, many acknowledging that indeed climate change is taking place. The bad news is that one member in particular—ExxonMobil—is still going full steam ahead in denying what the scientific body worldwide is screaming is a fact. And the other bad news is that Exxon is not only kicking millions to faux "think tanks" such as the Competitive Enterprise Institute to write articles and reports condemning "climate alarmism" and to run ad campaigns saying that the world is actually getting colder—but that Exxon and the Competitive Enterprise Institute are both advising the government on what stance to take. So it wasn't a big surprise that when President Bush took office in 2001, he promptly removed the United States from the Kyoto Protocol agreement. No big shock that he appointed Phil Cooney—a former lobbyist for the American Petroleum Institute—to head the White House Council on Environmental Quality. And, again, it's simply predictable that Cooney, not a scientist, took to editing the government's report on global warming—deleting and toning down anything that would give the impression that climate change is real or a real concern. And it was par for the course that when Cooney's whitewashing was exposed, he retired—to work as a lobbyist for Exxon, which, not surprisingly, was the corporation that Undersecretary of State for Democracy and Global Affairs Paula Dobriansky thanked for its "active involvement" in shaping the government's global warming policy.[16]

Despite all the misinformation gushing forth from the White House, despite the fact that every attempt to limit greenhouse gas emissions gets shot down in Congress, 94 percent of the American people stand united in their belief that the United States should do something to address climate change; 86 percent think the United States should sign the Kyoto Protocol.[17] Alas, unlike Exxon, those 86 percent aren't throwing millions into politicians' coffers. (Congress is now investigating the climate change cover-up.)

More Hot Air from the White House

Reporter at White House briefing: *"Scott, what message would the president like the rest of the world to take from the U.S. [dropping out] of the Kyoto treaty that kicks in tomorrow?"*

Scott McClellan, White House press secretary: *"Well, I think our views are very well known; they've been known for quite some time. In terms of the issue of climate change, let me step back and talk about that, because the United States has been a leader in advancing the science of climate change. Under this administration we have made an unprecedented commitment to reduce the growth of greenhouse gas emissions in a way that continues to grow our economy. . . . There's a lot that we are still learning about the science of climate change, but this administration is working to advance that science and to learn more about climate change itself, and its effect on the world. . . ."*

In this exchange, at a White House press conference on February 15, 2005, Scott McClellan could have summed it up much more succinctly with the more honest and direct, "Frankly, we don't give a hoot."

How many miles a car could squeeze out of a gallon wasn't a big deal in the 1980s and 1990s when the SUV first began rolling out of warehouses and gasoline cost a mere sixty cents a gallon; now, with prices near three dollars a gallon, it mattered. Car buyers switched to efficient Toyotas; the company that sold 7.7 million vehicles worldwide in 2005 couldn't keep its electric/gasoline hybrid Prius in stock.

As gas prices rose, sales of GM and Ford vehicles plummeted—since both heavily pushed SUVs. General Motors, the industry's leader since the 1930s, made nearly half of the cars sold in 1978 but barely a quarter of those sold in 2005; and, like Ford, its credit rating fell deep in the junkyard. In 2006, both companies made pitiful attempts to entice buyers by offering to help pay for gasoline: GM buyers in Florida and California could pump unlimited gas at $1.99 per gallon for a year if they bought certain model SUV's; Ford tossed in a $1,000 gas card to buyers of its models. By May 2006, you could get a $50 gas card simply to take an SUV for a test drive. The press lampooned the pathetic attempts, and *New York Times* columnist Thomas Friedman skewered the stunt, asking "Is there a company more dangerous to America's future than General Motors?"[18]

Worse, consumer groups and Congress began enunciating the four letters that the Big Three hated most, the four letters that over the past two decades they had spent billions in lobbying, advertising, and political contributions to prevent lawmakers from uttering: CAFE, or corporate average fuel efficiency. In other words, the pressure was on for Detroit to make cars that could squeeze out more than 27.5 miles per gallon—a standard that for cars has remained unchanged since 1987.

THE BIG THREE'S ANTI-CAFE SOCIETY

Nobody likes being told what to do, but the Big Three are really loud whiners. In 1965, when lawmakers forced carmakers to put in seat belts, the industry insisted that the safety items were "unreasonable" and "technically unfeasible" and the changes could very well shut them down.[19] Later forced to install air bags too, they screamed all the way to the Supreme Court. But they wailed the loudest over fuel efficiency, unsuccessfully battling the creation of CAFE standards in 1975. Despite their whimpers that if Congress forced them to make cars that could crank out at least 27.5 miles per gallon, their vehicles would be only slightly larger than matchboxes (CAFE would kill their van lines and even their midsize car business, they warned), they managed to pull through rather well. But they didn't want to go through it again. In 1990, when the issue of dependency on Middle Eastern oil arose yet again—this against the backdrop of the first Persian Gulf War (aka Desert Storm)—and Sen. Richard Bryan proposed that CAFE be boosted to 33 mpg in 1995 and 40 mpg by 2001, automakers wheeled out the same excuse about how they would be reduced to making compacts. That time (and every other time the subject has been raised since then) they won.[20]

The Big Three had their influential power boys in Congress, and they tossed millions into the election coffers. Among them:

- **Rep. John Dingell** (D-Michigan), who warned that increased CAFE regulations would cost hundreds of thousands of jobs and make America less competitive (and it probably had nothing to do with that $185,000 he pulled in from the transportation and auto industries in 2002 alone).
- **Rep. Tom DeLay** (R-Texas), who from 1995 to 1999 (during which time he received over $323,000 in contributions from the transportation and oil industries) successfully blocked all discussion of changing CAFE standards.
- **Sen. Trent Lott** (R-Mississippi), who (having received contributions of $136,000 from the transportation and automotive industries in the previous year's elections) declared in 2001 that "American people have a right to drive a great big road hog SUV . . . and I'm gonna get me one!"[21]

Lobbying individually and collectively, the Big Three found a new way to help shoot down laws. The car industry poured millions into the bank accounts of think tanks such as the Competitive Enterprise Institute to issue reports that smaller, more fuel efficient cars were dangerous—and the Big Three broadcast those findings in full-page advertisements whenever the CAFE issue reared its ugly head.

Like the student who bribes his teachers to pass school, only to graduate illiterate, car companies had figured out how to win hand after hand, but they screwed themselves and the American consumer in the process. And now they are losing the game: GM and Ford each laid off (or paid off) some forty thousand workers during 2006. Their stocks are junk status and they're getting killed by health-care costs and pension plans. Toyota, which didn't need laws to tell it to create cars that wring forty or more miles out of every gallon, or to develop hybrid (electric/gasoline) cars such as the 55 mpg Prius, is moving up in the world: 17 percent of the cars sold in the United States in 2005 were Toyotas and the company's credit rating is AAA.[22]

GM and Ford weren't the only ones that now appeared foolish. Congressional lawmakers looked like buffoons. They'd awarded hefty tax credits of $100,000 for buying SUVs in 2002—scaling the figure back to $25,000 in 2004: as a result, SUV sales skyrocketed. Meanwhile, those who bought alternative-fuel cars—such as hybrids—could claim a meager $250 to $3,400 as tax credit. The energy bill that Congress passed in 2005 dropped any requirements for increasing car fuel efficiency. Instead, it tossed billions in tax credits to oil companies—$2 billion for offshore drilling alone—and waived any requirements for the oil companies to pay royalties for new oil found on public lands.[23] And now, given that oil companies are the world's wealthiest companies, many were wondering why.

And what added even more spark to the powder keg: 2006 was an election year—one where Republicans looked likely to get clobbered. Forget all that cash that the oil industry (and their employees) had dropped into the campaign piggy banks of their cheerleaders in Congress; even House Speaker Dennis Hastert (R-Illinois) ($86,000 contributed in 2004) was among those calling for an investigation into oil company price gouging. Congress hauled in oil CEOs to drill them on wages, profits, and investments, and debated hitting them with higher taxes and slamming a lid on oil prices—but it was just a show.

In April 2006, as gasoline prices neared three dollars a gallon,

President Bush's approval rating dropped to a new low—32 percent, with 60 percent out-and-out disapproving.[24] In the case of his handling of energy, only 29 percent approved.[25]

Four days after hitting his new nadir, the president was hastily scheduled to speak before the Renewable Fuels Association—a group representing ethanol interests and farmers. Stunning backdrops of cornfields were quickly hung at the Marriott Wardman Park Hotel in downtown DC. "Ethanol is good for the environment," President Bush announced as he stood before panels of silos. "Ethanol is good for drivers. Ethanol is homegrown." And ethanol was also getting a fifty-one-cent-a-gallon subsidy, much of it going into the pockets of agricultural giant ADM. Thanks to upped demand for subsidized ethanol, analysts predict that ADM will make $1.3 billion from ethanol in 2007, doubling its already impressive take from 2006.

As government administrator, Joan Claybrook devised efficiency standard for cars in the 1970s. As president of Public Citizen she now urges Congress to update those rules. Writing hard-hitting reports about the Big Three's actions (or lack thereof) and testifying on matters from rollovers to upgrading auto safety and using alternative fuels, consumer advocate Claybrook is one of the few voices urging the car industry to get on it. (See http://www.citizen.org/autosafety.)

It can be made from sugar, stalks, straw, or other fibrous plants, but in the United States, ethanol—or grain alcohol—is made from corn, thanks to ADM cornering the market. Much gasoline in the United States has been blended with 10 percent ethanol (E10) for the last few years, but now there's increasing demand for the 85 percent blend (E85) and even the pure stuff, as flex-fuel and other engine types that can easily use it roll onto the market. Ethanol doesn't have quite the energy kick of gasoline, which means it burns more quickly. And there's endless debate about whether corn ethanol is really efficient, since plenty of petroleum gets used in the farming of corn; this is one reason why cellulosic ethanol—made from switchgrasses and sugarcane stalks—is seen as more attractive. Another problem with the corn and sugar varieties: they cut into the food supply, and should the price for those commodities go up, the supply of ethanol will go down, as producers find it a better deal simply to sell the potential fuel as food.

THE POWER OF CORN: ADM

For the past three decades, there has been only one way to spell ethanol in the United States: ADM, the mighty initials that stand for Archer Daniels Midland. Headquartered in Decatur, Illinois, the agricultural firm is a behemoth domestically and on the world stage: the agricultural buyer, shipper, and food processor is the supreme King of Corn—especially the corn we put in our cars.

No sooner had the words "alternative fuel" drawled out of Jimmy Carter's mouth in 1978 than Dwayne Andreas—ADM's president and friend of pretty much everybody who mattered, from Gorbachev to the pope—roared toward Washington in his private jet hoping to turn his extra cobs into green fuel—and moreover, green money. The first thing he did was look up his old pal Bob Dole, who soon became Mr. Ethanol in DC.

Showered with hoards of campaign money and offered free flights in ADM's private plane (Andreas also sold the Doles his Florida condominium at below market value), Senator Dole helped ADM win a 1979 tax exemption on blended fuel for refiners, which added ethanol into the gasoline mix—the one thing Andreas needed to jump-start ADM's ethanol industry. Dole fought for subsidies and tax credits that added billions to ADM's revenue. More important, Dole blocked foreign ethanol imports (such as Brazil's, now slapped with high tariffs) and successfully shielded ADM when its lifelines—the subsidies and credits—were repeatedly attacked for over two decades by politicians because they weren't accomplishing the intended goals of easing Mideast oil dependency or bettering the environment. With more endurance than you can crack a Viagra joke at, Dole played defense and saved ethanol every time—even when Ronald Reagan lumped it into a group of "ineffective business subsidies" that he planned to ax.

Reagan quickly backtracked, waking up to the muscle of the farm industry, particularly ADM, which was dumping millions into political campaigns. ADM is listed as being among the top 100 all-time political contributors, having given $7,775,889 to both parties between 1987 and 1998.[26] Andreas was such an influential political player that all of Congress knew when his plane was swooping into DC—and he stopped in for personal visits with the president. Reagan even dropped by ADM headquarters in 1984, and made a lasting impression: Andreas commemorated the visit by erecting a life-size bronze of Reagan in the company's parking lot.

However, when gas prices fell in 1987, ethanol's head was on the chopping block, particularly when news spread that ADM was reeling in record profits from 1986, when the Department of Agriculture had handed it 54 percent of the total subsidy payout for gasohol, a fuel mixture of 10 percent ethanol and 90 percent gasoline that can be used in most modern combustion engines.

The subsidies continued, although for a few years ADM's luck did not. The FBI raided the Decatur headquarters in 1995, although that actually had nothing to do with ethanol, but with the company's agricultural clout: ADM was subsequently fined $100 million for conspiracy to fix the price of lysine. Not to fret: the money would eventually find its way back home. After all, the subsidies remained—even after Dwayne's son Michael was thrown in prison, and despite the fact that ethanol, being more expensive than gasoline in those days, didn't contribute much to our energy needs.

Ignoring ethanol's troubled youth, President Bush pledged not to touch ADM's precious ethanol/blended-fuel subsidy. He stuck by that campaign promise. Bush's Energy Policy Act of 2005 virtually pulled ADM out from where it had been lying low since the 1995 price-fixing scandal: ethanol's production is now tripling—to 7.5 billion gallons by 2012—and the treasured fifty-one-cent-per-gallon tax credit appears to be a permanent ADM fixture. With a gargantuan 1.1 billion–gallon production capacity—25 percent of the U.S. ethanol market is currently stuffed into the company's overalls— ADM remains ethanol's single biggest American U.S. producer: with its record 2006 net earnings of $1.3 billion it quickly threw millions into new plant deals.

—Zac Petit

Ethanol does make at least a dent in our energy needs, although most gas stations don't carry it (some suspect that Big Oil is meddling), and many car owners don't even know that their cars will run on it, since the Big Three have largely neglected to designate which cars are in fact dual-fuel cars—while collecting the tax credits for making them. But now energy analysts are saying that a more efficient form of ethanol comes not from corn, but from switchgrass. We're betting that ADM ain't switching.

Yet, while President Bush was painting ethanol as the savior of the day, the energy speech he made at the end of April was mostly about helping out Big Oil. Initially, the president appeared to be snapping at the oil industry: he directed Congress to yank back the "unnecessary" $2 billion in tax credits offered to oil companies in the 2005 energy plan[27] (Big Oil had tipped off the government that it didn't need them). Warning that "this administration is not going to tolerate manipulation,"[28] he announced that the Federal Trade Commission was investigating price gouging (it subsequently announced there wasn't any). And he publicly implored oil companies to "reinvest their cash flows" in new refineries— a move that almost everyone agreed would increase supplies—well, at least a few years down the pike.

Nixing such ideas as putting a lid on oil prices or boosting oil industry taxes—both popular ideas in Congress—the president ticked off a number of ways to get through this bumpy patch, most of them greatly behooving the oil industry. Namely:

- President Bush lowered air pollution standards—"needless restrictions"—for oil refineries, a move he assured the nation would be temporary.[29]

- He told Congress to "simplify and speed up" the process to open refineries.[30] While opening more refineries is needed (and a move that oil companies delayed, contend their critics, simply to reduce supply and increase prices), one-stop licensing may result in shoddier, more polluting refineries.

- Most important, he demanded that we open up protected lands for oil exploration—bringing the whole Arctic National Wildlife Refuge issue back on the table. If Clinton hadn't blocked its opening a decade before, opined Bush, "America would be producing about a million additional barrels of oil a day"[31]—a stretch, since nobody is sure what the reserve holds.

In other words, under the guise of a crisis, President George W. Bush was simply pushing harder for what he'd been pushing all along.

The 2005 energy bill also directed Congress to hand out more tax credits for hybrid cars, but scarcely along the lines of the $100,000 previously offered for SUVs or even the current $25,000 SUV credit. Those who bought hybrids could claim $250 to $3,400 as tax credit. Not only was the amount puny, it also capped the number of cars eligible to sixty thousand per manufacturer; Toyota had reached the cutoff point within months.

The president's plan didn't have much of an immediate effect. The following week's poll showed his approval rating at only 31 percent. And within weeks, gas hit three dollars a gallon, and everybody was panicky. Not the least of whom were the CEOs of the Big Three: since Congress was considering new CAFE standards again, they zipped down to DC to jump through a few hoops, unveiling flashy new "flex-fuel" models on the lawn outside the Capitol and imploring Congress to make Big Oil offer ethanol at gas stations, only six hundred of which sold the fuel made from corn. President Bush, scheduled to meet with Detroit's big boys, canceled the meeting—twice. But he did wriggle the matter of auto fuel efficiency out of Congress' hands, requesting that the legislature grant him the authority to set the new standards. The Big Three shouldn't fear: in March, when the Bush administration decided to up the standards for light trucks, they increased it by a mere 0.3 miles per gallon.

As for the future of cars, the Bush administration points to the billions it's spending to help carmakers develop hydrogen fuel cells—a technological feat that many believe won't be feasible for a decade, although GM says it plans to have a model out in 2010 (no word on if it'll subsequently yank those back as well, as it did the electric cars). In the meantime, even with more ethanol being blended into gasoline, Big Oil reigns.

[**What You Can Do**]

- "Tell car companies, we're not interested in what they're offering," recommends Chris Paine. "Demand more efficient cars. Ask for plug-ins." ("Plug-in" cars are part electric, part gasoline/ethanol.) Or go electric: Tesla Motors will launch its first car—all electric—in mid-2007.

- Improve our cars' fuel efficiency. The Union of Concerned Scientist is one source that points consumers to new technology. (www.uscusa.org.)

- Buy green cars. They often cost more, but consumer experts say that hybrids and flex-fuel cars save thousands in gasoline costs.

- Work to change zoning standards. The reason we're dependent on cars is zoning: stores, banks, offices, and leisure places aren't typically within walking distance. The continuing trend among urban planners is to design "urban villages" that don't mandate hopping in the car every time you want a pint of milk, check out these pedestrian-oriented settlements for your next move.

- Support Public Citizen's Joan Claybrook and others who are demanding that carmakers quit stalling.

CHAPTER 6

Locking the Door

Immigration

The anonymous strawberry picker had a face that day. The unseen hotel maid was spotted. The mug behind the hammer, the man behind the crane, the dishwasher hidden in the restaurant kitchen, the janitor who sweeps at night—they all came out that day. And the reason wasn't all that hard to understand: they wanted to belong. The millions of Latinos who toil by day, plucking grapes for our fine wines, trimming the hedges on our manicured lawns, making beds and mopping floors and often living in a cutoff shadow society—they all spilled into the street not with anger but with pride and a noisy "We're here!"

And their announcement—in huge demonstrations across the United States in the spring of 2006—was met with bewilderment, surprise, and screaming epithets.

> *"[B]urn the Mexican flag on your street corner, show what you care about, show that you won't take it anymore, show that you're sick of everybody pushing us around like we are a pitiful, helpless giant of a nation. . . . Burn a Mexican flag for America, burn a Mexican flag for those who died that you should have a nationality and a sovereignty, go out in the street and show you're a man, burn ten Mexican flags. . . . Put one in the window upside down and tell them to go back where they came from."*
> —*Nationally syndicated radio host Michael Savage responding to the March demonstrations on his show* Savage Nation, *March 27, 2006*[1]

It wasn't surprising to hear radio shock jock Michael Savage having yet another vitriolic bigot fit. But given how integral immigrant workers (legal and not) have become to our society, and given our history as a land of immigration, and given the fact that he used to appear as such a dear, sensible man on a network that we'd come to trust, it was disconcerting to see the reaction of CNN host Lou Dobbs. Unlike smart-alecky Bill O'Reilly, who riles viewers up, comforting Dobbs used to calm viewers down: he was the Pillsbury Doughboy of anchors—soft, kind, authoritative, and above all trustworthy as he reported on new trends, be they the move toward outer space or India's boom in Information Technology. Harvard-educated but never haughty, Dobbs—well, you couldn't help but call him "Lou" back in the old days when he was like your favorite TV uncle—has changed. Lou Dobbs is now leading the hysteria parade of immigration foes, and feeding their righteous fear with conspiracies and misinformation. And his hundreds upon hundreds of shows spotlighting our "broken borders" and "exported jobs" are starting to sound like a broken record.

> *"Tonight, an astonishing proposal to expand our borders to incorporate Mexico and Canada and simultaneously further diminish U.S. sovereignty. Have our political elites gone mad? We'll have a special report. Border violence raging in Mexico. Assassins murder a Mexican police chief in cold blood. Yet, incredibly, the Mexican government declares U.S. warnings about border violence unnecessary. And massive population growth in our western states [from immigration] is straining already short water supplies. Twenty-six western states are in the grip of the worst drought ever. We'll have that report."*
> —Lou Dobbs introducing Lou Dobbs Tonight *on June 9, 2005. He's been airing essentially the same show since 2004, when he began his series "Broken Borders" as well as his series "Exporting America."*

> *"As many as 3 million illegal aliens continue to cross our border with Mexico each year."*
> —Lou Dobbs *citing stats that experts say are about 2 million higher than the real number (1 million) believed to be coming in illegally.[2] The Office of Homeland Security says, in fact, the number of undocumented immigrants is dropping.*

> *"[It's a] Mexican military incursion."*
> —Lou Dobbs' CNN *correspondent Casey Wian, reporting on Mexican president Vicente Fox's May 2006 visit to Utah[3]*

As the country's self-appointed immigration know-it-all, Dobbs heaps praise on the armed vigilantes who patrol the Southwest and has made them stars as he lauds their fine work as patriots. And in between giving the spotlight to known white supremacists and ranting paramilitaries, he spouts his beliefs about the "reconquista"—the reconquest of the southern United States by Mexico—as though it was verifiable fact instead of conspiracy theory that he reportedly pulled off of a neo-Nazi Internet site.[4] Illegal aliens sure look like aliens on Dobbs' show when he repeatedly airs infrared footage of them as green lights running in the far-off darkness. The numbers he spouts and his reports of plague-like diseases that illegal immigrants bring in are alarming—because they're frequently wrong; worse, Dobbs continues to broadcast inflated numbers and twisted facts even when notified of the errors.[5] But the most frightening thing is that now that Lou's true colors are showing, his ratings are skyrocketing: 800,000 watch him each night, and recent polls show that more people trust Lou Dobbs than they do President George W. Bush. And with the fastest rising ratings on the network, CNN ain't shutting him down—even if he's alarmist, he's inaccurate, and his griping doesn't make sense.

> *"On Monday, Tuesday, Wednesday, Lou Dobbs whines about immigrants," notes Grover Norquist, who has lectured that immigration is the issue that could most rip apart the Republican Party. "On Thursday, Friday, Saturday, he whines about outsourcing. Well, Lou, it's one or the other. If you keep the immigrants out, the companies are going to outsource."[6]*

Security zealots, social conservatives, and at least some Protestant evangelicals want to kick immigrants out, put up walls, and perhaps never let them back in. Meanwhile, businesses (some of whom have been happy to keep migrants illegal since it meant paying them less), along with economists and the Catholic Church, are pushing for guest worker programs that directly match foreign workers with domestic employers for stays up to six years; under this program as currently envisioned, guest workers would have to have a job or job offer before entering and they would be issued a guest worker ID card. Once the agreed-upon employment term was up, they would be required to leave. Immigration supporters also want amnesty for those working here without proper documents.

What Lou Dobbs seems to be forgetting, despite his degree in economics, is the government-documented fact that the American economy depends on some 21 million foreign-born workers[7]—making up one-seventh of the labor force. Whether they're the 6 million born in Mexico or the 2 million from India and the Philippines, whether they're farm workers or engineers, busboys or scientists, subtract many of those immigrants from the equation—as some very vocal groups would like to do—and a lot of wheels stop turning. Slam the door on the border (and turn back the 7 million Hispanics working in America without proper papers[8]), and crops won't get picked, nursing homes will be understaffed, and hotels, houses, and office buildings won't be built, landscaped, or cleaned—at least not at the prices that Americans are accustomed to paying.

> *Most illegal Latino workers use a borrowed Social Security card to gain employment. And the majority do pay Social Security and taxes, sending them in under the borrowed SSN and name.*[9]

Bolt the door to the East, and the United States would suffer a reverse brain drain—not by watching its leading scientists and inventors slip out, but by not allowing needed scientists and inventors from India, China, Japan, and Europe to come in, forcing companies such as Microsoft to reluctantly set up foreign shops to meet software needs.

NUMBERS, NUMBERS

With so many iffy numbers flying around, here are some we hope you can trust, since most are from the U.S. Census Bureau.

U.S. population in 2000: 282 million
U.S. population in 2006: 300 million
Hispanics living in the United States (2005): 42.7 million[10]
Percentage of U.S. population that is Hispanic: 15 percent[11]
Hispanics working in the United States without proper documents: 7.2 million[12]
Workers in the United States labor force (2006): 151 million[13]
Foreign-born workers (2004): 21 million[14]—about 14 percent of workers
Workers in the United States from Asia (2004): 5.4 million[15] (of this figure about 900,000 are from India and 900,000 are from the Philippines)
Number of immigrants admitted in 2003: 706,000[16]
Legal immigrants in the United States, as a portion of total population: 12.4 percent[17]
Estimated direct government spending for immigration reform (mostly security): $16 billion (2007–11); $48 billion over the 2007–16 period[18]

Immigration hasn't caused such a huge flap since 1954—when the U.S. government forcefully rounded up and deported at least a million Latinos in "Operation Wetback"—hauling them deep into Mexico on bus, train, and ship, an almost step-by-step repeat of the forceful booting of Mexicans during the Great Depression. From the 1960s on, however, immigration laws in the United States dramatically loosened. In 1965, Congress opened up immigration to non-Europeans; until then, Asians particularly had been barred from immigration, due to laws enacted during World War II. Congress went further in 1986, forgiving illegal workers and granting them amnesty—allowing millions to come out of the shadows and become naturalized citizens.

Some U.S. citizens, however, were watching the numbers of the foreign-born population inch up; they cloaked their concerns in population control and 1980s pro-English movements (to teach only English in schools, and ban Spanish from voting booths and public signs)—movements that typically never went too far on the floor of Congress. And during the boom years of the 1990s, most people stopped fretting about immigration, an issue that typically mirrors the state of the economy more than anything else.

Two crumbling towers, a smoldering Pentagon, and a plane smoking in a Pennsylvania field changed all that. The knee-jerk fear of foreigners that sprang up after 9/11 hasn't let up; combined with politicians digging for a hot-button issue to press in the 2006 election, it's slammed the door on immigration, much to the profitability of those in the defense business. Now in the name of keeping out undocumented workers—and anybody else who is lurking about—the heat is on to build a high-tech fortress along the Mexican-American border; some, including Rep. Tom Tancredo (R-Colorado)—who spearheaded the anti-immigration movement in Congress—want to seal out Canadians too. Foreigners, no matter their origins, make plenty of Americans jumpy these days and the issue is shredding the country. A 2005 *Wall Street Journal* poll showed that 45 percent thought immigrants "hurt more than helped" the economy, while 44 percent thought just the opposite.

A December 2005 bill out of the House called for criminalizing the 7 million foreign-born workers illegally in the United States; a May 2006 Senate bill had a plan for amnesty for those workers—and both bills caused a furor. Some Americans say that immigrants are stealing our jobs, while others, including President George W. Bush, say they're taking jobs that nobody wants; some fret that immigrants boost crime, and assert that our culture is getting "polluted"—immigrants sully the great mixed American bloodline, they say, introducing new languages, new customs and food, and having too many kids. Xenophobia and racism, church agendas and security, the cheap labor that is the underpinning of our economy, exploitation and desperation all churn about in the heated brew bubbling up under the banner of immigration.

Census figures show that with 14.5 percent of the U.S. population in 2005, Hispanic immigrants are "the fasting-growing minority group."[19] For those who trust population forecasts, the Census Bureau estimates that by 2050, "Hispanics will constitute 24 percent" of the population—with a projected population of 102 million in that future date.[20] Anti-immigrant and restrictionist groups have been blabbing that stat into any and all available mics ever since.

"In 2050, if they announce that 25 percent of the American population is of Hispanic origin, it will have the same impact as when they say today that 25 percent of the population is German."
    —Linda Chavez, author and columnist on immigration matters[21]

[Forces at Work]

- **Dr. John Tanton:** Publisher, population control activist, and compulsive frontman for anti-immigration groups, the retired eye doctor has a vision some call racist, others see as economically destructive, and others view as the cure to pretty much all social ills.

Columnist Linda Chavez is controversial, but often the voice of reason on immigration.

- **Rep. Tom Tancredo** (R-Colorado): Since 1999, loose cannon Tancredo has led the "get immigrants outta here" charge across Congress; hopes that he can ride it into the White House. Maybe Lou Dobbs will plug him.

- **Linda Chavez:** A Reagan administration mover (she was White House director of public liaison and staff director for the Commission on Civil Rights), the columnist and TV commentator resembles Mary Tyler Moore—but is far more fiery.

    Once a major player in the huge educators' union the American Federation of Teachers, Chavez has strong opinions: all immigrants need to learn English, schools should not teach Hispanics *en español*, and we need a guest worker program (to name but three). In her new book, *Betrayal*, she whips organized labor, and she is now heading her own think tank, the Center for Equal Opportunity. She really is in the middle of it all: as a Fox News talking head she's tried to bring better research to Lou Dobbs' table (mission not successful) and she previously worked for Dr. John Tanton and has worked with Tancredo on English-language education issues.

The reason her name sounds so familiar: Nannygate, the 2001 brouhaha that erupted when President George W. Bush nominated Chavez to be secretary of labor. Like Elaine Chao, who landed the position, Chavez is no friend of labor, regarding it as dictating the agenda of the Democratic Party. Chavez withdrew her nomination after being accused of employing an illegal immigrant, a charge she denied—and was later cleared of by the FBI. Decidedly conservative, she's proving to be one of the more even, steady voices in today's immigration debate.

- **Barbara Coe:** The West Coaster shrilly leading the "Stop the Invasion!" campaign as head of the California Coalition for Immigration Reform.

- **Vigilantes:** Members of volunteer border patrols are armed and zealous in their self-imposed duty to keep foreigners out. Some groups, including American Border Control, are reportedly linked to neo-Nazi and white supremacist organizations.[22]

- **Federation for American Immigration Reform (FAIR):** The original noisemakers on the immigration issue, this is a "restrictionist" group that wants immigration capped at 200,000 a year. An all-purpose get-results machine (even though until recently, it hasn't) it does it all—reports, numbers, lobbying, funding anti-immigration legislators, and civilian border patrols. Often gives testimony before Congress—it testifies more than anyone else. Given its slant and iffy numbers, that's not reassuring.

- **Business interests:** From winemakers, restaurateurs, and hoteliers to software and engineering companies, they are unified in their message: we need foreign-born workers.

- **La Raza:** The foremost Hispanic national group lobbying for Latino rights, La Raza pushes for amnesty and supports the president's guest worker program—and also draws big names to its conferences: Bill Clinton, Karl Rove, and Los Lobos were among those on the entertainment roster this year. The reason politicians are now keenly listening to what it is saying: La Raza influences much of the coveted Latino vote.

- **Catholic Church:** Cardinal Roger Mahony is the Church's immigrant-supporting face in the media and the Los Angeles diocese—but lobbyists for the Conference of Catholic Bishops work the congressional angle.

- **Hispanics:** About one in three Latino workers crossed over illegally, trekking across desert and mountain with the aid of "coyotes"—human smugglers who are generally regarded as dangerous characters. Most immigrants from anywhere end up in California, followed by New York and Texas.

[**Close-up**   ]

It was one hot spring.

In March 2006, students abruptly walked out of class and workers turned off their vacuums and put down their hoes. Alerted on their cell phones and via the Internet and beckoned by the calls from their radios, where several popular Latino DJs urged them "to let [Washington] know we're not criminals," Hispanics by the millions poured into the streets in numbers rarely, if ever, seen in this country. Waving American

Latino marches in spring 2006 brought the immigration issue into public view (for those who had missed Lou Dobbs).

flags and Mexican flags and controversially singing the national anthem in Spanish (an act later condemned by President George W. Bush), they marched through cities across the country—Los Angeles, New York, Houston, DC—protesting congressional moves to stamp undocumented workers as felons.

> *"If somebody does not agree with us, demonstrate [our good intentions] with work, with positive actions. We have to win the privilege of citizenship and we have to respect the laws."*
> —Eduardo "Piolín" Sotelo, Spanish-language radio host whose words helped mobilize 400,000 to march in Los Angeles on March 26, 2006[23]

Meanwhile, in growing numbers, thousands of ranchers, survivalists, and men who like guns have swelled the ranks of vigilante clubs in California, New Mexico, and Arizona. Clad in camouflage gear and toting sophisticated weapons, including M-16 assault rifles, they patrol the southern border, rounding up would-be illegal workers and sometimes collecting club "badges" for their missions.[24] Jim Chase, who formed California Border Watch, posted Internet ads calling for volunteers "who do not want their family murdered by Al-Qaeda, illegal migrants, colonizing illegal aliens, illegal alien felons, alien barbarians [and] Ninja-dressed drug smugglers"[25] to join his force, advising they bring "baseball bats, stun guns and machetes,"[26] or any other arms they had from assault rifles to nuclear weapons.[27] Highway billboards and signs in California, Florida, and the Southwest screamed "Stop the Invasion!" and "Something must be done!!!" Groups rallied outside Mexico's embassies, threatening armed conflict if Mexico didn't halt the "reconquista"—a supposed reconquest conspiracy that says Mexico plans to yank back the American Southwest.[28]

RACISMO AMERICAN-STYLE

The immigration issue highlights several problems, including border security, language proficiency, and our addiction to cheap labor to make economic wheels spin. But it also shines the spotlight on such unsavory topics as racism, white supremacy, xenophobia, and fanaticism—all qualities that lurk in our corners in the best of times and come flapping out in the worst. It's the racist element of the immigration debate that most concerns the Southern Poverty Law Center, which profiles the most vitriolic anti-immigrant organizations (condemning some as "hate groups"). Leaders it's keeping an eye on include:[29]

- **Glenn Spencer**, founder of Voice of Citizens Together, who patrols the Arizona border with an armed volunteer posse to scan the horizon with infrared glasses for fuzzy far-off green specks.

- **Chris Simcox**, who heads a group called the Minutemen; he's now a star of *Hannity & Colmes* ever since his April 2005 attempt to physically barricade Arizona from the Hispanic threat.

- **Erin Anderson**, who tours the country as a speaker and stands out for her fascinating theories, including that al-Qaeda and other Islamic terrorists go to special schools in Mexico where they learn to speak Spanish and pose as migrant workers to sneak up here and spread leprosy.[30]

- **Barbara Coe**, who is possibly the most rabid of the gang. Coe is enraged about the incursion of the "savages." Her lip curls in rancor as she implores groups of volunteers to join her battle to protect America from the invasion from the south; at the May 2005 "Unite to Fight" convention in Las Vegas, she stated that "we are suffering robbery, rape and murder of law-abiding citizens at the hands of illegal barbarians who are cutting off heads and appendages of blind, white, disabled gringos."[31] No surprise that she copped to being associated with the Council of Conservative Citizens—a white supremacy group.[32]

One unnerving question this bunch brings to mind: if theirs is the standard for pure American blood, perhaps it really is time we thoroughly dilute it.

Bill O'Reilly jumped in, reporting that a bill in the Senate "could lead to citizenship for more than 30 million illegal aliens"[33] (even though the total number of illegal aliens in the United States is believed to be at most 12 million); Fox's favorite heart attack maker rallied viewers to call the White House and demand that the president secure our borders.[34] In May 2006, the Senate passed a bill calling for 370 miles of high-tech fencing (price tag $2 billion) along the border; the bill out of the House of Representatives the previous December demanded construction of an 854-mile fence (price tag $2.5 billion). Under pressure, the president addressed the nation and unveiled a new immigration plan—one that called for temporary "guest workers" but also tossed a conciliatory $8 billion at a fancy-schmanzy fence and for six thousand National Guards to bolster the U.S. Border Patrol. Lockheed Martin and Raytheon queued up to design and construct what is envisioned to be a triple-walled barrier, electrified and monitored by satellite and unmanned aerial vehicles along the U.S.-Mexico divide—a move Mexico's government views as insulting.

"We're launching the most technologically advanced border security initiative in American history. We will construct high-tech fences in urban corridors, and build new patrol roads and barriers in rural areas. We'll employ motion sensors, infrared cameras, and unmanned aerial vehicles to prevent illegal crossings."
    —President George W. Bush, addressing the nation on May 15, 2006.[35] Congress appropriated $2 billion in emergency funding in August 2006 to get the fencing project rolling.

After Lou Dobbs made another on-air stink about how few employers had been popped for hiring undocumented workers In 2004, the feds made a show of stepping up crackdowns on factories employing illegal immigrants and the media lunged at the stories. The Heritage Foundation rushed out a hysterical report that a Senate bill under consideration (allowing guest workers) would balloon the number of new immigrants by an additional 103 million[36]—nearly the entire population of Mexico, and a number 2.5 times the population of Hispanics already here, most as legal citizens. Newspaper editorial boards and experts coast to coast machine-gunned the Heritage report, calling it "preposterous" and asking how the heck Heritage came up with those numbers, but the report did have an effect: the Senate slashed increases planned for the number of visas for guest workers. And good old Lou Dobbs kept tossing that 100 million figure around, even after the Heritage Foundation decreased it by a third[37]—a figure many still believed was grossly inflated.

From both sides of Congress came a flurry of calls that English be named the official language of the United States, including one inserted into a bill by Sen. James Inhofe (R-Oklahoma). And everywhere strange bedfellows embraced in fervent alliances: the country's weightiest business associations linked arms with the Catholic Church and farmer support programs to bring workers out of the shadows and legitimately into the workforce; some evangelical Protestants held hands with the nationalists, security fretters, and neo-Nazis to condemn the darker-skinned "barbarians" who threatened, they said, to discolor our world.

> *"Twenty-nine percent of all inmates in federal prisons are illegal aliens. No, Mr. Bush, they do not all come here to work. They come here to work the system, sell drugs, rape, and kill on contract."*
> —Radio host Michael Savage, spreading yet more brotherly love on his talk show Savage Nation, *March 27, 2006* [38]

> *"All immigrants are real Americans."*
> —White House political strategist Karl Rove, addressing members of the National Council of La Raza and, we suspect, calculating how many Republican votes that statement would bring

Behind the cacophony and the mass hysteria, the hand-wringing and border watching, was the hyperactive ticking of a metronome.

Dr. John Tanton, a Michigan ophthalmologist, likes to set it at 135 beats per minute—each tick signifying yet another birth in the world, or at least the world in 1969, when he first became intrigued with population control; today it would be ticking out about 300 beats every minute. Whenever he turns it on, it only takes a few minutes of hearing the rapid rhythm before visitors yelp, "Make it stop!"[39] With the help of his ticking torture device, used as a tool for media interviews or when giving speeches, Tanton has been orchestrating the buildup to this high-pitched debate for the past four decades—all from the tiny town of Petoskey, Michigan, better known for its fossils and boating than for what some call eugenics.

THE TANTON MACHINE

One person, indeed, can make a difference. From his modest home along Lake Michigan, John Tanton snapped together all the wheels of the "immigration restriction" machine—founding, cofounding, and funding more than a dozen groups that are huge noisemakers in to-day's immigration debate. Some lobby for closed borders, some focus on culture, and others endorse capping all immigration at 200,000 a year—about one-fifth of the current figure legally admitted annually as U.S. citizens. Hitting assorted angles of the immigration debate, they work together to solidly form an anti-immigration—or "restrictionist"—bloc. Among them:

- **Federation for American Immigration Reform (FAIR):** See page 196.

- **U.S. Inc.:** Founded by John Tanton in 1982 and funded through the Sarah Scaife Foundation and, until 1994, by donations from the old-time "genetic selection" club the Pioneer Fund, U.S. Inc. serves as the machine's financial motor. In turn, U.S. Inc. funds assorted "restrictionist" and "anti-immigration" groups, including those started by Tanton as well as border vigilantes and Barbara Coe's anti–Welcome Wagon.

- **U.S. English:** Cofounded with Japanese American senator S. I. Hayakawa (an immigrant who found political clout by playing the language card in California) in 1983, this English-only advocacy group kicked off the English-as-the-official-language movement—and ultimately kicked Tanton from the roster.

- **Pro English:** Another English-only group Tanton started, after being forced to resign from U.S. English.

- **Center for Immigration Studies:** Founded by John Tanton in 1985 and funded through other Tanton organizations, including U.S. Inc., this is the only American "think tank" that focuses exclusively on immigration matters. It says that it is "animated by a pro-immigrant, low-immigration vision that seeks fewer immigrants but a warmer welcome for those admitted." Right watchers bristle at its self-advertising of being independent, nonpartisan, and impartial.

- **NumbersUSA:** Founded by John Tanton in 1997, it's a voracious "immigration restriction" lobbying noisemaker that pawns itself off as a grassroots group. Overcrowded schools, gridlocked traffic, the difficulty of hiking or swimming in nature without seeing others—what's the cause of all these problems? Immigration, says NumbersUSA.[40]

With snowy white hair, wire frame glasses, and a ready smile, John Tanton hardly is the picture of back hills ignorance. The kindly eye doctor set out his shingle in north Michigan hideaway Petoskey—a fetching area brimming with good fishing lakes, woods for hunting, and quirky towns—where wealthy Midwesterners buy summer homes to boat on private lakes and the really well-to-do (like Madonna's papa) plant lush vineyards. Originally from the South (his father immigrated there from Canada), John Tanton's name soon became well known in these lush agricultural parts where migrant workers plucked apples and berries— and not only because of the beehives and beautiful flower gardens in his backyard or because his wife worked at the local history museum: Tanton, active in his Presbyterian church, where he ran Great Books study clubs, also opened up northern Michigan's first Planned Parenthood, dispensing low-cost birth control.

It was the late 1960s when intellectuals fretted over Paul R. Ehrlich's bummer of a book, *The Population Bomb*—which gravely forecast that billions would soon suffer from global famine. Upon reading it, Tanton, an avid conservationist and member of the Sierra Club's board of directors, became obsessed—not just with the idea that we needed to control our population before we did ourselves in, but with the idea of who exactly would be making up future America. And somewhere or another he got the number "150 million" lodged in his head. According to Linda Chavez, who met Tanton in the 1980s, he decided *that* was the ideal population for the United States. "Since we're at 300 million now," says Chavez, "I don't know what he was planning to do with the other 150 million."[41]

Zero population growth became his obsession: Tanton founded northern Michigan's first chapter of the group that brought the demographics and birth rate issues to the general public; he was so dedicated to the mission that he became the nonprofit's president. By 1975, the U.S. birth rate had dropped to "replacement level"—keeping the population steady. But the U.S. population kept rising, and Tanton knew why: immigrants. Through the 1970s, about 400,000 were coming in legally as permanent residents; tens of thousands more came in illegally. And Tanton, who thought the population should continue its slow growth, decided to do something about it.

SHAPING OUR FUTURE RACE

Mention eugenics and the image of Nazi Germany first comes to mind. But what's lost in the pages of many U.S. history books is that the control-the-gene-pool movement had strong and powerful proponents in the United States. "The early eugenicists were the intellectuals and the wealthy philanthropists," says Linda Chavez.[42] Nineteenth-century Harvard professors founded immigration restriction movements, and in the 1920s, do-gooder scientists, conservationists, and high society types formed the American Eugenics Society to promote a superior, pure American race. Holding "Better Baby" contests that awarded lily-white genes, the society sloganized—"Some are born to be a burden"—and tossed out alarming stats, including the one that a feeble-minded child was born every forty-eight seconds. They also convinced some government health departments to set up sterilization clinics for blacks, Mexicans, and others deemed racially inferior; one eugenics hotbed was wholesome Vermont. Hitler brought the demise of the movement, after the public learned of the loathsome experiments conducted in the name of a perfect race during the Holocaust.

At first glance Tanton may not have seemed more than simply conservative on the immigration issue, but upon closer inspection, as Linda Chavez soon discovered, he had an agenda that leaned a wee bit too close to Hitler's. In the '70s, he tried to convince the Sierra Club board to stand up and demand that America close its borders, particularly the southern ones, but 60 percent of the directors shot down that idea—and Tanton earned a reputation as an extremist. But he did have his recruits, among them the literary and famous who championed the idea of controlling population through squeezing immigration. Armed with statisticians, he formed the Federation for American Immigration Reform (FAIR)—even moving to DC to lobby legislators and get the power community to pull the door closed until there was but a small trickle of foreigners. Few were listening when the tiny organization first began making noise, but after meeting Senator Hayakawa, Tanton saw a new button to push—language. As he traveled around the country, casually polling people about what they thought about foreigners coming to America, some told him their fear was more about the language. They didn't like to see foreign languages in voter booths; it ticked them off that there was a "For Spanish, press 1" option when they called the phone company. They didn't like their kids learning Spanish, German, or French, and they didn't like their tax dollars going to teach immigrants' kids classes in their native languages. This was America, dammit, and here we speak English—or rather, American.

Intellectuals and immigration experts worried that foreigners weren't learning English—and some, such as Colorado junior high teacher Tom Tancredo, loudly opposed teaching classes in Spanish. Meanwhile, Tanton took his ideas to the highbrows on the East Coast and formed U.S. English, a group to ensure that English remained the main, preferably only, language of the United States. Walter Cronkite, Saul Bellow, Arnold Schwarzenegger, and neocon guru Norman Podhoretz were among the heavyweights that sat on the nonprofit's advisory board.

And that's where Linda Chavez enters the story. Tanton hired her to be the president of U.S. English. Chavez was the ideal person to push in front of the cameras to assure the public that no, this wasn't an anti-Hispanic group; this was about immigrants learning to assimilate. But then, about a year into the project, just as momentum was building and Chavez was becoming a frequent face on the national news, everything exploded.

It began in 1988, when Chavez was looking for a book in the U.S.

English library and with horror came across a bound galley called *The Camp of Saints* by French writer Jean Raspail. She knew it well: the novel about a darker-skinned race fornicating madly and overtaking a lighter-skinned civilized people was one of the most racist and vitriolic of the twentieth century—as she had noted years before in her published review of the book, which she'd panned. Perplexed at what it was doing in the U.S. English library, she noticed that this new edition—a rerelease—was published by Social Contract Press, out of Petoskey, Michigan. She hadn't yet figured out that Social Contract was yet another Tanton enterprise, when Chavez received a disturbing phone call. On the line was a reporter she knew well, James Crawford from *Education Week*. He had some papers he wanted her to see.

And when she read the papers—copies of a memo Tanton had written and a financial record showing donations from a group called the Pioneer Fund, it all came together: hidden under the guise of intellectual philanthropist, Chavez says she realized Tanton was really promoting a whole different agenda, one that had the ideology and thinking of the eugenics movement, and one that she felt was riddled with Nazi-like implications and pure racism.[43]

The memo was addressed to a member of a small group he belonged to called WITAN—short for the old English *witenagemot*, or council of wise men. Written by Tanton, it slammed Catholics and Hispanics and immigrants in general. Hispanics were not educable, he opined, and they bred like bunnies. The Catholic Church was a danger, he said, because of its influence on Hispanics and its views on birth control. And in underscoring the danger, Tanton wrote that he was worried that Hispanics would soon overtake the population of whites, who, he opined, were more likely to use birth control. Chavez's face was burning with anger when she read, "Perhaps this is the first instance in which those with their pants up are going to get caught by those with their pants down."[44]

Chavez had already decided what she was going to do when she came to the final page: the reporter had also uncovered that funding for Tanton groups was coming from the Pioneer Fund, an old eugenics (some would say white supremacist) organization.

Chavez called an emergency meeting of the U.S. English board. She passed out copies of the WITAN memo. And she quit. Most of the board's other big names quickly followed, with Walter Cronkite among those most red-faced in embarrassment.

Tanton was so shaken that he soon resigned as well.

But he didn't stop.

A clever strategist and tireless advocate, if an extremist, he kept the wheels of his machine grinding out the same message. "We're in this for the long haul," he wrote in a 2002 message to his group FAIR, outlining a new strategy with points such as "Infiltrate the Judiciary Committees." So Tanton sat back and waited for just the right legislator to come along.

Soon a short, balding, round-faced Italian-American from Colorado walked into the picture. Tom Tancredo looked like a used-car salesman, but in fact he'd headed Colorado's Department of Education—a department he believed should be eliminated, and he certainly deleted many names from the roster in his region, shrinking the number of employees by two-thirds, while endorsing moves to transform it into a "truly Christian educational system." Like Tanton, he was a Presbyterian (in Tancredo's case evangelical) and he had no qualms about dueling with the Catholic Church.

Proof that if you don't shut up, somebody will finally listen, Rep. Tom Tancredo (R-CO), is head of the movement to lock the door.

A former teacher, Tancredo didn't much care for the dual-language push of the 1970s and '80s, and coming from the Southwest, he was well aware of a populist zeal in scapegoating immigrants. Elected to the state legislature in 1976, he was branded by Governor Dick Lamm as one of the "crazies" for his attempts to deflate budgets for social services, but by the time he made it to Congress in 1999, Representative Tancredo had pinpointed the issue that would make him famous.

After first flipping off the Clinton administration (rejecting the invitation to the freshmen Welcoming Party because, he announced, Clinton didn't deserve to be president), Tancredo formed a new caucus—this one on immigration reform. By the end of the year, fewer than a dozen members had signed up—a sign of how unimportant the issue was regarded. But like Tanton, Tancredo let nothing—including reality—faze him. Most other congressmen avoided him, lest they be subjected to yet another monologue about kicking out illegal aliens and shutting the borders, the only issue he cared about.

The friendless congressman struck a tragicomic presence, staying in the House Chamber until 2 or 3 a.m. for his chance in front of the C-SPAN camera, droning on and on about the immigration invasion. He had enemies, too—especially after President George W. Bush took office. The president's all-important advisor Karl Rove called Tancredo a traitor and warned him not to "darken the White House door" by decrying the president's immigration plans. Tancredo indeed was a loose cannon—refusing to back the president's plan for guest workers, announced in the first months of his presidency, and lambasting the White House for the porous Mexican-American border.

Then, on Wednesday, September 12, 2001, an extraordinary thing happened. The number of congressmen who wanted to join Tancredo's Immigration Reform Caucus ballooned from 12 to 147. Suddenly, plenty of congressmen were happy to talk about border security and preventing unwanted persons from slipping in. To top things off, the chairman of the House Judiciary Committee, F. James Sensenbrenner, gave Tancredo a boost. After Tancredo's bill, the 2005 Mass Immigration Reduction Act (that called for a wall along the border) was shot down, Sensenbrenner revived the cause. And in November 2005 the House passed a bill turning illegal immigrants into felons.

The Catholic Church did not like the bill. By and large, Hispanics are Catholic, and lobbyists were sent out to ensure the Senate didn't pass such a draconian act. Agribusiness likewise loathed it. So did associations of restaurants and hotels—and they formed assorted coalitions to support the guest worker program. The U.S. Chamber of Commerce weighed in, also demanding a guest worker program and forming a coalition with two labor groups.

Business leaders, including Bill Gates, got their two cents in. But the Microsoft founder didn't want to talk about Hispanics—he wanted to discuss the Indians and other Asians who came in on H1B visas to work as scientists and engineers. And what Gates said was pretty clear: either let more of the highly skilled workers come or we will go to their countries.

Indeed, usually entirely excluded from the immigration debate are the incoming Asians.

THE OTHER KIND OF IMMIGRANT

While many immigrants work as crop pickers, hotel maids, and janitors, Asians—particularly Indians—are often employed as scientists, engineers, and software programmers; their contributions range from creating the famous Pentium chip to devising Hotmail. This elite fills jobs that the American workforce can't, since U.S. colleges are turning out far fewer scientists and engineers—and nearly a third of Silicon Valley workers are Indian. Typically entering on a different sort of work visa—the H1B—the numbers fluctuate with the political tide and are now capped at 65,000 a year. Microsoft, for one, has stated that if the United States won't let the brainy sorts they need into the United States they'll simply set up in India. And while Americans fume that foreign-born sorts are taking high-paying high-tech positions in the United States—even becoming CEOs—Indians are ticked too: many of these engineers were educated at their country's leading engineering universities—and they say India is subsidizing American business.

Over the summer, House members took the three-ring circus on the road—holding public forums where Americans flocked to speak their minds about the immigrant "invasion." But all those in the know shook their heads in disgust: this was but a show. Because Big Business—in the form of the U.S. Chamber of Commerce—had signaled its preference. And these days what the Chamber wants, the Chamber gets. And the Chamber wanted guest workers.

[**What You Can Do**   ]

Get your facts straight and watch your sources:

- Among government sources, reports from the Congressional Research Services, Government Accountability Office, U.S. Census Bureau, and Congressional Budget Office are generally trustworthy.

- Reliable think tanks include the RAND Corporation, Brookings Institution, Cato Institute, Pew Hispanic Center, and Council on Foreign Relations.

- Consider a few more factors in the immigration issue: the creation of NAFTA—the 1992 North American Free Trade Agreement—lifted tariffs and promoted more trade between the United States, Canada, and Mexico, but Mexico lost hundreds of thousands of jobs (some put the figure in the millions). And that's just one factor never mentioned in the immigration debate.

- Write to Fox News, and ask them to hire Lou Dobbs.

CHAPTER 7

Battles of the Titan
The U.S. Chamber of Commerce and Friends

F orget the president. Forget Congress. More than ever, Big Business is dictating the American agenda, both here and abroad. At home, those massive corporate contributions to politicians' war chests and the swarms of lobbyists unleashed on the Capitol have helped decide everything from how much money the Treasury takes in to our rights in the courts; the inroads Big Biz makes overseas, whether outsourcing services in India or offshoring manufacturing in China, sends ripples across the U.S. economy. And the corporate world's most fearsome vehicle—essentially an all-purpose tank—is the U.S. Chamber of Commerce.

Indicative of the cheerily pro-business mood in the government, a largely unknown federal office, the White House Office of Information and Regulatory Affairs now has the job of ensuring that laws and regulations don't financially harm corporations. Among the regulations deleted because this office deemed their cost to business too steep: requirements to install in cars sixty-six-dollar sensors that would alert drivers when tire pressure was low, thereby preventing blowouts such as those that killed over forty people in 2000 from defective Firestone tires.[1] The office is also relaxing worker safety standards, including how many hours a truck driver could stay behind the wheel without a break, enabling companies to keep costs down by employing fewer drivers.

Fashioned in the neoclassical style of our most revered government symbols, the U.S. Chamber of Commerce's DC headquarters is a stately, heavily columned building that one might imagine parked on the back of a hundred-dollar bill. Spreading out on H Street, the three-story structure sits almost directly in front of the White House, its presence hidden by the trees of Lafayette Park. With the weight the Chamber of Commerce is throwing around, however, one might wonder if the White House—as well as the Capitol, rising a mile away—are transforming into little more than stages for conducting Chamber business. Despite its nonprofit status, the U.S. Chamber of Commerce is all about enhancing profits: the world's "largest business federation representing more than three million businesses and organizations of every size"[2] is now the biggest lobbying force on the planet—it doled out over $244 million to lobbying firms between 1998 and 2005,[3] and that's just the money that can be followed. The Chamber has created a maze of nonprofit institutes, subgroups, councils, and special accounts that make tracking money a tricky affair. In some ways, the Chamber itself is a cover: the secretive association keeps its lips sealed about who its members are—thus allowing businesses to campaign for controversial issues without damaging their reputations. And if it doesn't get what it wants, the Chamber doesn't shirk from character assassination or otherwise machine-gunning any impediments in Big Business' way—whether through litigation (it often sues government regulatory agencies), issuing questionable reports (including "Reality Check: Straight Talk About the Kyoto Protocol"), or masterminding smear campaigns run by fake groups made possible by Chamber funding.

Gathered together under the USCC banner you'll find most of the big boys, from Lockheed Martin to Xerox, Wal-Mart to GE, holding hands with trade associations like the Nuclear Energy Institute and American Petroleum Institute. Their combined force is one reason the power wielded by this nonprofit group is jaw-dropping, and their success in changing the government into a business is alarming.

> Grover Norquist, who worked for the USCC in the 1980s, gave the
> keynote speech at a May 2005 Chamber forum (where members cel-
> ebrated victories in loosening environmental regulations). He con-
> gratulated the Chamber (and underscored its immense power) for its
> "success in reforming government."[4]

These days, the Chamber, whose motto is "Fighting for your business,"
wins most of its battles—be they for slashed corporate taxes, easier
conquests of foreign markets, or shredded rights for Americans if those
rights hinder making a buck. Dictating foreign policy, loosening environmental laws, and profoundly affecting our prices—be they for drugs or
oil (the mighty Chamber opposes government-imposed ceilings on
either)—the organization that spends tens of millions on attacking its
enemies (and tosses as much or more into lobbying[5]) is certainly helping lawmakers pick their priorities and decide when to yea and nay.

> Heel, boy. In July 2005, a bill concerning slapping trade sanctions on
> countries that peddle arms to China was just about to pass in a
> House floor vote, when a last-minute notice was delivered to con-
> gressmen: the Chamber of Commerce opposed the bill. At the news,
> one hundred representatives immediately switched their vote.[6]
> That's how closely our lawmakers, to whom the Chamber threw over
> $174,000 during the 2004 election,[7] heed the USCC whistle.

CHINESE AWAKENING

In the 1990s, when China made what might be called its "second
great leap"—from a closed state-run communist economy to one that
allowed capitalist foreigners in to exploit it—American Big Business
cheered. For years the Chamber, along with the likes of GE, Boeing,
and Bechtel, had been trying to pry open that distant cash cow, which
held over a billion potential consumers and a vast pool of labor whose
weekly paychecks wouldn't buy a chopstick around here.

Checks from corporations such as GE and Boeing began winging
toward K Street as the corporate high rollers leaned on Congress and

the Clinton White House to allow the giant from the east into the global trading club; China soon lumbered into the World Trade Organization and was granted tariff-free trading status, while the corporations and manufacturers plunged into the Far Eastern market, able to produce goods at such low prices that they were quickly gobbled up by savings-obsessed Wal-Mart; in fact, Wal-Mart was a driving force in manufacturers hightailing it to the East. Another plus for importing Chinese goods into the United States: China's currency, the yuan, was and remains undervalued—allowing purchasers to get more bang for their buck. Dominated by huge Fortune 500 companies, the Chamber of Commerce lauded the arrival of American businesses in China, although it sometimes makes a half-assed show of wagging its finger at the undervalued yuan that makes China so enticing. American workers, however, weren't so thrilled when their factories took their jobs overseas where goods could be produced at a fraction of the cost. Small- and medium-sized factories were slammed as cheap Chinese goods flooded the market. The National Association of Manufacturers—the Chamber's business association competitor, which represents more of these smaller companies—has ratcheted up its presence in DC, pitching more into lobbying and election campaigns, and pressuring the government to clamp down on China to revalue the yuan; some are even calling for tariffs, which the Chamber vehemently opposes. But while a showdown over China seems imminent, there's a new star on the Chamber's horizon: India, which U.S. Big Business is ushering into the world trading club, and where American companies already outsource billions of business a year. The further opening of India—until 1991 a closed economy like China's—and the upcoming deal for U.S. companies to sell India nuclear plants and warplanes, sound to U.S. retailers and the Chamber like a very loud, melodious ka-ching. Some American workers, however, won't be hearing that music at all, only the thud of the other shoe falling.

While keeping business a well-oiled machine and the American economy chugging along, the Chamber's most dramatic moves have often simultaneously whittled away rights, from the consumers' in the courtroom to the stockholders' in the boardroom to the employees' in the workplace, where the Chamber endorses "more reasonable" standards.

"The U.S. Chamber of Commerce is pulling out all the stops to ensure that big business won't be held accountable for the faulty, often dangerous, sometimes deadly merchandise it puts on the market. The Chamber is working in all 50 states and at the federal level to dismantle the civil justice system."
    —Bill Straub, Association of Trial Lawyers of America's deputy
       director of communications, writing in the association's magazine,
       Trial.[8] The Chamber and the association are at each other's throats.

Now the Chamber is touching up our courts and even our political system. It has already helped Congress decide in exactly which courts class action suits (involving a number of parties) can be heard. The Chamber is also influencing who will hear the cases: it's running snarling attack ads (without identifying that the Chamber is behind them) that slam pro-consumer groups—while lavishly funding "issue ad" campaigns that favor pro-business judges and attorney generals.

> *Big Business–wise, John Kerry's choice of 2004 presidential running mate John Edwards was a dicey call. Edwards was formerly a trial lawyer, and on principle alone, the Chamber dumped millions into blasting Edwards—via the November Fund, a well-monied front group that hid its connection to the Chamber.[9]*

More alarming, the Chamber is taking a whack at our two-party system. Nonpartisan through its history, the Chamber is now a cheerleader for Republicans, throwing millions into campaigns and millions more into mudslinging opponents.[10] Like the Bush administration itself, the Chamber is also trying to drain the bank accounts of the two groups who most "hinder" business. Coincidentally, they just happen to be the two biggest donors to the Democratic Party: namely, organized labor and trial lawyers.

> *In the 2004 elections, labor gave $90 million to Democrats and $7 million to Republicans. Lawyers and law firms contributed $137 million to Democrats and $46 million to Republicans. Exactly how much the USCC forked over to candidates via its assorted institutes, non-*

profit organizations, and front groups is hard to track—but the Chamber threw some $200 million into everything from "issue ads" and lobbying to election contributions during the 2004 campaign. And that doesn't reflect the many millions handed over by its individual member companies such as drugmakers and manufacturing giants.

Forces at Work

- **U.S. Chamber of Commerce (USCC):** The Rolex-watched, Hermès-tied, Ferragamo-heeled heads of virtually all U.S.-based Fortune 500 companies lock arms with CEOs of 3 million businesses and hundreds of trade associations to give the USCC unsurpassable clout—as well as a very hefty yearly budget. The Chamber usually tops the lobbying charts, throwing over $53 million at outside firms in 2004[11] alone, much of it directed at minimizing liability and damages to businesses from lawsuits. Officially a trade association—as well as a lobbying, funding, advocacy, and advertising machine—the multi-tentacled Chamber has numerous arms, including the Litigation Center, which tries to get business-hostile rulings overturned, and powerful business forums, such as the United States–India Business Council. The Chamber is also behind aggressive front groups running rabid ads against judges who have ruled favorably for consumers in class action suits, and trying to take down legislators who have ever sided with labor.

- **Association of Trial Lawyers of America:** The association of fifty-six thousand lawyers professionally squeezes businesses where it hurts while representing the wronged and the injured in the courtroom. Big moneymakers for both plaintiffs and their lawyers: tort cases involving tobacco, asbestos, malpractice, and lately, mold. Trial lawyers Ron Motley (of Charleston law firm Ness Motley) and Richard Scruggs of Mississippi (whose firm reportedly made $1.4 billion from tobacco settlements[12]) are two kingpins regularly targeted by business interests. Under fire and trying to wriggle free of accusations leveled by the Chamber and a growing disfavor from the public, the Association of Trial Lawyers took a bizarre PR tact: it suddenly changed its name to the American Association for Justice—which just gave more fodder for attack.

- **Organized labor:** The brawn of industry and mighty Democrat boosters, the unions, representing 13 million U.S. workers, still have some muscle—in body count and influencing power—but they're getting flabby. Some unions are dropping out of labor's backbone, the AFL-CIO, and as membership shrinks (one in three workers were unionized in 1950; now the figure is closer to one in eight) so does clout. Some want leaders to stop dumping so much money into lobbying (over $40 million a year—most of it for Democrats) and spend more money on recruitment.

- **Thomas Donohue:** When Donohue, the former president of the American Trucking Associations, walked into the Chamber of Commerce as its new CEO in 1997, he amped up its visibility, which had been getting blurry under Clinton, and revved up its lobbying budget (as well as hiring over four dozen in-house persuaders, many of them former congressional chiefs of staff).[13] The group began streamrolling anything that it viewed as impeding business, whether it was consumers "whining" about flipping cars and exploding tires, the indebted crushed under credit card bills, or patients upset by medical malpractice. Through his reign, the Chamber has turned political and rather militant.

- **Eliot Spitzer, Governor of New York State:** When he was New York attorney general, some wondered if he was fighting for the common man or overstepping his job boundaries. He has substantially more room between those job boundaries now. The man, who took the New York's governor chair in 2006, threatens Big Business, bringing the giants to heel by using state law to bring down all aspects of Wall Street corruption—taking on investment banks, brokers, mutual funds, and insurance companies with jaw-dropping results. Lord knows what the U.S. Chamber of Commerce is thinking now that he's moved into the Governor's Mansion, and we're all waiting to see how he'll tidy up the state.

- **Sen. Charles E. Grassley** (R-Iowa): With Grassley, one of Big Biz's faves, chairing the Senate Finance Committee, the Chamber has reaped rich harvests: its man on the hill (to whom it contributed almost $2 million since 1989)[14] introduced a successful $137 billion corporate tax cut bill in 2004 and a legal reform bill that passed the next year, marking two of the Chamber's most delicious victories ever.

[## Close-up]

When a cup of coffee spilled onto Stella Liebeck's lap in February 1992, nobody knew that the fifty-nine-cent contents of that Styrofoam cup would become an international emblem. Liebeck, a seventy-nine-year-old Albuquerque resident, who at that moment was sitting in the backseat of her son's car, had no idea that day that she was going to become a symbol in a nasty showdown—one where Big Business and trial lawyers clobbered each other in a battle that threatened to crush the American political system. All Stella was thinking about at that moment was the searing pain as the scalding coffee, at 180 degrees, scorched her thighs and crotch. At the hospital, doctors said she had third-degree burns, and Stella was in the hospital for eight days for skin grafting on 6 percent of her body.

Stella hit up McDonald's, where she had purchased that cup of coffee at the drive-through window, to pay $20,000 for the hospital bill; McDonald's offered her $800. Stella sued. And when a jury—shown photos of the red blisters and oozing wounds as well as hearing testimony that McDonald's knew of hundreds of burn cases from its coffee but wouldn't deviate from the industry-recommended temperature—awarded her $2.7 million in punitive damages,[15] the American public began to swing toward a view long held by some 3 million businesses nationwide: that in its pursuit of protecting consumers, courts were rewarding greed. And the U.S. Chamber of Commerce has done everything it can to help that idea along, including embracing the Stella Awards—the annual outrage-a-thon over ludicrous complaints and inconceivable victories.

> *From billboards and full-page ads, the Chamber of Commerce is publicly ridiculing trial lawyers. Among the most unsightly: billboards that read "Please don't feed the trial lawyers"—and show a porcine-faced man with cash spewing out of his mouth. Trial lawyers, on the defensive, are in turn running ads attacking corporate greed.*

Groups critical of trial lawyers say awards in court cases for tort-related damages topped $200 billion in 2001; trial lawyers say the figure is grossly inflated.[16]

TRYING TRIAL LAWYERS

In an odd alliance, tobacco companies, doctors, fast-food sellers, petrol giants, and most businesses that sell to the public stand united in their hatred of trial lawyers, particularly those courtroom dramatists who slap businesses with dreaded class action suits—when dozens, maybe hundreds or thousands, collectively sue for damages under tort law (which essentially means "somebody got hurt, and somebody else is going to pay"). Favorable rulings result in megabuck settlements—averaging over a million per plaintiff, and a quarter or more of the collective booty goes into lawyers' pockets. The hazards of asbestos rose up as the first highly profitable class action issue in the 1970s, ultimately closing down some seventy companies, says the Chamber; in the 1990s, awards for suits against tobacco companies—even individual suits—soared above the billion-dollar mark. New potential big ka-chingers: cases resulting from Merck's heart attack–inducing drug Vioxx and drinking water contaminated from gasoline additive MTBE (which is why oil companies have pres-sured lawmakers—unsuccessfully—to shield them from liability). Trial lawyers insist tort laws are needed to keep business in line; business interests insist it's time for reform—and are aiming to put caps on damages—$250,000 for most malpractice suits, for instance. They're also trying to install more business-friendly judges—and to make suing a stigma, while stamping the idea in the public's head that the legal system is in need of emergency revamping.[17]

Watchdog group Public Citizen, for one, doesn't buy it. "We think this crisis is manufactured," says head researcher Taylor Lincoln. As for physician claims that malpractice suits are killing them with skyrocketing malpractice insurance rates, and even regarding those widely publicized laughable lawsuits, Lincoln says, "We think a lot of this is myth."[18]

Pundits say "tort reform" is less about law and more about shaving the awards and thus the wads of money that lawyers hand to Democrats. The clever ploy—to kill the opposition, while appearing to be fighting greed—blossomed in 1990s Texas, and was masterminded by current White House top dog Karl Rove. By pushing through tort reform, and tightening the purse strings to the "other" party, he helped transform Texas from a heavily Democratic to a heavily Republican state. Rove's pal Grover Norquist (along with Rep. Tom DeLay, Sen. Rick Santorum, and others) took a different tact: they tried to force both lobbying firms and the businesses that use them to hire only Republican lawyers, for the same result. Both plays aim to shrink the money that ends up in the hands of Democrats or in their election accounts.

Never mind that he's well past retirement age. Thomas Donohue is a force to be reckoned with, coupling the ruthless drive of an out-to-make-his-name whippersnapper with the eloquence of a scholar, the cunning of a general, and the connections of a veteran power monger. The U.S. Chamber of Commerce CEO and president brandishes a thick Rolodex that he can drop open like an accordion wallet of platinum credit cards—and the high-placed friends listed there don't flinch at dropping a million or two into the collection plates he often passes around for everything from ad campaigns to new legal adventures. Taking the reins a decade ago, Donohue quickly boosted the Chamber's profile, shoving aside other business groups such as the Business Round-table and the National Association of Manufacturers to make the Chamber the king of business hill—starting by bolstering its lobbying force and by transforming the association (traditionally nonpartisan) into an openly Republican-supporting machine that churns out millions of dollars for political campaigns.[19]

> *"The Chamber hasn't previously played such an important role in elections and issues. They have political chips to trade in. They're like partners with the Republican party in making laws."*
> —Taylor Lincoln of consumer group Public Citizen[20]

With a long face capped by snowy white hair, Donohue resembles Gregory Peck, the actor most famous for his role as a trial lawyer in *To Kill a Mockingbird*—a clear case of genetic miscasting, as Donohue detests the legal breed, at least if they're not working for him. No one better ex-emplifies all he loathes about lawyers than Eliot Spitzer, New York's knock-'em-sock-'em ex–attorney general, who went after drugmakers and insurers and even took on investment firm Merrill Lynch. Donohue views him as a symbol of all that's gone awry in the legal department.

> *"[Spitzer appoints himself in the roles of] the investigator, the prosecutor, the judge, the jury and the executioner. . . . It's the most egregious and unacceptable form of intimidation that we have seen in this country in modern times."*
> —Thomas Donohue on Eliot Spitzer[21]

> *"I think he's a shill for guilty people, and Tom Donohue has never once found a crime that he couldn't justify, as long as it was committed by one of his dues-paying members."*
> —Eliot Spitzer on Thomas Donohue[22]

For the past decade—ever since Tom Donohue started barking out orders—the Chamber has been obsessed with lassoing trial lawyers and hog-tying their ability to try cases in state courts (believing they were more likely to award high damages than federal courts). The Chamber attacked on numerous fronts: it launched campaigns about

Swinging at trial lawyers and labor, Tom Donohue—president of the U.S. Chamber of Commerce—has led the mighty business group into the Republican bed.

"frivolous" lawsuits, like the guy who sued McDonald's because he was fat—implying that most lawsuits are just as trivial. The Chamber even snuck in as silent publisher of at least two newspapers—the *Madison County Record* in Illinois and the *West Virginia Record*—that trumpet what the Chamber believes are absurd litigation cases.[23]

More pointedly, Donohue created a new, powerful, and nasty Chamber organ—the Institute for Legal Reform—and pumped it up with a fat budget for reports and advertising campaigns to sway public opinion and rein in trial lawyers and the "runaway" courts. And he sent out hundreds of lobbyists to spread the word on the urgency of legal reform: the institute spent $9.5 million in the first six months of 2005 paying lobbyists to push the Chamber's views on the three legal issues before Congress in 2005, and the Chamber backed it up with $8.6 million of additional lobbying during that period.[24]

In 2003, Senate Minority Leader Tom Daschle blocked Chamber-endorsed legislation to limit class action suits, thereby signing his political death warrant. "We put dozens of people and a million dollars into the [2004] effort to defeat Senate Minority Leader Tom Daschle . . . who enjoyed strong union support [and] was a major obstruction to business-backed priorities in the U.S. Senate," the Chamber reports on its site.[25]

But the Chamber hasn't stopped there. It's also taking jabs at the other major moneybag for the Democrats—organized labor, which over the twentieth century forced passage of numerous worker safety laws, and through strikes and collective bargaining had made America's blue-collar workers among the world's best paid, a fact that Big Business did not relish. How to take on unions—about 12 percent of U.S. workers are members—was a more delicate matter: touchingly, the Chamber and the big labor unions had called a truce after September 11—vowing to work together as patriotic Americans. Despite the handshakes and smiles, hostility remained behind the scenes. In between stomping out every attempt to boost the minimum wage, the Chamber champions causes such as crippling workers' legal rights and lowering on-the-job safety regulations. Meanwhile, organized labor is trying to entice Wal-Mart workers to unionize—a thought that terrifies Wal-Mart, the country's biggest private employer. In 2006, when unions were lobbying heavily to push the Employee Free Choice Act through Congress—a bill that would make union organizing easier—Big Business wasn't pleased. Nor were restaurant owners, who typically pay waiters minimum wage with the opportunity to make more in tips.

As the bill began gaining momentum, DC's professional mudslinger Rick Berman stepped up. As is his forte, Berman created an "Astroturf" group—or fake grassroots front group that hides who created and funds it—namely, the Center for Union Facts, now a source of anti-labor propaganda, which funds nasty ad campaigns and runs a website. Melanie Sloan of the Citizens for Responsibility and Ethics in Washington (CREW) says that a big chunk of Berman's $8 million budget for his latest hack job came from the Chamber, formerly Berman's employer.[26] Whoever was funding it, Berman, a bald, super-sized magician with facts—hey, where did they go?—was doing what he does best: distort reality, blur the issue, and organize biting information blitzes and searing ad campaigns that seek to confuse voters and consumers. And in this case, the goal was to slam organized labor, to dissuade legislators from supporting the employees' rights bill, and to persuade the public that labor was a monster.

RICK BERMAN: KING OF DISINFORMATION

Obesity is not a major threat to health—and junk food, huge portions, and sugar-riddled drinks don't have anything to do with being fat or ailments such as diabetes. Americans have been "force-fed a steady diet of obesity myths" by "lawyers licking their chops in search of their next super-sized payday." If indeed there is mercury in fish, it ain't gonna hurt you. Mothers Against Drunk Driving—well, they are another of those wacko fringe groups who are "using junk science, intimidation tactics and even threats of violence to push their radical agenda." Welcome to the twisted Center for Consumer Freedom, just one of the many faux consumer groups set up by Rick Berman, the PR whiz who does to facts what a clown does to balloons when he shapes them into funny animals. Professional doubt-caster Berman must be getting a great laugh out of making oodles from nonprofit, tax-exempt fronts that attack anyone who has a finding that might hurt the food and beverage industry, cigarette makers, or other Big Business—all of whom have been his clients. In his latest creation, the Center for Union Facts, he's taking out full-page ads attacking state employees as snarling time-wasters (led by teachers and police, about a third of government employees are in unions, more than any other sector); and to emphasize that organized labor was obsolete, the front group erected a fifteen-foot dinosaur in front of the AFL-CIO headquarters in DC.[27]

Big Business and the restaurant industry haven't been the only forces working to weaken labor. So is government. Upon entering office in 2001, President George W. Bush started cracking the anti-labor whip almost immediately, reversing labor-friendly moves initiated by the Clinton administration and signing executive orders lashing out at unions, including issuing a directive that all government contractors inform workers that they aren't obligated to join a union—while negating the need to tell them they have the right to do just that.[28] Demanding new accounting procedures of unions that cost them millions, Bush approved a budget that slashed money for enforcing workplace safety and investigating complaints of corporate wrongdoing—while boosting the money for investigating union activities. And his administration has made a point of hiring non-union workers—farming out jobs ordinarily done by unionized state employees, and demanding that collective bargaining rights be denied to the airport workers employed through the Department of Homeland Security.[29] And the crowning glory was when he appointed anti-labor Elaine Chao as Secretary of Labor, where she appears to plot how to further take them down.

The Republican-dominated Congress had mirrored such efforts to steamroll unions and workers' rights, passing legislation that shredded a requirement for ergonomically correct computers, stripped rights to litigate against employers, and kept the federal minimum wage at $5.15 (although under legislation enacted by the Clinton administration, individual states can set their minimum wage above the federal level).

As if the picture weren't grim enough, lately organized labor is fraying from the inside as well: seven unions split off from labor's backbone, the AFL-CIO, in 2005, and there's bickering about whether dues should go to boosting memberships or trying to get results out of Democrats. There's even a debate on whether labor is fully behind the Democratic Party anymore. In 2004, after being trounced by the clearly anti-union Bush administration and the 108th Congress, the AFL-CIO announced it was going to sock it to Republicans in that year's elections. But despite throwing some $90 million into contributions and voter registration drives, workers failed to make much of a dent. One problem: at least a third of the workers voted Republican—specifically for Bush.

And while labor was being attacked, the White House and Congress were greenlighting nearly every Chamber demand—from establishing free trade areas in Central America to restricting citizens' rights in court, a cause that the Chamber has championed for a decade. The Chamber was rewarded for its diligence: in February 2005, President Bush happily signed the Legal Reform Act into law—pushing class action cases where awards could total over $5 million to the more conservative federal courts, which are less likely to give plaintiffs large awards. But the Chamber is not content: it wants to further minimize (some say erase) business liability, cap damage amounts, and strangle the ability to try many cases in *any* courts.

MODESTY: AN OUTDATED VIRTUE?

Most major legislation coming out of Congress over the past few years has been Chamber-approved (and often Chamber-initiated)— including the $286 billion Transportation Act, the 2005 Energy Policy Act, the drastic rewriting of bankruptcy laws, and the limitation of state-level class action suits. A few more "victories":

- After years of relentless lobbying, "in 2005, the Chamber secured Senate approval for oil and gas exploration and production in the Arctic National Wildlife Refuge"[30] and "achieved House passage of legislation that [allows] oil and natural gas exploration in the Outer Continental Shelf "[31] in the Gulf of Mexico
- Led "industry coalition to successfully oppose passage of legislation that would have [set caps on] emissions of greenhouse gases" from power plants and factories[32]
- "Achieved Senate passage of comprehensive immigration reform legislation" (increasing numbers of visas for high-tech and seasonal workers)[33]
- "Won House approval of four separate bills designed to help small businesses contest alleged [worker safety] violations"[34]
- "Successfully defended against attempts to increase the federal minimum wage"[35]
- "Secured enactment of legislation" that forces the bankrupt to pay up under Chapter 13, "rather than file under Chapter 7, where debts are erased"[36]
- "Helped U.S. negotiators secure . . . free trade agreements with Colombia and Peru"[37]—and helped push through passage of Central America Free Trade Agreement
- "Secured enactment of HR 4297" (an act to prevent tax hikes) and "helped to block $13 billion in proposed tax increases"[38]
- "Promoted the expansion of nuclear energy" and helped "educate Americans about the benefits of nuclear energy"[39]

In no area has the U.S. Chamber of Commerce been more influential than in embracing India.

At the behest of Big Business—including the Chamber, Lockheed Martin, Boeing, Bechtel, and GE, as well as the thousands of lobbyists who represent the Big Boys—the U.S. government is welcoming Delhi into the backslapping nuclear club. In July 2006, the House passed the United States and Indian Nuclear Cooperation and Promotion Act; in November it got a green light from the Senate.

A crucial component of the selling of India to American businesses— and vice versa—has been the United States–India Business Council (USIBC), an offshoot of the U.S. Chamber of Commerce. As president of the USIBC, Ron Somers has been busy, very busy. It's his job to pave the way between American businesses and the Indian frontier. The council formed in 1975, but Somers, who arrived a decade later, made it soar. Representing the top-shelf players of both countries—here is the place where the CEOS from Citigroup and Dow strategize with India's private sector stars such as billionaires Ratan Tata and Mukesh Ambani—his group has pushed agendas that only a few years ago looked laughably impossible. The USIBC helped coax the Indian government into lifting restrictions to foreign investments in retail—a rather astounding accomplishment that brought retailers from Nike to Swarovski swooping in.

Along with an army of hundreds upon hundreds of lobbyists representing everyone from Boeing to Westinghouse, Somers persuaded the White House to drop the U.S. ban on selling nuclear equipment to India—a ban imposed in 1974 after India tested its first nuclear weapon, when the United States realized that the bomb had been made with the help of nuclear equipment sold by GE. President Bush is all for it and after his March 2006 visit to Delhi, he, too, joined the lobbying song and dance to get Congress to give India a nuclear nod.

It wasn't such a hard sell, particularly in the post-2001 era: for several years now, the United States has been militarily palsy-walsy with its "War on Terror" recruit, running huge joint military exercises and grooming India as its potential partner to counter any future threats from China, Pakistan, or anyone else in that neck of the woods. India, Somers pointed out in weekly meetings with dozens of companies, is a peaceful country, democratic, and mature (never mind the 1998 two-week nuclear test-a-thon alongside its enemy Pakistan), and the subcontinent is filled with 1.1 billion potential consumers (many itching to buy American designer goods) and a rising middle class, which some say is 300 million strong.

There was a hellacious amount of money to be made, any way you looked at it. But the figures were even more compelling when Ron Somers was telling the story, in between warning that the smell of money shouldn't be the sole "driver" in approving the deal to again sell India nuclear plants. Who could say no when enthusiastic Somers let such Sweet numbers roll off his tongue?

Those 126 fighter planes that India was itching to buy, well, those alone would ring up at more than $12 billion, Somers told lawmakers; the nuclear reactor sales could easily shoot another $100 billion (more than 10 percent of India's 2005 GDP) to U.S. businesses, he added. If you totaled up all potential energy sales from U.S. companies, he told *CQ Weekly*, it would be $200 billion. In fact, he added, U.S. companies stood to gain over a trillion dollars by 2025 if the nuclear deal went through. And with a trillion dollars waving in the breeze of the near future, legislator after legislator signed on.

> *"[T]he U.S. business community is betting on India to become one of our closest economic and geopolitical partners. . . . For nearly 60 years, India has nurtured an extraordinary pluralistic and secular democracy that embraces a vibrant and free press, free and fair elections, and a transparent legal system based on English common law. . . . There is another area that calls for cooperation between India and the United States, and that's the development of safe, clean, and reliable energy resources."*
> —Thomas Donohue, at the 2006 U.S.-India Partnership Summit,[40] *illustrating that he too knows the NEI's nuclear branding method*

And nobody knew the joys, headaches, and potential profits to be had in India better than General Electric.

GENERAL ELECTRIC: U.S. FOREIGN POLICY DIRECTOR?

From toasters to hydropower turbines, solar cells to desalination plants, GE is the global titan of manufacturing, and it's always been revolutionary. The company that resulted when Edison's electric company merged with a rival in 1892, GE has introduced us to the cutting-edge technology of the day—first lighting our homes with newfangled voltage, then using that novelty to power refrigerators and air conditioners, dishwashers and self-cleaning ovens, computers and high-tech climate-controlled wine vaults. The first to set up a research and development lab in 1900, GE also introduced business novelties, from twenty-four-hour customer service to sending that customer service overseas, being the leader in outsourcing. Now nearly half of the $150 billion it pulls in each year comes from financial services—leading some to refer to GE as a lender that makes things,[41] although the things it makes now are even more diversified, ranging from neuron image devices to wind machines.

And along the way, GE has taken a number of controversial turns, many of them related to matters atomic: its botched handling of the Hanford Nuclear Reservation in Washington made that land the most toxic place in our country; its longtime refusal to clean up decades' worth of PCBs it had dumped into the Hudson River (legal at the time) was defiantly accompanied by deceptive ads claiming the river had pretty much self-cleaned; its cruel (government-condoned) radiation experiments on the reproductive organs of prisoners in the 1950s and its deliberate release of radioactive materials to study to the public health effects, as well as GE's active development of nuclear weapons, all contradict the corporate theme of "bringing good things to life." As the company has grown ever more diversified, it's grown ever more powerful: General Electric's whiz lawyers and top-notch lobbyists helped to whittle the corporate tax rate to a pittance, one reason the U.S. Treasury is in the red. And the corporation continues to scout out new locations that best suit its business needs regardless of the consequences to those back home—consequences that were quite dire under "Neutron Jack" Welch, who slashed the company's workforce drastically boosting profits thirtyfold.

But where GE becomes most potentially dangerous is when it steps in to influence or determine foreign policy. The company helped crack open China, but its most dramatic effects have played out in India, for good and for bad. The company that built the subcontinent's first hydroelectric dam in 1902 was quite active in hooking India into the Atoms for Peace program—setting up the country with plants, nuclear fuel, and, through GE Canada, reactors that yielded high-grade plutonium. The effects of GE's nuclear salesmanship played out in India's Pokharan Desert in May 1974, when, much to the shock of the rest of the world, India set off a nuclear device in a test called Smiling Buddha, which prompted everyone else to glare back. The Atoms for Peace program died the next day, GE was forced to pull out of the Indian nuclear business, and the world became preoccupied with nuclear weapons proliferation; the United States slapped on harsh sanctions, cut economic aid, and banned nuclear technology sales to India. GE helped form the Chamber of Commerce's United States–India Business Council shortly thereafter, but two decades would pass before "Neutron Jack" brought GE back to India, setting up tens of thousands of Indian employees in its new call centers and R&D labs. But the real attraction to India for GE has always been its electrical market—which still needs plenty of help since half the country is still unlit and major cities experience blackouts sometimes a dozen times a day. Now headed by Jeffrey Immelt (who not only deigned to finally help clean up the Hudson but unveiled "Ecomagination," a host of "green energy" technologies to produce electricity), GE is now moving in to finish up what it started in the 1970s. The question becomes whether GE will sign up India for a wide smattering of its lower-priced alternative energy devices or if it will more persuasively push the big-money nuclear plants. Thus far, it sure looks like the latter.

Even though GE helped make India's nuclear weapons possible, the U.S. government shouldn't have been shocked by India's nuclear tests. Recently declassified documents show that the CIA and State Department knew that India was developing nuclear weapons way back in 1964.[42] That knowledge didn't stop the government from approving even more plants. In fact, one might wonder if DC was giving India's weapons program a silent nod.

CHAPTER 8

What You Can Do

The story of the appearance of humans on the planet was never Professor Lawrence Krauss' passion; the acclaimed physicist is more intrigued with the origins of the universe and what forces control it—and he writes books and hundreds of articles unwinding the mysteries of our physical world, trying to put them in terms that mere mortals can understand. But in 1996, his mouth dropped open when he read one line in the newspaper—a line that would shoot his life onto a different course and eat up his spare time, with some 20 percent of his waking hours from that point being suddenly consumed by a project he'd never before realized was needed.

The one line that rearranged Krauss' life had been uttered by one of the year's presidential candidates, Pat Buchanan, who opined, in Krauss' words, that "he wasn't descended from an ape, and children shouldn't be taught that they are either."[1] Instead, Buchanan believed schools should teach children about intelligent design (ID)—a fancily packaged take on creationism that holds that the universe is so complex that a

Esteemed physicist Lawrence Krauss says business, government, and conservative religious groups are rewriting science—and he's fighting back.

superior being must have created it. Upon reading Buchanan's plea to change our science programs, Krauss, a physics professor at Case Western Reserve University in Cleveland, thought, "This is truly amazing"—not simply because Buchanan said it, but because the media was barely questioning this stance while harpooning him on most every other.[2] Krauss' amazement would soon grow.

> *Science is not the strong suit of twenty-first-century America. Students who might have once studied sciences now are lured by the big bucks of business. The result is that we have to import many of our top-end scientists and scientific scholars, often from Asia. More alarming: when asked in the national science surveys whether it is true or false that the earth revolves around the sun and takes a year to do it, a majority of Americans consistently answer "false."*

Throughout the 1990s, groups such as the Christian Coalition had been strategizing, as had evangelical think tanks such as Seattle's well-moneyed Discovery Institute and the Institute for Creation Research in California, and they'd developed a stealth plan of attack: the Christian Coalition's Ralph Reed helped the ground-level evangelicals infiltrate the school boards that decide the district's and state's curricula. And the institutes devised strategies to get intelligent design into the school—including using that successful tactic of confusing the issue.

> *Whatever one thinks about the push from the Religious Right to incorporate intelligent design in science classes, they have illustrated the power of organized grassroots movements.*

And little by little, election by election, Reed's flock stacked the boards in cities and towns, from Pennsylvania to Kansas, Florida to Washington. They formed groups with misleading names like Citizens for Science, whose goal in fact was to insert theology into biology. And across the United States, school boards were suddenly calling for stickers to be added to textbooks to notify that evolution is a controversial idea, and mandating that teachers instruct on intelligent design. In Tennessee, it became illegal to even assert that evolution is true. Every time a school board was reviewing its science curricula—which school boards were suddenly doing more often—the Discovery Institute would send in expert witnesses and lobbyists to work with the ground-level Christian soldiers. In 2002, the Ohio School Board announced it, too, would be reviewing how science was taught in the state, and Krauss rallied fellow scientists to appear at the meeting. But what the ID supporters did then, says Krauss, "was really ingenious."[3] The Discovery Institute expert who spoke that night noted that they were willing to compromise and weren't insisting that students be taught ID instead of evolution. What he wanted, instead, was for schools to "teach the controversy." The ID promoters wanted students to learn about how scientists come to their conclusions, and, taking it one step further, they wanted students to learn about the "evolution debate." On the surface that sounds fair enough. Except for one thing—there was no scientific debate about evolution. It wasn't controversial to scientists who've studied it for a century and a half, and who have used the model for everything from predicting how pathogens mutate to creating drugs to fight them. "Evolution," says Krauss, "is no more controversial than Newton's law of gravity."[4]

But by presenting their idea in that innocuous package, "their public relations campaign" worked. The school board decided that a committee should devise a course in which students unwrap science and study the debate. "They tried to make it appear that evolution was controversial," says Krauss, "that scientists were trying to keep it in schools even though it was flawed."[5] And that just wasn't the case.

The problem, says Krauss, is that many hard-core evangelicals denounce science because it doesn't directly acknowledge God, and therefore the hard-right Christians consider it evil.[6]

And what was happening to evolution was just one indication of how science was being eroded, altered, and deleted from the American landscape. Another that left Krauss open-mouthed was the "debate" about global warming, a phenomenon that virtually the entire scientific body worldwide agreed was happening—and they agreed it was caused by humans. Krauss was one of sixty scientists—a bipartisan panel of scholars, including twenty Nobel laureates—who'd sent a letter to President George W. Bush notifying him that global warming is real and human-caused, and we need to take immediate action, only to have the Bush administration shrug it off as yet another matter about which the jury is still out, another matter about which there is controversy and debate. "What is happening in the United States is extreme and extremely worrisome," Krauss says. "There's been a systematic, comprehensive effort to censor scientists, to pad scientific review panels, and to remove people who are competent from their positions. We've never seen anything like this before in any administration, Republican or Democrat."[7] Krauss fought back: he wrote hundreds of pieces for the op-ed pages. He attended meetings and testified that no, evolution isn't controversial, it is, as far as we could tell, the truth. He organized groups of scientists and he encouraged qualified people to take on the increasingly important task of sitting on school boards. The National Center for Science Education also publicized the issue and finally people realized what was happening to their schools.

"Because Darwin's Theory is a theory, it continues to be tested as new evidence is discovered. The Theory is not a fact. Gaps in the Theory exist for which there is no evidence. A theory is defined as a well-tested explanation that unifies a broad range of observations.

Intelligent Design is an explanation of the origin of life that differs from Darwin's view. The reference book Of Pandas and People is available for students who might be interested in gaining an understanding of what Intelligent Design actually involves.

With respect to any theory, students are encouraged to keep an open mind. The school leaves the discussion of the Origins of Life to individual students and their families. As a Standards-driven district, class instruction focuses upon preparing students to achieve proficiency on Standards-based assessments."
—Addition to Dover, Pennsylvania, science books, added at insistence of school board[8]

It all came to a head in 2005, when parents of pupils in the Dover, Pennsylvania, school district sued the school board for teaching their

kids intelligent design. In November of that year, the eight school board members who'd supported the intelligent design addition to school books were voted out. And the next month, a judge ruled ID couldn't be taught in Dover.

Beyond science, beyond ID, something greater is at stake: the facts and the truth. They've been disappearing in government spin, and in the mirrors and smoke of corporate public relations firms who think up appealing lines and set up front groups funded by corporations and pretending to be grassroot movements. And a number of journalists, investigators, and citizen activists are taking them on—many using the Internet. Take for instance the Center for Media and Democracy, a small outfit out of Wisconsin that took on the government in revealing the use of "fake news"—television segments in which actors pose as reporters praising government programs. The center, manned by investigative journalists John Stauber and Sheldon Rampton, revealed that the "news" was manufactured by public relations firms paid by the government. Beyond that, the center has put together a comprehensive list of "front groups"—organizations that sound like something they're not, and are funded by corporations or trade groups to take out confusing advertisements and further cloud issues. Take the Advancement of Sound Science Coalition: according to SourceWatch this industry-funded organization attacks environmental groups for promoting "junk science." Or what about the Coalition for Vehicle Choice? It's funded by the Alliance of Automobile Manufacturers and its goal is to shoot down efforts to increase car efficiency. And although Hands Off the Internet sounds like it'd be for keeping the Internet the way it is—free and open—it's funded by telecoms, such as AT&T and BellSouth, that want to inflict tiered prices to Internet access.[9] And these misinformation groups go hand in hand with corporate-sponsored experts and think tanks that, under the guise of telling the truth, gush the messages that industry wants us to hear. "The public needs to be skeptical consumers of information," says Sheldon Rampton. "These groups make it hard to figure out" who's behind them. And the media, says Rampton, is doing a poor job of deciphering for us exactly who is standing for what.[10]

Jimmy Wales, who introduced revolutionary Wikipedia—the free

Jimmy Wales brought the common man into the information web—launching Wikipedia, the free online encyclopedia that anybody can edit (wikipedia.org).

online encyclopedia that Everyman can contribute to—has started a virtual wiki empire, now extending from travel to politics. The Florida-based visionary, who travels the world meeting with Wikiites from Europe to Asia says, "My dream is that every single person on the planet can have free access to the sum of all human knowledge. And by 'free' I mean not only 'no cost' but also 'free as in free speech'—that is, the ability to take our work, modify and adapt, and redistribute it."[11] He says we ain't seen nothing yet as far as the changes that will be brought as more and more of those in poor countries go online. "We think the Internet has done a lot to transform the developed world, but what it is doing and will do for the developing world will be even more profound."[12]

Progressive organizations such as the International Relations Center (IRC) boast a handy information tool in the form of Right Web (http://rightweb.irc-online.org), which tells you exactly who is who in the world of U.S. politics on the global level. Looking up, say, Stephen Hadley's work experience and groups he's been in one finds a number of links not discernible to the naked eye—and links to articles. Nobody does a better job of untangling this administration's web. And nobody's done more to open up our access to classified information than the National Security Archive of the George Washington University, which posts a treasure trove of recently declassified government documents on its fascinating site (www.gwu.edu/~nsarchiv/).

Bloggers are playing a crucial role in ripping off the veil of deceit: Russ Kick (http://www.thememoryhole.org) first forced the government

to show photos of the war dead by writing numerous Freedom of Information Act requests, and posting the resultant photos on his website. Suddenly the shamed media, which had just accepted the government ban, started running them too. TPMmuckraker—"They've got muck. We've got rakes"—serves up some of the finest reporting on the ongoing scandals (http://www.tpmmuckraker.com/) as does the racy Wonkette (http://www.wonkette.com), where the motto is "Politics for People with Dirty Minds"; from *Harper's* reporter Ken Silverstein's blog Washington Babylon (http://www.harpers.org/WashingtonEditor.html) to War and Piece (http://www.warandpiece.com/), which rounds up progressive news, it's getting harder to pull a fast one on Americans, at least if they have access to the Internet.

Beyond simply getting the information, however, we need the will to take action. And in the same way that Lawrence Krauss spent most of his spare time over the past decade writing op-eds, organizing groups, and making noise, we need to organize ourselves to be counted.

[What You Can Do]

- "Half of Americans don't vote," points out Grover Norquist.[13] So if you vote, convince three of your friends to vote with you, and you've just quadrupled your voice, he says. Adds Lawrence Krauss: vote in the tiny elections—as in for school boards, where a few hundred, even a few dozen votes can make the difference.

- Call up talk radio, Norquist suggests, "You can talk to tens of thousands—even millions at one time."[14] But be sure to have your three-minute spiel practiced and polished.

- Do like Grover: start a Wednesday networking meeting of motivated people to talk about the issues of the day and figure out how to act on them.

- Demand the ear of your representative, says Joan Claybrook of Public Citizen. They're easier to reach at the district level. And don't overwhelm them with e-mails; better to hit them up with a handwritten letter, she says.

- "People can have a huge impact on energy policy simply by weighing in on the debate and getting their friends, family, and neighbors engaged," says Michele Boyd of Public Citizen. "People can call into and write to their senators' and representatives' offices regularly, and especially when there are energy-related votes. People can meet with their elected officials when Congress is on recess. People can make individual choices about reducing their energy consumption."[15]

- Let us not forget the success of Tom Tancredo. Take an issue that you're passionate about. And just keep hammering it home.

- And, above all, think of David Sickey: "Don't think you don't have a part in the system," he urges. "Stop sitting on the sidelines." Even if we're just the little people, he says, "We do have the ability to affect change."[16] And Jack Abramoff—and a few dozen quivering-in-their-boots politicians—can now testify to the truth of Sickey's words.

Notes

Unless otherwise noted, all figures for lobbying and contributions are provided by the Center for Responsive Politics (www.opensecrets.org).

Chapter 1: Something Stinks

1. "Merry Christmas, Tom DeLay," CBS News, Nov. 17, 2004 (http://www.cbsnews.com/stories/2004/11/19/politics/main656728.shtml).
2. Figures from U.S. Treasury for Fiscal Year 2005.
3. Judy Bachrach, "Washington Babylon," *Vanity Fair*, Aug. 2006.
4. "Porter Goss Resigns . . ." CNN Transcript, May 5, 2006 (interview with former rep. Bob Barr).
5. *USA Today*/Gallup poll, Oct. 6–8, 2006 (http://www.pollingreport.com/CongJob.htm).
6. Lichtman/Zogby International poll, "U.S. Public Widely Distrusts Its Leaders," May 23, 2006.
7. Paul Blumenthal, "The Do-Nothing Congress," The Sunlight Foundation, Aug. 2006 (http://www.sunlightfoundation.com/files/Days_Im_Session_109th.pdf).
8. Ibid.
9. Christopher Drew, "In Case Against Politician, a Tale of Friendship, Ambition, Betrayal," *New York Times*, Sept. 16, 2006.
10. "Supreme Court Decision on Child Pornography," Justice Department Press Conference, Attorney General Transcript, May 1, 2002 (http://www.justice.gov/archive/ag/speeches/2002/050102ag-transcriptchildpornography.htm).
11. Roxana Tiron, "Defense Cash Focuses on Lobbying," *The Hill,* Oct. 18, 2005.

12. Jeff Zeleny, "Hastert, a political survivor, vows to overcome scandal," *New York Times*, Oct. 6, 2006 (http://www.iht.com/articles/2006/10/06/america/web.1006hastert.php).

13. Press Briefing by Scott McClellan, White House press release, Jan. 4, 2006 (http://www.whitehouse.gov/news/releases/2006/01/20060104-1.html).

14. "Bush Ranger and Pioneer Appointees," Public Citizen, Aug. 8, 2004 (http://www.whitehouseforsale.org/contributorsandpaybacks).

15. See Public Citizen's White House for Sale site for a damning assessment (http://www.whitehouseforsale.org).

16. Thomas Edsall, Sarah Cohen, and James V. Grimaldi, "Pioneers Fill War Chest, Then Capitalize," *Washington Post*, May 15, 2004 (http://www.washingtonpost.com/wp-dyn/articles/A29142-2004May15.html).

17. Michael A. Hafken and G. Calvin Mackenzie, "Campaign Contributions and Presidential Appointments: A Fact Sheet Analyzing Campaign Contributions from Nominees in the Administrations of George W. Bush and William J. Clinton." Brookings Institute, Presidential Appointee Initiative, Sept. 6, 2001 (http://www.appointee.brookings.org/events/sept6 2001_transcript.htm; http://www.appointee.brookings.org/events/contributionsappts.pdf).

18. Ilan Levin, Eric Schaeffer, Conor Kenny, and Frank Clemente, "America's Dirtiest Power Plants: Plugged into the Bush Administration," Public Citizen Congress Watch, March 2004.

19. Walter F. Roche Jr., "Bush removal ended Guam investigation," *Los Angeles Times*, Aug. 8, 2005.

20. Michael A. Hafken and G. Calvin Mackenzie, op. cit.

21. Campaign Finance Improprieties and Possible Violations of Law, Hearings Before the Committee on Government Reform and Oversight, House of Representatives, Oct. 8, 1997 (http://commdocs.house.gov/committees/gro/hgo281.000/hgo281_0.HTM).

22. Jeffrey H. Birnbaum, "The Road to Riches Is Called K Street," *Washington Post*, June 22, 2005.

23. Elizabeth Brown, "More Than 2,000 Spin Through Revolving Door," Center for Public Integrity, Apr. 7, 2005 (http://www.publicintegrity.org/lobby/report.aspx?aid=678#).

24. R. Jeffrey Smith, "The DeLay-Abramoff Money Trail," *Washington Post*, Dec. 31, 2006.

25. Jackie Koszczuk with Alan K. Ota, "The Slow Decline of a GOP 'Godfather,'" *Congressional Quarterly*, Oct. 3, 2006. See also: Dean Calbreath

and Jerry Kammer, "Contractor 'knew how to grease the wheels,'" *San Diego Union-Tribune*, Dec. 5, 2004 (http://www.pulitzer.org/year/2006/national-reporting/works/copley09.html).

26. Anne E. Kornblut and Glen Justice, "U.S. lobbying inquiry shifts to second firm," *New York Times,* Jan. 8, 2006.

27. Source: Center for Public Integrity (http://www.publicintegrity.org).

28. Frank Bruni, "Donors Flock to University Center. . .," *The New York Times*, May 8, 1999.

29. Brian Ross, "DeLay's Lavish Island Getaway," ABC News, Apr. 6, 2005 (http://abcnews.go.com/WNT/Investigation/story?id=647725& page=1).

30. Lara Chausow, Tom Scherer, Craig Holman, Taylor Lincoln, et al., "The Bankrollers: Lobbyists' Payments to the Lawmakers They Court (1998–2006)," Public Citizen Congress Watch, May 2006 (http://www.citizen.org/documents/BankrollersFinal.pdf).

31. Mark Benjamin, "Golfing with Tom DeLay," Salon.com, May 2, 2005 (http://dir.salon.com/story/news/feature/2005/05/02/delay/index.html).

32. Ibid.

33. R. Jeffrey Smith, "Former DeLay Aide Enriched by Nonprofit," *Washington Post*, Mar. 26, 2006 (http://www.washingtonpost.com/wp-dyn/content/article/2006/03/25/AR2006032501166_pf.html).

34. Ibid.

35. Ibid.

36. "Frist's Charity Under Scrutiny," CBS News, Dec. 17, 2005 (http://www.cbsnews.com/stories/2005/12/17/politics/main1134721.shtml).

37. Jonathan Katz and John Solomon, "Frist Charity Had Big Donors . . ." Associated Press, Dec. 18, 2005.

38. Michael Grunwald, "Pork by Any Other Name," *Washington Post*, Apr. 30, 2006.

39. "Statement by Senator John McCain before the Senate Rules Committee Hearing to Examine Procedures to Make the Legislative Process More Transparent," Feb. 18, 2006 (http://truthlaidbear.com/porkbusters/2006/02/mccain_announces_earmark_refor.php).

40. Ibid.

41. Ibid.

42. Ibid.

43. Ibid.

44. Ibid.

45. Ibid.

46. Ibid.

47. Michael Judge, "The Incredible Shrinking Rainforest," *Wall Street Journal*, Mar. 9, 2006.
48. Awarded between 2001 and 2005; from May 17, 2006, testimony of Thomas Schatz, president of Citizens against Government Waste before Senate Rules Committee Hearing to Examine Procedures to Make the Legislative Process More Transparent.
49. Tom Finnigan, "All About Pork: The Abuse of Earmarks and the Needed Reforms," Citizens Against Government Waste report, May 13, 2006 (http://www.cagw.org/site/DocServer/PorkFinal.pdf). See also: (http://www.duckworthforcongress.com/free_details.asp?id=27).
50. Highlights of the Pig Book (http://www.cagw.org/site/PageServer?pagename=reports_pigbook2006#criteria; see also (http://www.duckworthforcongress.com/free_details.asp?id=27).
51. David Kirkpatrick, "Earmarks Find Way into Spending Bill," Sept. 30, 2006 (http://select.nytimes.com/search/restricted/article?res=FA0C15FA3C540C738FDDA00894DE4044482).
52. Congressional Research Service Appropriations Team memorandum, "Earmarks in FY2006 Appropriations Acts," Congressional Research Service, Mar. 6, 2006 (http://demint.senate.gov/news/EarmarksFY2006.pdf).
53. Chuck Neubauer and Richard T. Cooper, "Senator's Way to Wealth Was Paved with Favors," *Los Angeles Times*, Dec. 17, 2003, (http://www.commondreams.org/headlines03/1217-05.htm).
54. "Ponying Up for Ted," *Washington Post*, Mar. 5, 2004.
55. Chuck Neubauer and Richard T. Cooper, op. cit.
56. Ibid.
57. Ibid.
58. Michael Winship, "King Crab, King Pork," *Messenger Post*, Jan. 24, 2006.
59. "FBI Raids Office of Alaska Senate president Ben Stevens . . ." Alaska Report, Aug. 31, 2006 (http://www.alaskareport.com/news11012.htm).
60. See: "Series of Tubes," Wikipedia (http://en.wikipedia.org/wiki/Series_of_tubes).
61. Congressman Jerry Lewis statement in response to *Los Angeles Times* allegations, May 12, 2006 (http://www.house.gov/jerrylewis/may112006.html).
62. Sources include: Dean Calbreath and Jerry Kammer, "Contractor 'knew how to grease the wheels,'" *San Diego Union-Tribune*, Dec. 5, 2004 (http://www.pulitzer.org/year/2006/national-reporting/works/pley09.html).

63. Judy Bachrach, "Washington Babylon," *Vanity Fair*, July 5, 2006, (http://www.vanityfair.com/features/general/articles/060705fege01).

64. "Jerry Lewis on the F-22," *Air Force Magazine*, Feb. 2000, (http://www.afa.org/magazine/Feb2000/0200jerry.asp).

65. Judy Bachrach, op. cit.

66. "Chairman Lewis Praises Leaderships' Commitment to Comprehensive Earmark Reform," press release from U.S. House of Representatives Committee on Appropriations, Apr. 27, 2006.

67. Jerry Kammer, "A close-knit circle of money, power," Copley News Service, June 24, 2006, (http://www.signonsandiego.com/uniontrib/20060624/news_1n24cozy.html).

68. Peter Perl, "'Absolute Truth,'" *Washington Post*, May 13, 2001, (http://www.washingtonpost.com/ac2/wp-dyn?pagename=article&node=&contentId=A6825-2001May9&no).

69. Juliet Eilperin, "House Whip Wields Fund-raising Clout," *Washington Post*, Oct. 18, 1999 (http://www.washingtonpost.com/wp-srv/politics/campaigns/keyraces2000/stories/delay101899.htm).

70. "DeLay Must Go," *The Nation*, May 9, 2005 (http://www.thenation.com/doc/20050509/editors).

71. "DeLay Inc.: A Democracy 21 Report on House Majority Leader Tom DeLay and His Money Machine," Democracy 21, July 22, 2003 (http://www.democracy21.org).

72. Peter Perl, op. cit.

73. Brody Mullins, "The Affair That Shook Washington," *Wall Street Journal*, Apr. 3, 2006.

74. Jonathan Weisman, "Speaker Largely Silent Amid Scandal," *Washington Post,* Jan. 17, 2006 (http://www.washingtonpost.com/wp-dyn/content/article/2006/01/16/AR2006011600997.html).

75. Ibid.

76. David Rose, "An Inconvenient Patriot," *Vanity Fair*, Sept. 2005, (http://www.vanityfair.com/commentary/content/printables/051003roco01?print=true). Also see: "Did Speaker Hastert Accept Turkish Bribes . . ." Democracy Now, Radio transcript, Aug. 10, 2005, (http://www.democracynow.org/article.pl?sid=05/08/10/1346254).

77. Ted Barrett, "Ethics Complaint Filed Against DeLay," CNN, June 15, 2004.

78. Ibid.

79. "CREW Demands DeLay Bribery Investigation," CREW Press Release, Mar. 31, 2004; Pete Yost, "Lawmakers Deny Westar Quid Pro

Quo, *AP*, June 6, 2003; Thomas B. Edsall, "Firm Fined for Channeling Funds to GOP," *Washington Post*, Aug. 19, 2005.

80. CREW: "Summary of Complaint Against Rep. Tom DeLay," filed by Chris Bell, June 8, 2004.
81. Ted Barrett, op. cit.
82. Ibid.
83. Ibid.

Chapter 2: Lobbying Pays

1. "Members of Congress Increasingly Use Revolving Door to Launch Lucrative Lobbying Careers," Public Citizen Press Room, July 27, 2005, (http://www.citizen.org/pressroom/release.cfm?ID=1999).
2. Susan Milligan, "Back-room dealing a Capitol trend," *Boston Globe*, Oct. 3, 2004 (http://www.boston.com/news/nation/articles/2004/10/03/back_room_dealing_a_capitol_trend?pg=full).
3. Jim VandeHei, "GOP Whip Quietly Tried to Aid Big Donor," *Washington Post*, June 4, 2003.
4. "Family Members Who Are Lobbyists," Public Citizen, May 9, 2006.
5. Ellen Nakashima, "Ashcroft finds private sector niche," *Washington Post*, Aug. 12, 2006.
6. "Members of Congress Congress Increasingly Use Revolving Door to Launch Lucrative Lobbying Careers," op. cit.
7. "The Bankrollers: Lobbyists' Payments to the Lawmakers They Court," Public Citizen's Congress Watch, May 2006 (http://www.citizen.org/documents/BankrollersFinal.pdf).
8. Ibid.
9. According to the Center for Responsive Politics (http://www.open secrets.org).
10. Craig Aaron, et al., "The Medicare Drug War," Public Citizen Congress Watch, June 2004 (http://www.citizen.org/documents/Medicare DrugWarReportREVISED72104.pdf).
11. Jim VandeHei and Juliet Eilperin, "Drug Firms Gain Church Groups' Aid," *Washington Post,* July 23, 2003.
12. Nick Confessore, "Bush's Secret Stash," *Washington Monthly*, May 2004.
13. Craig Aaron, et al., op. cit.
14. "Congressional Watchdog Agency Finds Claims of Malpractice Insurance 'Crisis' Not Substantiated," Public Citizen press release, Sept. 4, 2003 (http://www.commondreams.org/news2003/0904-10.htm).

15. Michael Isikoff and T. Trent Gegax, "Where's There's Smoke," *Newsweek*, Mar. 26, 2001.

16. "The Bankrollers: Lobbyists' Payments to the Lawmakers They Court," op. cit.

17. Ibid.

18. Ibid.

19. Donald L. Barlett and James B. Steele, "The Great Energy Scam," Time.com, Oct. 4, 2003 (http://www.time.com/time/magazine/article/ 0,9171,1101031013-493241,00.html).

20. "The Bankrollers: Lobbyists' Payments to the Lawmakers They Court," op. cit.

21. Ibid.

22. Ibid.

23. Ibid.

24. Ibid.

25. Edmond L. Andrews, "Suits Say U.S. Impeded Audits for Oil Leases," *New York Times*, Sept. 21, 2006.

26. David Sickey interview with author, Sept. 2006.

27. Ibid.; also from memo of Coushatta accountant.

28. Ibid.

29. "Thanks to Steady Casino Cash . . . ," *Casino* magazine, Sept. 21, 2003 (http://casinomagazine.com/ManageArticle.asp?C=540&A=2178).

30. Susan Schmidt, "A Jackpot from Gaming Interests," *Washington Post*, Feb. 22, 2004 (http://www.washingtonpost.com/ac2/wp-dyn? pagename=article&contentId=A60906-2004Feb21).

31. David Sickey interview with author, Sept. 2006.

32. Jonathan D. Salant, "Abramoff Sought Bush Officials' Aid in Indian-Tribe Fee Dispute," Bloomberg, Nov. 29, 2005 (http://www.bloomberg .com/apps/news?pid=washingtonstory&sid=aSn4ZmIPPIpw).

33. Lou Dubose, "The Coushatta Connection," *Gambit Weekly,* Jan. 11, 2005.

34. Mark Hemingway, "My Dinner with Jack," *The Weekly Standard*, Apr. 3, 2006.

35. Dele Olojede and Timothy Phelps, "Front for Apartheid," *Newsday*, July 16, 1995.

36. David Margolick, "Washington's Invisible Man," *Vanity Fair*, Apr. 2006.

37. Ibid.

38. "Behind Unravelling of DeLay's Team, a Jilted Fiancée," *Wall Street Journal*, Mar. 31, 2006.

39. Susan Schmidt, "A Jackpot of Indian Gaming Tribes," *Washington Post*, Feb. 22, 2005.

40. Ibid.

41. Nonpartisan and nonprofit, the Center for Responsive Politics' site (www.opensecrets.org) shows "who gives" and "who gets" with regard to political contributions, and also tracks lobbying, PACs, and much more. A veritable treasure trove of figures.

42. Brian Ross, "DeLay's Lavish Island Getaway," ABC News, Apr. 6, 2005 (http://abcnews.go.com/WNT/Investigation/story?id=647725&page=1).

43. Erica Werner, "Receptionist-turned-lobbyist gets attention of federal investigators," Associated Press, Aug. 28, 2006.

44. Ibid.

45. Jerry Kammer, "A Steady Flow of Financial Influence," *Copley News Service/San Diego Union-Tribune*, Dec. 23, 2005 (http://www.signon sandiego.com/news/politics/20051223-9999-lz1n23lewis.html).

46. Jerry Kammer, "A close-knit circle of money, power," *Copley News Service/San Diego Union-Tribune*, June 24, 2006 (http://www.signon sandiego.com/news/politics/20060624-9999-1n24cozy.html).

47. Ibid.

48. Ibid.

49. David Johnston and David D. Kirkpatrick, "Deal Maker Details the Art of Greasing the Palm," *New York Times*, Aug. 6, 2006.

50. "The USA's FY 2007 Defense Budget," *Defense Industry Daily*, Feb. 18, 2006.

51. Jim Lobe, "Spy Probe Scans Neocons," Inter Press Service, Sept. 1, 2004 (http://www.commondreams.org/headlines04/0901-20.htm); Stephen Green, "Serving Two Flags," *Counterpunch*, Feb. 28, 2004.

52. Ibid.

53. Ibid.

54. Ibid.

55. James Risen, "FBI Said to Reach Official Suspected of Passing Secrets," *New York Times*, Aug. 28, 2004.

56. Anne Hessing Cahn, "Team B: The Trillion Dollar Experiment," *Bulletin of Atomic Scientists*, 1993.

57. John B. Judis, "Minister Without Portfolio," *The American Prospect*, Jan. 1, 2003 (http://www.prospect.org/print/V14/5/judis-j.html).

58. Karl Grossman and Judith Long, "Star Wars Boosters," *The Nation*, Jan. 29, 2001 (http://www.thenation.com/doc/20010129/grossman).

59. Jeffrey St. Clair, "Lockheed and Loaded," *Counterpunch*, Jan. 22, 2005.

60. Source: Center for Responsive Politics (www.opensecrets.org).
61. Jeffrey St. Clair, op. cit.
62. Ibid.
63. Also see: Richard Girard, "Lockheed: The Weapons Manufacturer That Does It All," Polaris Institute, Oct. 2004.

Chapter 3: Party Matters

1. Morris P. Fiorina, "Ask This: Is the Culture War a Myth?" Nieman Watchdog, Nieman Foundation for Journalism at Harvard University, Aug. 24, 2004, (http://www.niemanwatchdog.org/index.cfm?fuseaction =ask_thls.view&askthisid=0046).
2. A. J. DiCintio, "Think the Culture War Is a Myth," MichNews.com, Sept. 19, 2006, (http://www.michnews.com/artman/publish/article_14134 .shtml).
3. "Remarks of Karl Rove at the New York Conservative Party," *Washington Post*, June 22, 2006.
4. John Soloma, *Ominous Politics*, New York: Hill and Wang, 1984.
5. Steven Kull, "Americans on Climate Change 2005," The PIPA/Knowledge Networks Poll, July 5, 2005.
6. Source: 2004 Republican Party Platform, p. 7 (see: www.ontheis sues.org for both parties' platforms, divided by issues).
7. Ibid, p. 86 (see www.ontheissues.org for both parties' platforms, divided by issues).
8. AP-Ipsos, March 2006 (http://www.msnbc.msn.com/id/11795147/).
9. August 2006 Newsweek Poll: Arian Campo-Flores, "Split Remains," *Newsweek*, Aug. 26, 2006 (http://www.msnbc.msn.com/id/14527419/ site/newsweek/).
10. "Strong Support for Abortion Rights," CBS News Poll, Jan. 22, 2003.
11. Ibid.
12. "Keep Feeding Tube Out," CBS News poll, Mar. 23, 2005 (http://www .cbsnews.com/stories/2005/03/23/opinion/polls/main682674.shtm).
13. "Democrats hold solid lead," Pew Research Center for the People and the Press, Sept. 14, 2006 (http://people-press.org/reports/pdf/289.pdf).
14. Joseph Carroll, "Gallup Poll: Who Supports the Death Penalty," The Gallup Organization, Nov. 16, 2004.
15. Michael Dimock, "Both Reds and Blues Go Green on Energy," Pew Research Center for the People and the Press, Feb. 28, 2006 (http:// pewresearch.org/obdeck/?ObDeckID=8).
16. Ibid.

17. "Bush grade on environment falls," *Bloomberg/Los Angeles Times* poll, Aug. 4, 2006 (http://www.organicconsumers.org/2006/article_1431.cfm).
18. Michael Dimock, "Maximum Support for Minimum Wage," Pew Research Center for the People and the Press, Apr. 19, 2006 (http://pewresearch.org/obdeck/?ObDeckID=18).
19. Fourth National Survey on Religion and Politics, Ray C. Bliss, Institute of the University of Akron, May 2004.
20. Ibid.
21. "National Annenberg Election Survey," Annenberg Public Policy Center of University of Pennsylvania, Nov. 2004.
22. Interview with Morris Fiorina, Director's Forum, Hoover Institute, Dec. 2, 2005.
23. "Majority in U.S. Favors Stricter Gun Control," Harris Poll #42, June 6, 2004 (http://www.harrisinteractive.com/harris_poll/index.asp?PID=471).
24. Ibid.
25. "Gun Laws and Women," Gallup poll, May 12, 2000.
26. "Gun Legislation in the 109th Congress," Congressional Research Service, May 6, 2005.
27. "U.S. Adults' Attitudes on Iraq Polarized by Political Party," Harris Poll #72, Sept. 22, 2006 (http://www.harrisinteractive.com/harris_poll/index.asp?PID=699).
28. Dana Milbank, "A Reprise of GOP Line," *Washington Post*, Sept. 13, 2006.
29. William M. Welch, "Daschle Condemns Bush on Iraq Debate," *USA Today*, Sept. 25, 2002.
30. Dana Milbank, op. cit.
31. Press release from Rep. John Murtha's office, Nov. 17, 2005.
32. Press release/statement from White House in response to Murtha's press release, Nov. 18, 2005.
33. Interview of vice president with Wire Service Reporters, Aug. 9, 2005 (see http://www.whitehouse.gov/news/releases/2006/08/20060809-2.html).
34. Morris Fiorina interview with author, Sept. 2006.
35. Newt Gingrich speech to College Republicans, Atlanta Airport Holiday Inn, June 24, 1978.
36. Grover Norquist interview with author, Sept. 2006.
37. Speech by Grover Norquist of Americans for Tax Reform, given Oct. 5, 2005 (http://www.atr.org/content/html/2005/oct/101505spch-dllslcr.html).
38. Paul Weyrich, "Congressional Challenge," Townhall.com, Sept. 7,

2006 (http://www.townhall.com/columnists/PaulWeyrich/2006/09/07/
a_congressional_challenge).

39. Grover Norquist, interview with author, Sept. 2006.
40. Grover Norquist, September 1995 speech, Council for National Policy
(http://www.policycounsel.org/18856/35101.html).
41. Ibid.
42. Some Democrats split from the party and supported Lincoln's war effort against the rebel South, becoming known as War Democrats.
43. Pat Buchanan, Republican national convention speech, Aug. 17, 1992.
(see www.buchanan.org)
44. Jeffrey H. Birnbaum, "Going Left on K Street," *Washington Post*, July 2,
2004 (http://www.washingtonpost.com/wp-dyn/articles/A21972-2004
Jul1_3.html).
45. Kate Ackley, "Parties Vie for Edge on K Street," *Roll Call,* Aug. 18, 2006.
46. "Religious Right Leaders Blame Iraqi Prison Abuse Scandal on MTV,"
Americans United for Separation Between Church and State, May 13,
2004.
47. Interview with author, Aug. 2006.
48. Interview with author, Sept. 2006.
49. Mary Jacoby, "House Divided," Salon.com, May 24, 2004 (http://div
.salon.com/story/news/feature/2004/05/24/armey/index1.html?ph=1).
50. Interview with author, Sept. 2006.
51. Ibid.
52. Ibid.
53. Ibid.
54. Ibid.
55. John Soloma, Ominous Politics, New York: Hill and Wang, 1984.
56. David Grann, "Robespierre of the Right," *The New Republic*, Oct. 27,
1997.
57. Source: Sourcewatch, Center for Media and Democracy, "Heritage
Foundation."
58. Abramoff, like many a PR firm, paid experts (including one from Cato
Institute) to place op-eds in newspapers that were favorable to his
clients.
59. Thomas B. Edsall, "Think Tanks Ideas Shifted as Malaysia Ties Grew,"
Washington Post, Apr. 17, 2005 (http://www.washingtonpost.com/
wp-dyn/articles/A59539-2005Apr16.html).
60. "Moral Majority," Wikipedia, The Free Encyclopedia (en.wikipedia.org),
Jan. 4, 2007.

61. Interview with author, Sept. 2006.

62. Thomas B. Edsall, "College Republican Fundraising Criticized," *Washington Post*, Dec. 26, 2004.

63. Sidney Blumenthal, "Republicans Gone Wild," Salon.com, Jan. 19, 2006 (http://www.salon.com/opinion/blumenthal/2006/01/19/abramoff/index_np.html).

64. "Ralph Reed: The Crash of the Choir Boy," People for the American Way (www.pfaw.org), drawing from the book of Nina J. Easton, *Gang of Five* (New York: Simon and Schuster, 2002).

65. Thomas B. Edsall, "Abramoff Allies Keeping Distance," *Washington Post*, Nov. 8, 2004.

66. "The Long March of Newt Gingrich," *Frontline,* PBS, Jan. 16, 1996 (http://www.pbs.org/wgbh/pages/frontline/newt/newtscript.html).

67. Ibid.

68. Sources include: Rick Stoff, "Learn to speak 'Republican,'" *St. Louis Journalism Review*, Apr. 1, 2005; Jennifer Lee, "A Call for Softer, Greener Language," *The New York Times*, Mar. 2, 2004; *Luntz Political Playbook,* Luntz Research Companies.

69. Luntz Political Playbook, Luntz Research Companies.

70. Ibid.

71. Ibid.

72. Interview with author, Sept. 2006.

73. Ibid.

74. Interview with author, Aug. 2006.

75. Ibid.

76. E-mail response to author, Aug. 2006.

77. Jeff Brady, "Colorado Springs: A Mecca for Evangelical Christians," National Public Radio broadcast, Jan. 17, 2005 (http://www.npr.org/templates/story/story.php?storyid=4287106).

Chapter 4: Going Nuclear

1. All figures from this dire scenario from Edwin S. Lyman, "Chernobyl on the Hudson?" Union of Concerned Scientists, commissioned by Riverkeeper, Aug. 2004 (http://www.ucsusa.org/global_security/nuclear_terrorism/impacts-of-a-terrorist-attack-at-indian-point-nuclear-power-plant.html).

2. William B. Scott, "Exercise Jump-Starts Response to Attack," *Aviation Week and Space Technology*, June 3, 2002 (http://911research.wtc7.net/cache/planes/defense/aviationnow_jumpstart.htm).

3. "Homeland Unsecured," Public Citizen, Oct. 2004 (http://www.citizen.org/documents/ACF1B7.pdf).

4. Barbara Starr, "NRC memo warns of attacks on nuclear plants," CNN, Jan. 31, 2002 (http://edition.cnn.com/2002/US/01/31/ret.terror.threats/).

5. The National Academy of Sciences is among them.

6. According to the Congressional Research Service, Capitol Hill's information gathering arm.

7. Deborah Halbers, "NRC Commissioner sees nuke role expanding," *MIT Tech Talk*, Mar. 8, 2006.

8. According to the GAO.

9. Statement of Sen. James Jeffords, U.S. Senate Committee on Energy, May 20, 2004.

10. As advocated by the Department of Energy.

11. "Public Support and Five Ways to Keep the Momentum," Speech by Dr. Ann Bisconti at the American Nuclear Society Winter Meeting, Nov. 14, 2005 (http://www.nei.org/index.asp?catnum=4&catid=863).

12. Ibid.

13. Ibld.

14. "Survey: Americans Not Warming up to Nuclear Power," Opinion Research Corporation, May 31, 2006 (http://www.resultsforamerica.org/calendar/files/053106%20CSI%20renewables%20survey%20release%20FINAL.pdf).

15. "Public Support and Five Ways to Keep the Momentum," speech by Dr. Ann Bisconti.

16. Ibid.

17. Ibid.

18. Cora Daniels, "Meet Mr. Nuke," *Fortune*, May 11, 2006 (http://money.cnn.com/magazines/fortune/fortune_archive/2006/05/15/8376894/index.htm).

19. Katharine Q. Seelye, "Nuclear Gains in Status After Lobbying," *New York Times*, May 23, 2001.

20. "Data Shows Industry Had Extensive Access to Cheney Energy Task Force," Natural Resources Defense Council press release, May 21, 2002 (http://www.nrdc.org/media/pressreleases/020521.asp).

21. James Ridgeway, "Mondo Washington: GOP Patron Gets Nod for Alaska Pipeline," *Village Voice*, Feb. 27, 2002 (http://www.villagevoice.com/news/0209,ridgeway,32635,6.html).

22. "The National Commission on Energy Policy," Public Citizen, Dec. 2006.

23. "Data Shows Industry Had Extensive Access to Cheney Energy Task Force," Natural Resources Defense Council press release, May 21, 2002 (http://www.nrdc.org/media/pressreleases/020521.asp).

24. "Bush's Rangers and Pioneers Enjoy Their Share of Energy Bill Booty," Public Citizen Congress Watch, Nov. 2003 (http://www.whitehousefor sale.org/documents/EnergyBillBooty.pdf); see also: "The Best Energy Bill Corporations Could Buy," Public Citizen, Aug. 2005 (http://www .citizen.org/documents/aug2005ebsum.pdf).

25. Katharine Q. Seelye, op. cit.

26. Jon Lamb, "The Global Nuclear Energy Partnership," *Alexander's Oil and Gas*, Mar. 22, 2006.

27. "The Best Energy Bill Corporations Could Buy," Public Citizen, Aug. 2005 (http://www.citizen.org/print_article.cfm?ID=13980).

28. Ibid.

29. Ibid.

30. Source: The Center for Responsive Politics (www.opensecrets.org).

31. Rep. Edward Markey's report for the House, Committee on Energy and Commerce Subcommittee on Energy Conservation and Power, "American Nuclear Guinea Pigs: Three Decades of Radiation Experiments on U.S. Citizens," oddly never received much press attention; see Geoffrey Sea, "The Radiation Story No One Would Touch," *Columbia Journalism Review*, Mar./Apr. 1994 (http://www.cjr.org/year/94/2/ radiation.asp).

32. "Cheney Energy Task Force Documents Feature Map of Iraqi Oilfields," Judicial Watch, July 17, 2003 (http://www.judicialwatch.org/iraqi-oilfield -pr.shtml).

33. "Global Nuclear Energy Partnership," Foreign Press Center briefing with Clay Sell, Feb. 16, 2006 (http://fpc.state.gov/fpc/61808.htm).

34. Figures from Center for Responsive Politics as reported in Public Citizen press release. "Bill of Sale . . . ," May 20, 2003.

35. Bill Mesler, "Springtime for Nuclear," *The Nation*, July 23, 2001 (http:// www.thenation.com/doc/20010723/mesler).

36. Mike Stuckey, "From Senate job to nuclear lobbyist—twice," MSNBC .com, Mar. 22, 2006 (http://www.msnbc.msn.com/id/11845981/).

37. Ibid.

38. "Bush Puts FirstEnergy First—Consumers Last," Statement of Public Citizen, Aug. 19, 2003 (http://www.citizen.org/pressroom/release.cfm ?ID=1527).

39. "Besse troubles bring big fine," *The Cleveland Plain Dealer*, Apr. 22, 2005.

40. Jeff Birnbaum, "Big Money Contributors Line Up for Inauguration," *Washington Post*, Jan. 13, 2005.

41. All of the following points from "The Best Energy Bill Corporations Could Buy," Public Citizen (http://www.citizen.org/print_article.cfm?ID=13980).

42. Interview with author, Aug. 2006.

43. Darren Goode, "Funding for Global Nuclear Program Facing Opposition," *Congress Daily*, Mar. 9, 2006.

44. Ibid.

Chapter 5: Quit Stalling

1. Chris Paine, interview with author, July 2006.

2. Ibid.

3. Martin Zimmerman, "Movie Casts the Electric Car as Hero . . .," *Los Angeles Times*, July 15, 2006.

4. Chris Paine, interview with author, July 2006.

5. Ibid.

6. Ibid.

7. Ibid.

8. Source: Center for Responsive Politics. See: "Auto Safety Legislation Rolled by Special Interests," Public Citizen, Oct. 2006.

9. CNN Poll, taken Apr. 21–23, 2006; see: "Bush takes aim at rising gasoline prices," CNN.com, Apr. 25, 2006.

10. Chris Isidore, "ExxonMobil sets profit record," CNNMoney.com, Jan. 30, 2006.

11. Jeff Wilson and Joe Carroll, "Exxon Mobil CEO calls for an end to ethanol subsidies," *Bloomberg/Detroit Free Press*, Mar. 9, 2006.

12. "The New Oil Crisis," *The Guardian* (London), Dec. 8, 1998.

13. "This is ExxonMobil," ExxonMobil fact sheet at Exxonmobil.com.

14. All figures in preceding two sentences from "This is ExxonMobil," fact sheet on ExxonMobil.com

15. Paul Krugman, "Enemy of the Planet," *New York Times*, Apr. 17, 2006.

16. John Vidal, "Revealed: How Oil Giant Influenced Bush," *The Guardian* (London), June 8, 2005.

17. "Overwhelming Majority of Americans Favors US Joining with G8 Members to Limit Greenhouse Gas Emissions," Program on International Policy Attitudes Survey, Jul. 5, 2005.

18. Thomas Friedman, "A Quick Fix for the Gas Addicts," *New York Times*, May 31, 2006.

19. Senator John Kerry, "Auto industry should stop roadblocks to CAFE," *The Hill*, Mar. 13, 2002.

20. Bryan Gruley, "Mideast crisis fuels CAFE war," *Ward's Auto World*, Oct. 1990.

21. As *Roll Call* reported in March 2001.

22. "Toyota Passes Ford in U.S. Vehicle Sales," *The New York Times*, Aug. 2, 2006.

23. Edmund L. Andrews, "U.S. Royalty Plan to Give Windfall to Oil Companies," *New York Times*, Feb. 14, 2006.

24. CNN Poll, taken Apr. 21–23, 2006; see: "Bush takes aim at rising gasoline prices," CNN.com, Apr. 25, 2006.

25. According to a Gallup poll released Apr. 18, 2006 which put his approval rating at 36 percent. Joseph Carroll, "Bush Reaches New Lows on Ratings of Terrorism, Energy," Gallup.com poll, Apr. 18, 2006.

26. Speech, "President Discusses Energy Policy," Apr. 25, 2006.

27. Ibid.

28. Ibid.

29. Ibid.

30. Ibid.

31. Ibid.

Chapter 6: Locking the Door

1. "Savage: Burn the Mexican Flag," Media Matters, Mar. 31, 2006 (http://mediamatters.org/items/200603310008).

2. "Dobbs' immigration reports marked by misinformation, extreme rhetoric, attacks on Mexican president . . . ," Media Matters, May 24, 2006 (http://mediamatters.org/items/200605240011).

3. Ibid.

4. Ibid.

5. Numerous sources, including Media Matters and Linda Chaveze.

6. Interview with author, Sept. 2006.

7. Congressional Budget Office estimate is 21.4 million foreign-born workers in 2004: "The Role of Immigrants in the U.S. Labor Market," The Congress of the United Status, Congressional Budget Office, Nov. 2005.

8. Pew Hispanic Center estimated 7.2 million. The Congressional Budget Office uses the figure of 6.3 million unauthorized workers as of March

2004, as estimated by Jeffrey Passel in his paper, "Unauthorized Migrants: Numbers and Characteristics."

9. Source: Congressional Budget Office.

10. "The estimated Hispanic population of the United States as of July 1, 2004, making people of Hispanic origin the nation's largest ethnic or race minority. Hispanics constituted 14 percent of the nation's total population. (This estimate does not include the 3.9 million residents of Puerto Rico.)" "Hispanic Heritage Month," Press Release, U.S. Census Bureau, Sept. 8, 2005 (http://www.census.gov/Press-Release/www/releases/archives/facts_for_features_special_editions/00538.html).

11. Ibid.

12. Pew Hispanic Center figure.

13. As of May 2006. "Labor Day 2006," U.S. Census Bureau, July 6, 2006 (http://www.census.gov/Press-Release/www/releases/archives/facts_for_features_special_editions/007125.html).

14. "The Role of Immigrants in the U.S. Labor Market," Congressional Budget Office, Nov. 2005.

15. Ibld.

16. Gordon H. Hanson, "Why Does Immigration Divide America?" The Center for Comparative Immigration Studies, University of California, San Diego, Dec. 2005.

17. As of 2005. "Census Bureau Data Shows Key Population Changes Across Nation," U.S. Census Bureau (http://www.census.gov/Press-Release/www/releases/archives/american_community_survey_acs/007287.html); Gordon H. Hanson, "Why Does Immigration Divide America?" The Center for Comparative Immigration Studies, University of California, San Diego, Dec. 2005.

18. Congressional Budget Office Cost Estimate S. 2611, Comprehensive Reform Act of 2006, CBO, Aug. 18, 2006 (http://www.cbo.gov/ftpdocs/75xx/doc7501/s2611spass.pdf).

19. "Hispanic Heritage Month," Press Release, U.S. Census Bureau, op. cit.

20. Ibid.

21. Interview with author, Sept. 2006.

22. Zoe Hammer-Tomizuka and Jennifer Allen, "Hate or Heroism," Border Action Network (Tucson), Dec. 2002.

23. Sara Catania, "Making Radio Waves," *Mother Jones*, July/August 2006.

24. Zoe Hammer-Tomizuka and Jennifer Allen, op. cit.

25. Susy Buchanan and Tom Kim, "The Nativists," Intelligence Report, Southern Poverty Law Center, 2006.

26. Ibid.

27. Ibid.

28. Zoe Hammer-Tomizuka and Jennifer Allen, op. cit.

29. Susy Buchanan and Tom Kim, op. cit.

30. Ibid.

31. Ibid.

32. Susy Buchanan and Tom Kim, op. cit.

33. Website for *O'Reilly Factor*, Apr. 12, 2006 show (http://billoreilly.com/show?action=viewTVShow&showID=766).

34. Source: Media Matters.

35. "President Bush Addresses the Nation on Immigration Reform," White House press release, June 15, 2006 (http://www.whitehouse.gov/news/releases/2006/05).

36. Robert Rector, "Senate Immigration Bill Would Allow 100 Million New Legal Immigrants over the Next Twenty Years," The Heritage Foundation, May 15, 2006.

37. "Dobbs again cited discredited Heritage immigration figures," Media Matters, July 18, 2006.

38. "Savage: Burn the Mexican Flag," Media Matters, op. cit.

39. Christopher Hayes, "Keeping America Empty," *In These Times*, Apr. 24, 2006 (http://www.inthesetimes.com/site/main/article/2608/).

40. "Our goals," NumbersUSA.com. "Since 1976, virtually all the increase in student enrollments in the U.S. has been due to the rise in the number of children of immigrants—immigrants who on average don't begin to earn enough money to pay the taxes to cover the education costs of their children . . ." (see: www.numbersusa.com/about/wearefor.html).

41. Interview with author, Aug. 2006.

42. Ibid.

43. Ibid.

44. "The Puppeteer," Intelligence Report, Southern Poverty Law Center, Summer 2002 (http://www.splcenter.org/intel/intelreport/article.jsp?aid=93). Also see memo to Witan VI from John Tanton posted on Southern Poverty Law Center site (http://www.splcenter.org/intel/intelreport/article.jsp?sid=125); see also other memos, info: (http://www.splcenter.org/intel/intelreport/article.jsp?aid=93).

Chapter 7: Battles of the Titan

1. Rebecca Adams, "Regulating the Rule Makers," *CQ Weekly*, Feb. 23, 2002.

2. U.S. Chamber of Commerce self-description (http://www.uschamber
    .com).
3. Source: Center for Responsive Politics (http://www.opensecrets.org).
4. "Environment, Technology and Regulatory Affairs: Annual Report 2005,"
    U.S. Chamber of Commerce, Environment, Technology and Regulatory
    Affairs Division (http://www.uschamber.com/publications/reports/
    environment_technology_regulatory_affairs_05ann_report+.htm).
5. Source: PoliticalMoneyLine, as reported by Jonathan D. Salant and
    Jeff St. Onge, Bloomberg, July 7, 2006.
6. "House Rejects Sanctions Bill on Sales of Arms to China," *Congress-
    Daily*, July 14, 2005.
7. Source: Center for Responsive Politics (http://www.opensecrets.org).
8. "The myth of the litigation crisis," *Trial*, July 2006 (http://www.atla.org/
    Publications/trial/0607/straub.aspx).
9. Jeffrey H. Birnbaum, "A Quiet Revolution in Business Lobbying,"
    Washington Post, Feb. 5, 2005.
10. Laurie Beacham, "The Secret Chamber: The Inner Workings of the
    U.S. Chamber of Commerce and the Hijacking of an Election," Center
    for Justice and Democracy, July 2006 (http://centerjd.org/private/
    papers/secretchamberstudy.pdf).
11. Source: Center for Public Integrity (http://www.publicintegrity.org).
12. "Trial Lawyers, Inc." Center for Legal Policy at the Manhattan Institute
    for Policy Research, 2003.
13. Jim VandeHei, "Major Business Group Wins Back Its Clout . . . ," *Wall
    Street Journal*, Sept. 11, 2001.
14. Center for Responsive Politics (http://www.opensecrets.org).
15. "McDonald's Scalding Coffee Case," Association of Trial Lawyers,
    ATLA Press Room (www.atla.org/pressroom/FACTS/frivolous/
    McDonaldsCoffeecase.aspx).
16. T. R. Goldman, "Tort lobby sharpens its aim on hill," *Legal Times*, June
    20, 2005.
17. See: Peter H. Stone, "Trial Lawyers on Trial," *The National Journal*, July
    12, 2003.
18. Interview with author, Aug. 2006.
19. "What's Happened to the Chamber of Commerce," Center for Democ-
    racy and Justice, March 2005.
20. Interview with author, Aug. 2006.
21. Michelle Bates Deakin, "The Equalizer," *Harvard Law Bulletin*, Spring
    2005.

22. Interview with Neal Cavuto, Fox News, Feb. 15, 2005.
23. Jeffrey H. Birnbaum, "Advocacy Groups Blur Media Lines," *Washington Post*, Dec. 6, 2004.
24. Figures from PoliticalMoneyLine.com.
25. "President's Update, May 2005," Memo from Tom Donohue to U.S. Chamber Board of Directors, June 1, 2005.
26. Interview with author, July 2006.
27. Kim Chapman, "New group launches anti-union drive," Bloomberg News, Feb. 14, 2006.
28. Robert Borosage, "Class Warfare, Bush-Style," *The Prospect*, March 1, 2003.
29. Ibid.
30. "Environment, Technology, and Regulatory Affairs: Annual Report 2005," U.S. Chamber of Commerce, Environment, Technology, and Regulatory Affairs Division (http://www.uschamber.com/publications/reports/environment_technology_regulatory_affairs_05ann_report.htm).
31. "Recent Victories 2006," U.S. Chamber of Commerce (www.uschamber.com).
32. "Environment, Technology, and Regulatory Affairs: Annual Report 2005," op. cit.
33. "U.S. Chamber of Commerce Policy Accomplishments for 2005," U.S. Chamber of Commerce (www.uschamber.com).
34. Ibid.
35. Ibid.
36. Ibid.
37. Ibid.
38. Ibid.
39. Ibid.
40. The U.S.–India Partnership Summit, "Rising India—The Alignment of Two Great Democracies for the 21st Century." Remarks by Thomas J. Donohue, president and CEO, U.S. Chamber of Commerce, The Palace Hotel, New York, May 3, 2006.
41. "General Electric," Wikipedia, The Free Encyclopedia, (http://en.wikipedia.org/w/index.php?title=General_Electric&oldid=105241885).
42. State Department documents from Oct. 1964 make mention of this. See A. G. Noorani, "U.S. Espionage in India," *Frontline*, Aug. 12–25, 2006 (www.hinduonnet.com).

Chapter 8: What You Can Do

1. Interview with author, Sept. 2006.
2. Ibid.
3. Ibid.
4. Ibid.
5. Ibid.
6. Ibid.
7. Ibid.
8. "Intelligent design," Wikipedia, The Free Encyclopedia (http.//en .wikipedia.org/w/index.php?title-Intelligent_design&oldid=105721091).
9. See PRwatch.org for more examples of front groups.
10. Interview with author, July 2006.
11. Interview with author, Aug. 2006.
12. Ibid.
13. Interview with author, Aug. 2006.
14. Ibid.
15. Interview with author, July 2006.
16. Interview with author, Sept. 2006.

Bibliography

Books

Alterman, Eric and Mark Green. *The Book on Bush*. New York: Penguin, 2004.

Angell, Marcia. *The Truth About the Drug Companies*. New York: Random House, 2004.

Armstrong, Jerome and Markos Moulitsas. *Crashing the Gate: Netroots, Grassroots, and the Rise of People-Powered Politics*. New York: Chelsea Green Publishing Company, 2006.

Baer, Robert. *Sleeping with the Devil: How Washington Sold Our Soul for Saudi Crude*. New York: Three Rivers Press, 2003.

Barsamian, David and Noam Chomsky. *Propaganda and the Public Mind*. London: Pluto Press, 2001.

Boehlert, Eric. *Lapdogs: How the Press Rolled Over for Bush*. New York: Free Press, 2006.

Bonner, William and Addison Wiggin. *Empire of Debt: The Rise of an Epic Financial Crisis*. Hoboken, NJ: John Wiley & Sons, 2005.

Brock, David. *The Republican Noise Machine: Right-Wing Media and How It Corrupts Democracy*. New York: Crown Publishers, 2005.

Canterbery, E. Ray. *Wall Street Capitalism: The Theory of the Bondholding Class*. Singapore: World Scientific Publishing Company, 2000.

Cohen, Jay S., M.D. *Overdose: The Case Against Drug Companies*. New York: Penguin, 2004.

Continetti, Matthew. *The K Street Gang: The Rise and Fall of the Republican Machine*. New York: Doubleday, 2006.

Cooper, David. *Broken America*. Lincoln, NE: iUniverse, Inc, 2006.

Domhoff, G. William. *Who Rules America?* Mountain View, CA: Mayfield Publishing Company, 1998.

Goodman, Amy. *The Exception to the Rulers*. New York: Arrow, 2001.

Greenwald, Glenn. *How Would a Patriot Act? Defending American Values from a President Run Amok*. San Francisco: Working Assets Publishing, 2006.

Hartung, William. *How Much Are You Spending on the War, Daddy?* New York: Nation Books, 2003.

Herman, Edward S. and Noam Chomsky. *Manufacturing Consent: The Political Economy of the Mass Media*. New York: Vintage, 1994.

Hightower, Jim. *Thieves in High Places*. New York: Penguin, 2003.

Johnston, David Cay. *Perfectly Legal: The Covert Campaign to Rig Our Tax System to Benefit the Super Rich—and Cheat Everybody Else*. New York: Penguin, 2003.

Juhasz, Antonia. *The Bush Agenda: Invading the World, One Economy at a Time*. New York: HarperCollins, 2006.

Kamenetz, Anya. *Generation Debt: How Our Future Was Sold Out for Student Loans, Bad Jobs, No Benefits, and Tax Cuts for Rich Geezers— And How to Fight Back*. New York: Riverhead/Penguin, 2006.

Kean, Thomas H., and Lee H. Hamilton, vice chair, *The 9/11 Report, The National Commission on Terrorist Attacks Upon the United States*. New York: St. Martin's Press, 2004.

Kennedy, Robert F., Jr. *Crimes Against Nature: How George W. Bush and His Corporate Pals Are Plundering the Country and Hijacking Our Democracy*. New York: Harper Perennial, 2005.

Klare, Michael. *Blood and Oil*. New York: Hamish Hamilton, 2004.

———. *Resource Wars*. New York: Henry Holt and Company, 2002.

Lapham, Lewis. *Gag Rule*. New York: Penguin, 2004.

Ledeen, Michael A. *The War Against the Terror Masters: Why It Happened. Where We Are Now. How We'll Win*. New York: St. Martin's Press, 2003.

Lessig, Lawrence. *Free Culture*. New York: Penguin, 2004.

Levy, Joel. *Secret History: Hidden Forces that Shaped the Past*. London: Vision Paperbacks, 2004.

Lewis, Tom. *Divided Highways*. New York: Penguin, 1999.

Mann, James. *Rise of the Vulcans: The History of Bush's War Cabinet*. New York: Penguin, 2004.

Mann, Michael. *Incoherent Empire*. London: Verso, 2003.

Marrs, Jim. *Rule by Secrecy*. New York: HarperCollins, 2000.

Micklethwait, John, and Adrian Wooldridge. *The Right Nation: Why America Is Different*. London: Allen Lane, 2004.

Morris, Langdon. *The War for America: Morality, Ideology, and the Big Lies of American Politics.* Lincoln, NE: iUniverse, Inc, 2006.

Palast, Greg. *Armed Madhouse: Who's Afraid of Osama Wolf?* New York: Dutton/Penguin, 2006.

Palast, Greg. *The Best Democracy Money Can Buy.* New York: Plume, 2003.

Perkins, John. *Confessions of an Economic Hit Man.* San Francisco: Berrett-Koehler, 2004.

Peterson, Peter G. *Running On Empty: How the Democratic and Republican Parties Are Bankrupting Our Future and What Americans Can Do About It.* New York: Farrar, Straus and Giroux, 2004.

Phillips, Kevin. *American Dynasty.* New York: Viking, 2004.

Phillips, Kevin. *American Theocracy: The Peril and Politics of Radical Religion, Oil, and Borrowed Money in the 21st Century.* New York: Viking/Penguin, 2006.

Rampton, Sheldon and John Stauber. *Toxic Sludge Is Good for You.* London: Constable and Robinson, 2000.

Rampton, Sheldon and John Stauber. *Trust Us, We're Experts: How Industry Manipulates Science and Gambles with Your Future.* New York: Tarcher/Penguin, 2002.

Rifkin, Jeremy. *The Hydrogen Economy.* New York: Tarcher/Penguin, 2003.

Rossi, Melissa. *What Every American Should Know About Who's Really Running the World.* New York: Plume/Penguin, 2005.

Rothkopf, David J. *Running the World: The Inside Story of the National Security Council and the Architects of American Power.* New York: Public Affairs/Perseus Group, 2005.

Sands, Philippe. *Lawless World: America and the Making and Breaking of Global Rules—From FDR's Atlantic Charter to George W. Bush's Illegal War.* New York: Viking, 2005.

Sirota, David. *Hostile Takeover: How Big Money and Corruption Conquered Our Government—and How We Take It Back.* New York: Crown Publishers, 2006.

Snow, Nancy. *Information War, American Propaganda, Free Speech and Information Control Since 9-11.* New York: Seven Stories Press, 2003.

Snow, Nancy. *Propaganda, Inc.* New York: Seven Stories Press, 2003.

Soros, George. *The Bubble of American Supremacy.* New York: Public Affairs/Perseus Group, 2004.

Suskind, Ron. *The Price of Loyalty.* New York: Simon & Schuster, 2004.

Thomas, Helen. *Watchdogs of Democracy? The Waning Washington Press Corps and How It Has Failed the Public.* New York: Scribner, 2006.

Todd Whitman, Christine. *It's My Party Too: The Battle for the Heart of the GOP and the Future of America*. New York: Penguin, 2006.

Tudge, Colin. *So Shall We Reap: What's Gone Wrong with the World's Food—And How to Fix it*. London: Allen Lane, 2003.

Unger, Craig. *House of Bush, House of Saud*. New York: Scribner, 2004.

Resources

Newspapers

Dailies

The Boston Globe (www.boston.com/news/globe/)

The Chicago Tribune (www.chicagotribune.com/)

The Christian Science Monitor (www.csmonitor.com)

The Toronto Globe and Mail (www.theglobeandmail.com/)

The Guardian/Observer (www.guardian.co.uk and
    www.observer.guardian.co.uk)

The Los Angeles Times (www.latimes.com)

The Madison Capital Times (www.madison.com/tct)

The New York Times (www.nytimes.com)

Philadelphia Inquirer (www.philly.com/mld/inquirer)

Rocky Mountains News (www.sptimes.com/home.shtml)

The San Francisco Chronicle (www.sfgate.com/chronicle/)

The Seattle Post-Intelligencer (seattlepi.nwsource.com)

St. Louis Post-Dispatch (www.stltoday.com)

St. Petersburg Times (www.sptimes.com/home.shtml)

USA Today (www.usatoday.com)

The Washington Post (www.washingtonpost.com)

Business

The Financial Times (www.ft.com/home/us)

The Wall Street Journal (www.wsj.com)

Magazines

Business and News
Business Week (www.businessweek.com)
The Economist (www.economist.com)
Forbes (www.forbes.com/forbes/)
Fortune (www.cnn.com/fortune)
Newsweek (www.msnbc.msn.com/id/3032542/site/newsweek)
Time (www.time.com
US News and World Report (www.usnews.com)

Society
Harper's (www.harpers.org)
Mother Jones (www.motherjones.com)
The New Statesman (www.newstatesman.com)
The New Yorker (www.newyorker.com)
The New York Times Magazine (www.nytimes.com/pages/magazine)
Rolling Stone (www.rollingstone.com)
Utne Reader (www.utne.com)
Vanity Fair (www.vanityfair.com)
The Washington Post Magazine (http://www.washingtonpost.com)

Politics
The American Prospect (www.prospect.org)
The American Spectator (www.spectator.org)
Atlantic Monthly (www.theatlantic.com/)
Congress Daily (nationaljournal.com/pubs/congressdaily)
Congressional Weekly (www.cq.com)
The Hill (www.hillnews.com)
The Nation (www.thenation.com)
The National Review (www.nationalreview.com)
National Journal (nationaljournal.com)
The New Republic (www.tnr.com)
Roll Call (www.rollcall.com)
Washington Monthly (www.washingtonmonthly.com)
The Weekly Standard (www.weeklystandard.com)

Specialty and Reports
Science (www.sciencemag.org)

Standard & Poor's Industry Surveys (http://sandp.ecnext.com/coms2/
   page_industry)
Time Higher Education Supplement (www.thes.co.uk)

Academic
Columbia Journalism Review (www.cjr.org)
CQ Researcher (library.cqpress.com/cqresearcher)
Foreign Affairs (www.foreignaffairs.org)
Foreign Policy (www.foreignpolicy.com/story/index.php)
Nature (www.nature.com/nature)

Web-Based Sources

Political Magazines and Sites
AlterNet (www.alternet.org)
Buzzflash (www.buzzflash.com/)
Common Dreams (www.commondreams.org)
Counterpunoh (www.counterpunch.org)
Daily Kos (www.dailykos.com)
Huffington Post (www.huffingtonpost.com)
Salon (www.salon.com)
Slate (www.slate.com)
Tompaine.com (www.tompaine.com)
Townhall.com (www.townhall.com)

News Providers
Air America Radio (www.AirAmericaRadio.com)
BBC (news.bbc.co.uk)
CNN (edition.cnn.com)
Common Dreams (www.commondreams.org)
C-SPAN (www.c-span.org)
Frontline (www.pbs.org/wgbh/pages/frontline)
Inter Press Service (www.ips.org)
Jim Lehrer Newshour (www.pbs.org/newshour)
MSNBC (www.msnbc.msn.com)
NPR (www.npr.org)
PBS (www.pbs.org)
Wikipedia (en.wikipedia.org/wiki/Main_Page)

Government Sources

Executive Branch
Congressional Budget Office (www.cbo.gov)
Department of Energy—Energy Information Administration
 (www.eia.doe.gov)
Federal Election Commission (www.fec.gov)
U.S. Environmental Protection Agency (www.epa.gov)
U.S. Nuclear Regulatory Commission (www.nrc.gov)
White House (www.whitehouse.gov)

Legislative Branch
Committee on Government Reform—Minority Office (www
 .democrats.reform.house.gov)
Congressional Research Services (www.opencrs.com or
 fpc.state.gov/c4763.htm)
The Government Accountability Office—GAO (www.gao.goc)
The Library of Congress (www.loc.gov)
THOMAS—Legislative information (www.thomas.gov)
United States House of Representatives (www.house.gov)
United States Senate (www.senate.gov)

Think Tanks

Brookings Institute (www.brookings.org)
Cato Institute (www.cato.org)
Center for Strategic and International Studies (www.csis.org)
Council on Foreign Relations (www.cfr.org)
Institute for Policy Studies (www.ips-dc.org)
New America Foundation (www.newamerica.net)
Pew Research Center for the People and the Press (www.people-
 press.org)
The Urban Institute (www.urban.org)
World Resources Institute (www.wri.org)

Watchdogs

Americans United for Separation of Church and State (www.au.org)
Arms Trade Resource Center (www.worldpolicy.org/projects/arms)

Bulletin of Atomic Scientists (www.thebulletin.org)

Center for Democracy and Technology (www.cdt.org)

Center for Media and Democracy—PR watch (www.prwatch.org)

Center for Responsive Politics (www.opensecrets.org)

Center for Science in the Public Interest (www.cspinet.org)

Center for Public Integrity (www.publicintegrity.org)

Citizens Against Government Waste (www.cagw.org)

Citizens for Responsibility and Ethics in Washington (www
.citizensforethics.org/index.php)

Consumer Federation of America (www.consumerfed.org)

Demos Institute (www.demos.org)

Electronic Frontier Foundation (www.eff.org)

Fairness and Accuracy in Reporting (www.fair.org)

Foreign Policy In Focus (www.fpif.org)

International Relations Center (www.irc-online.org)

Media Matters for America (mediamatters.org)

Judicial Watch (www.judicialwatch.org)

OMB Watch (www.ombwatch.org)

People for the American Way (www.pfaw.org)

Public Citizen (www.citizen.org)

Polaris Insititute (www.polarisinstitute.org)

PoliticalMoneyLine (www.fecinfo.com)

Project for Excellence in Journalism (www.journalism.org)

Public Agenda (www.publicagenda.org)

Southern Poverty Law Center (www.splcenter.org)

Spinwatch (www.spinwatch.org/index.php)

Union of Concerned Scientists (www.ucsusa.org)

United States Public Interest Research Group (www.uspirg.org)

Worldwatch Institute (www.worldwatch.org)

Photo Credits

Page 3 courtesy of United States House of Representatives (www.house.gov)
Page 5 courtesy of F. Malotaux, Wikimedia Commons (www.commons.wikimedia.org)
Page 9 courtesy of United States China Commission
Page 17 from Corbis
Page 26 from Corbis
Page 28 from Corbis
Page 31 from Corbis
Page 35 courtesy of Chris Bell
Page 54 courtesy of David Sickey
Page 56 courtesy of United States Senate (www.senate.gov)
Page 61 from Corbis
Page 67 from Terry Ashe/Getty Images
Page 97 courtesy of U.S. National Archives and Records
Page 103 courtesy of Americans for Tax Reform
Page 110 from Reuters
Page 114 from Getty Images
Page 150 from Corbis
Page 154 courtesy of United States Senate (www.senate.gov)
Page 155 courtesy of Woodrow Wilson International Center for Scholars
Page 181 courtesy of Public Citizen (www.citizen.org)
Page 195 courtesy of Linda Chavez
Page 198 from Reuters
Page 208 from Getty Images
Page 226 courtesy of United States Chamber of Commerce
Page 237 courtesy of Lawrence Krauss
Page 242 courtesy of Jimmy Wales

Index